ISUAL STORIES

BEHIND THE LENS WITH **VINCENT LAFORET**

VISUAL STORIES: BEHIND THE LENS WITH VINCENT LAFORET

Vincent Laforet with Ibarionex Perello

New Riders
1249 Eighth Street
Berkeley, CA 94710
(510) 524-2178
Fax: (510) 524-2221

Find us on the Web at www.newriders.com
To report errors, please send a note to errata@peachpit.com
New Riders is an imprint of Peachpit, a division of Pearson Education

Senior Editor: Karyn Johnson
Writer and Development Editor: Ibarionex Perello
Copy Editor: Jacqueline Aaron
Production Editor: Tracey Croom
Proofreader: Elizabeth Welch
Composition: WolfsonDesign
Indexer: Valerie Perry
Interior Design: WolfsonDesign
Cover Design: Charlene Charles-Will
Cover Photo: Vincent Laforet

NOTICE OF RIGHTS

NOTICE OF LIABILITY

TRADEMARKS

ISBN 13: 978-0-321-79392-8
ISBN 10: 0-321-79392-7

9 8 7 6 5 4 3 2 1

Printed and bound in the United States of America

ACKNOWLEDGMENTS

I would like to thank the people who are captured within these images for their trust, time, and often very gracious hospitality. I would like to thank all the photographers and photo editors who came before me, who inspired me with their work, the stories they shared, and often for their mentorship.

Specifically, I would like to thank my father, Bertrand Laforet, for handing me his camera when I was 15, the moment that forever changed my life. I would like to thank my mother, Dominique Bazin, for being unwavering in her support of my career. I'd like to thank Justin Jaeckin for suggesting I find more "craziness" in my work. Thanks to Amber Laforet for her help in shaping my vision for close to a decade. Also I'd like to thank Kenneth Irby for nearly throwing me out of his office nearly two decades ago only to become one of my closest mentors. Kenneth gave me the most amazing gift by challenging me to share this craft with others and teach people much older and experienced than I was. As a result, he led me to do a lot of important introspection during the mid-point of my career.

Thank you to Ibarionex Perello for a fantastic series of interviews and incredible effort in making sense of everything. To Karyn Johnson for staying on top of me to ensure this book made it to print. To Justin Hamilton and Sophie Thall for their help in getting everything out the door from our studio.

Finally, "thank you" to an endless series of teachers, mentors, acquaintances, fellow photographers, photo editors, readers, competitors, critics and most importantly, to my family—I would have never gotten here without you.

I'd like to dedicate this book to my daughter, Eliana, and son, Noah, who give meaning to my life every day.

Vincent Laforet
Tuesday, October 18, 2011

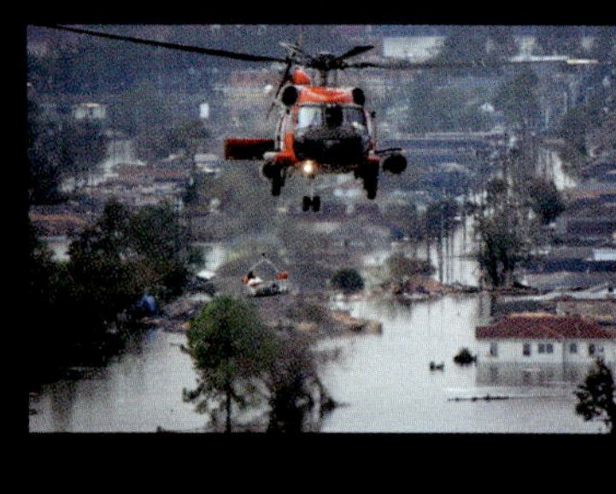

CHAPTER 1

THE VALUE OF AN IMAGE 3

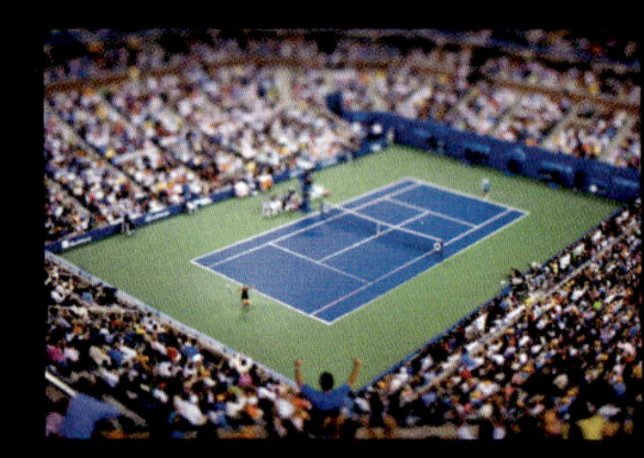

CHAPTER 2

A STORY IN A SINGLE IMAGE 17

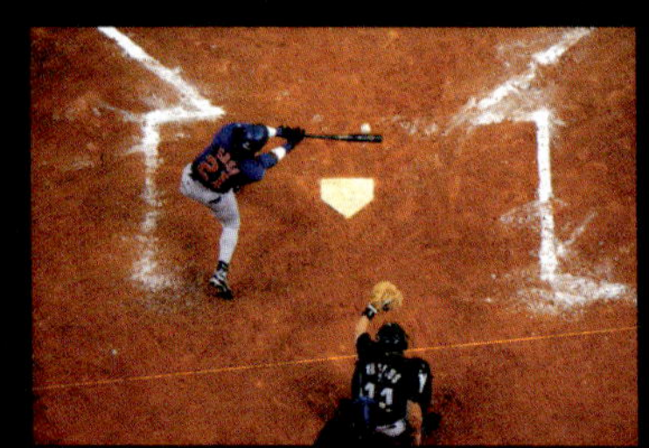

CHAPTER 3

MARRYING THE STORY WITH THE AESTHETIC 35

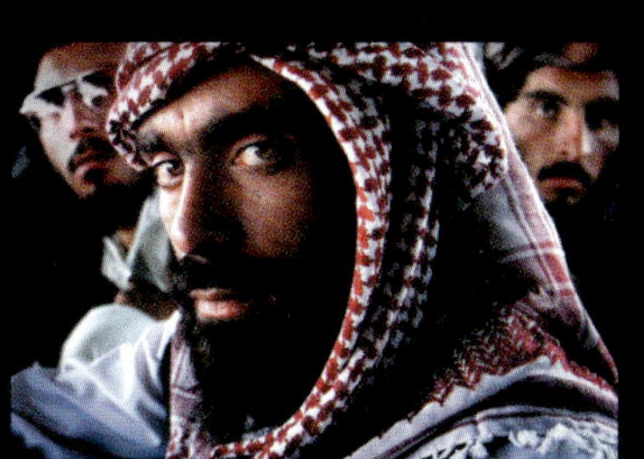

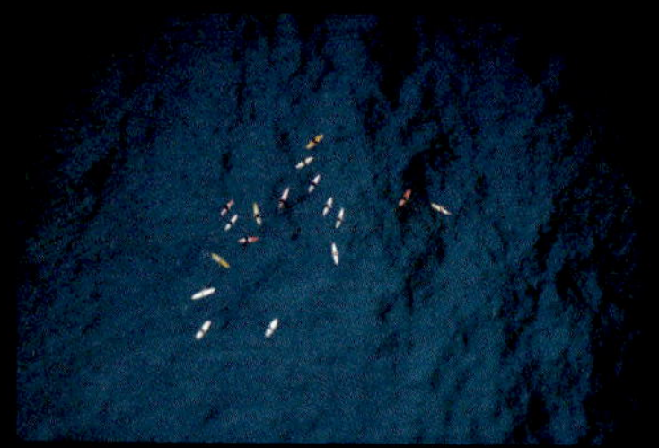

CHAPTER 6

KISS (KEEP IT SIMPLE, STUPID

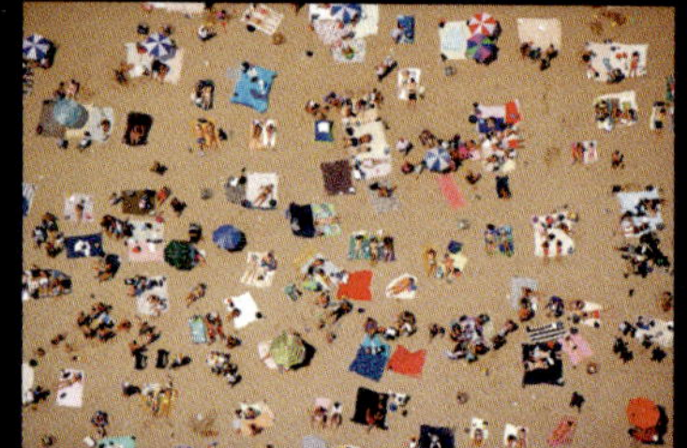

CHAPTER 7

IN THE AIR

CHAPTER 8

A LOVE AFFAIR WITH NEW YORK 129

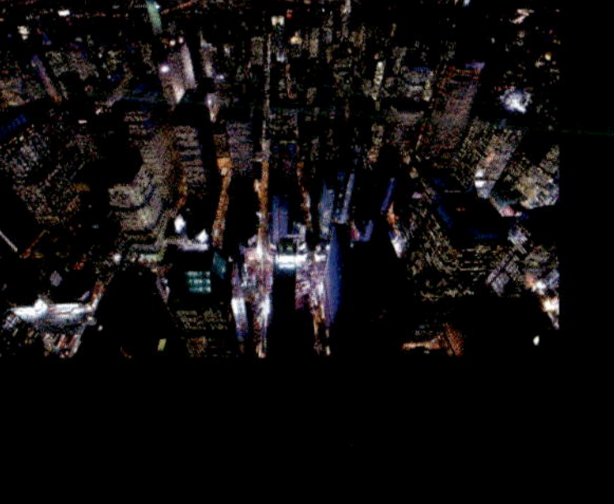

CHAPTER 9

THE ART OF LENS CHOICE 139

CHAPTER 10

THE WORLD THROUGH A TILT-SHIFT LENS 153

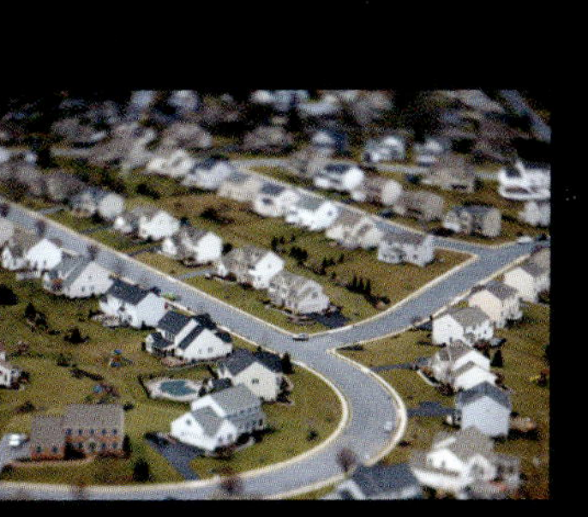

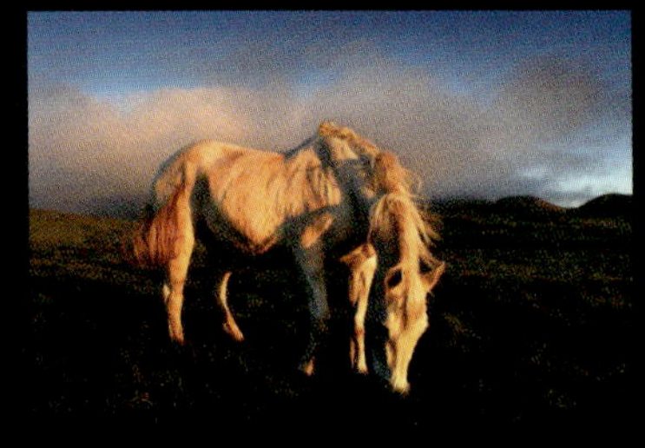

CHAPTER 11

SEEING AND USING LIGHT 171

CHAPTER 12

THE PANIOLO 191

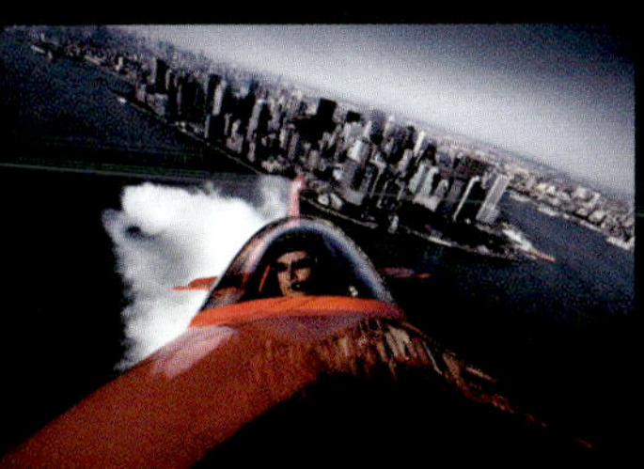

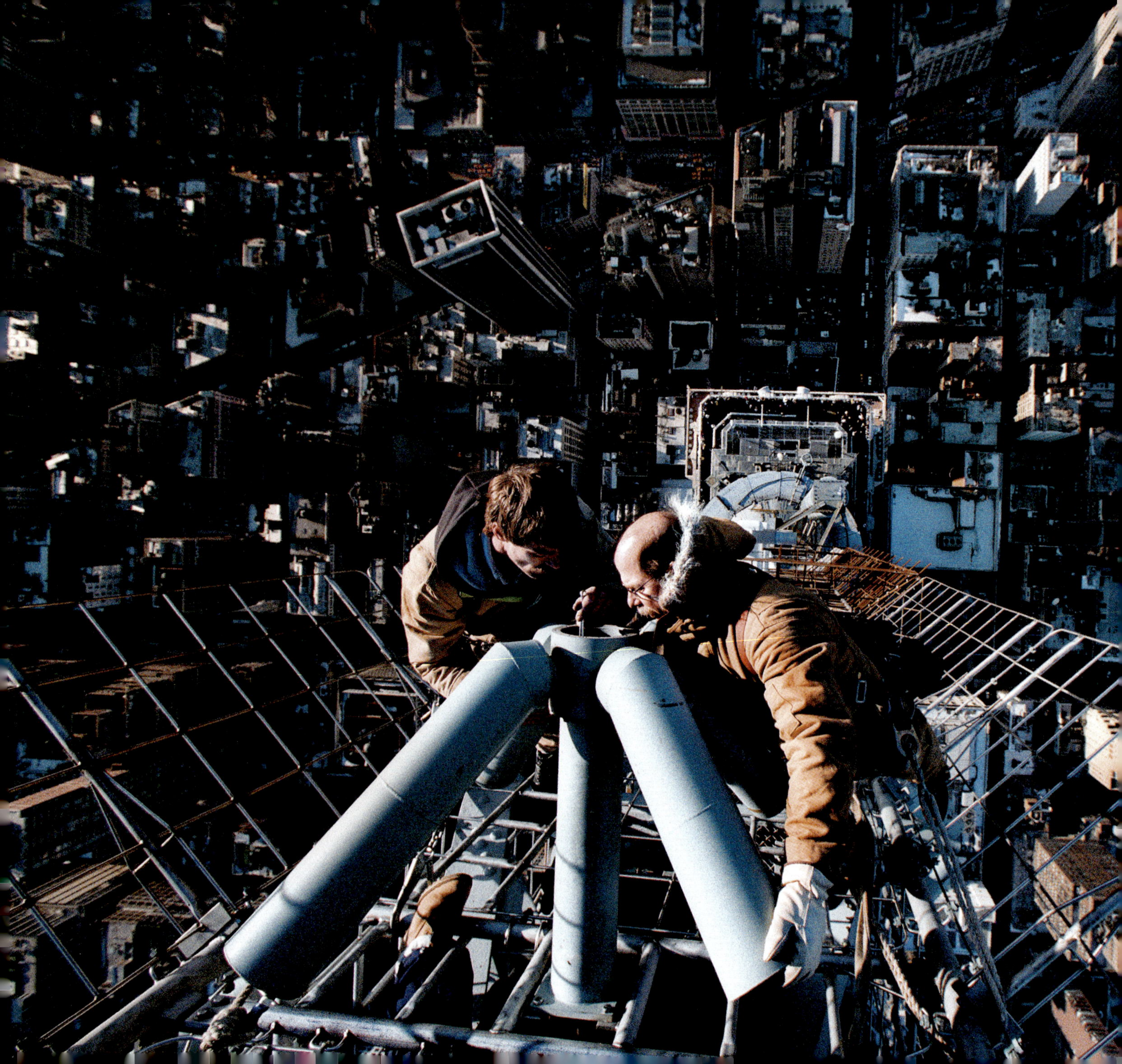

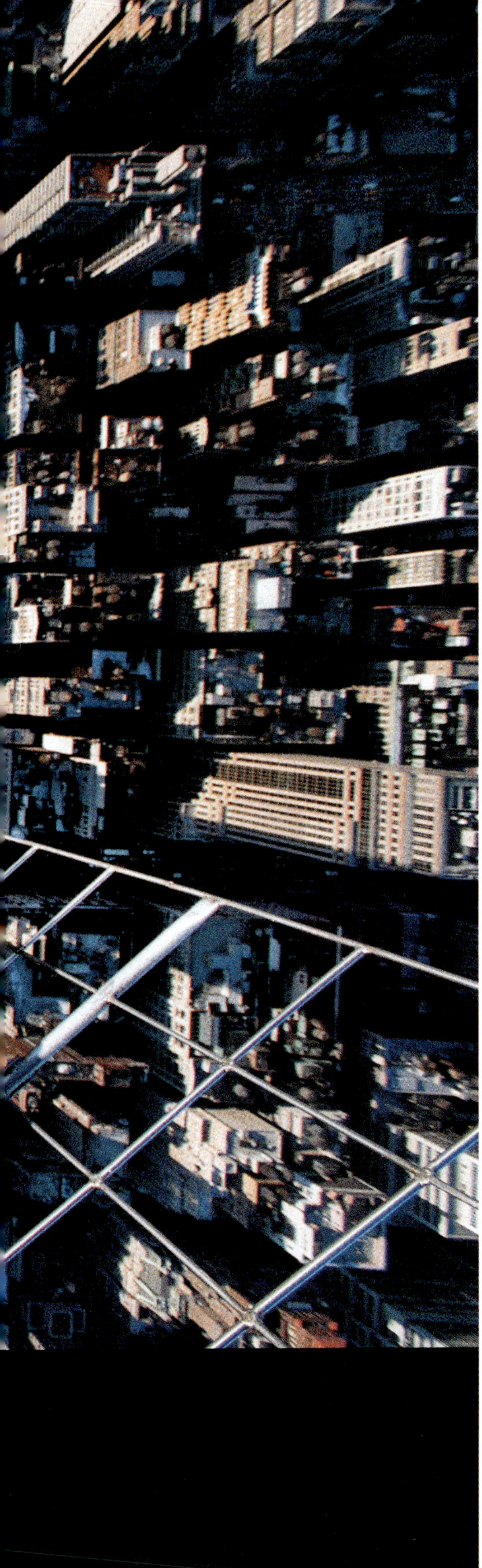

INTRODUCTION

I have been given a chance to witness and experience many different lives, occupations, and realities, thanks to the many generous people who've allowed me to document them with a camera.

I have hung from the needle of the Empire State Building, nearly 1,500 feet above New York City. I have witnessed the launch of the Second Gulf War from the deck of the *USS Abraham Lincoln* aircraft carrier. I have seen people uprooted from their lives in Afghanistan, and witnessed Americans devastated by the aftermath of Hurricane Katrina in New Orleans.

◀ Workers repair the antenna atop the Empire State Building in 2001.

ISO 200 f/5.6 1/1000 14mm

I have photographed a U.S. president in the White House in the morning, and, later that very afternoon, a homeless man on the street. I have photographed major sporting events including the Olympics, the Super Bowl, and the World Cup.

But some of my favorite moments in photography—of my career—have been the intimate moments spent with everyday people. Granted, some were Nobel Prize winners, industry titans, or billionaires, but others were fascinating, regular people from small towns or villages who made tremendous contributions to their local community—or sometimes simply to their loved ones.

Most of the time, human beings are extremely complex. I have witnessed some of the very best of humanity with my own eyes, and some of the very worst behavior imaginable, as well.

Photography has given me the opportunity to be in awe of a child reacting to being photographed for the first time. On the other end of the spectrum, I've witnessed the joy on someone's face when they make a great photograph of a flower or of the game-winning touchdown and realize they've captured that moment for eternity.

That is the ultimate beauty of photography, as with any art: its ability to make us very happy.

One of the most important photographic lessons I learned came from my father, Bertrand Laforet, who is also a photographer. I was 16 years old, sitting in his office at a magazine in Paris. He walked in and looked at me.

"You know what I love about photography?" he said. "I've been doing this for close to 30 years now, and every day I still learn something completely new."

My father was referring to the endless world out there for photographers—and the endless opportunity to learn, to take chances, to experiment. I never forgot those words. I came to understand what he meant, and did my best to live and practice photography accordingly.

A surfer makes his way into the water at sunrise at San Buenaventura Beach in Ventura, California.

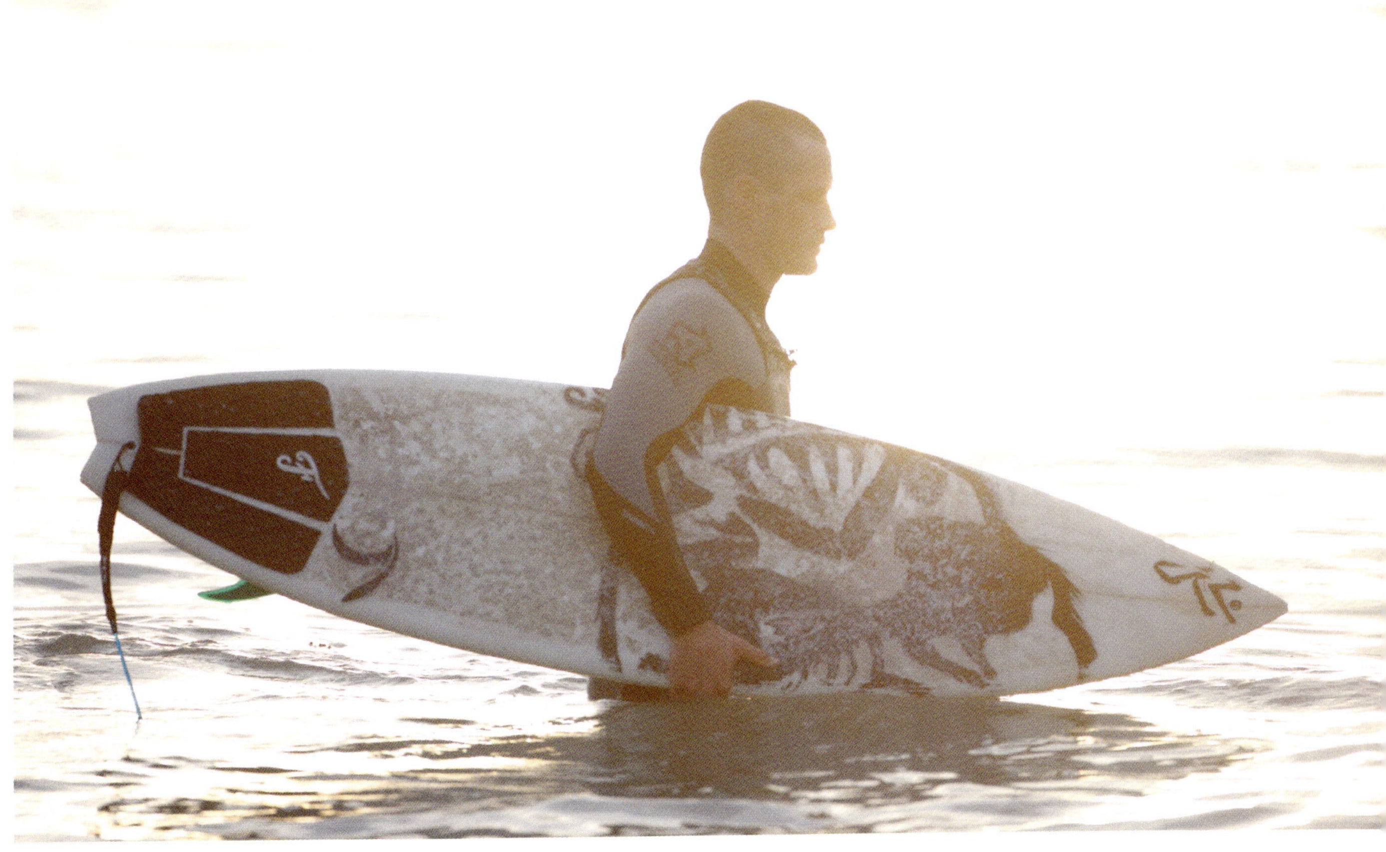

ISO 50 f/100 1/100 500mm

This book is meant to be a collection of some of my most successful images from my career that has spanned nearly 18 years. On the DVD that accompanies the book, I discuss some of these photographs and others in greater detail in over 60 videos. The book and DVD come at an interesting time for me, as I am starting to focus almost exclusively on being a director.

That being said, my first love will always be the photograph. I find it to be one of the purest artistic pursuits. The artist is always held back by reality in some ways (by what he or she can actually photograph, Photoshop excluded) but is also challenged to produce a work of art and to push creative boundaries to new levels.

One of the things I discuss in the book is technique. I believe that just as a musician must learn her scales before tackling whole works of music, a photographer must master the basic technical aspects of photography in order to create works of art. Technique doesn't generally lead to great photographs, but poor technique can prevent a photographer from creating great images.

As we all know, it's far too easy to become frustrated with an out-of-focus image, one that was made a split-second too late or early. As much fun as photography can be, it is by no means easy. We should remember that if we end up missing a photograph, even a historical one we were supposed to capture for a major publication, no one died on the operating table. In other words, the stakes are not as high as they are with a surgeon or a judge making critical decisions that will alter someone's destiny.

Nevertheless, the right photograph taken at the right moment can change the path of a war by changing people's perceptions of it. An example is Eddie Adams' photograph of the Vietcong execution during the Vietnam War. Who knew that the act of focusing a lens and pressing a button could change the course of history?

There is one thing I deeply believe in when it comes to documentary photography: it's not about *you*; it's about the stories of the people you are photographing.

And yet I can honestly say that making a living taking pictures is one of the greatest guilty pleasures any human being can get away with.

If you go back to what my father told me when I was 16, photography is for everyone. You need not aim to be a photojournalist; you need not aim to change the world. All I recommend you do is to have fun along the way. And take chances.

An aerial photograph of the devastation caused by Hurricane Katrina.

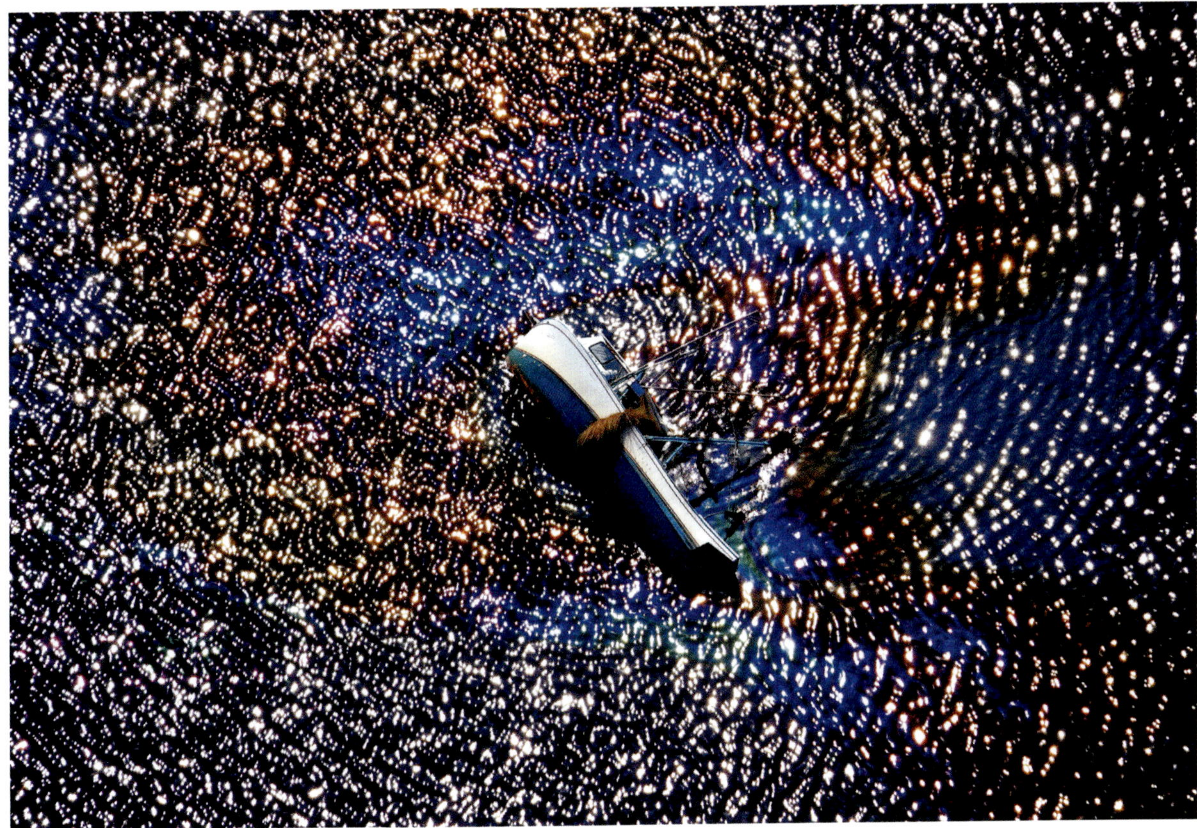

ISO 250 f/7.1 1/2000 180mm

While many of you may not yet know what your style or vision is (I certainly didn't), the best way to discover them is to go out there, take chances, and see what images draw you in—see what errors lead to surprisingly successful images.

If you find that the image you are about to take doesn't excite you, don't take it. Doing so will almost guarantee that you will miss a much better photograph. After all, if you waste time making a mediocre image, you will likely run out of time to make the great image that may just be a few steps, or inches, away.

The photograph is a powerful thing. Regardless of the thousands of images and videos that are available to us out there, the still image holds a very important place in the media at large, no matter what anyone says.

As long as you follow your heart, as long as you are true to your subjects, and as long as you strive to make an image that you think captures something special or interesting either to yourself or to others, it is hard to fail.

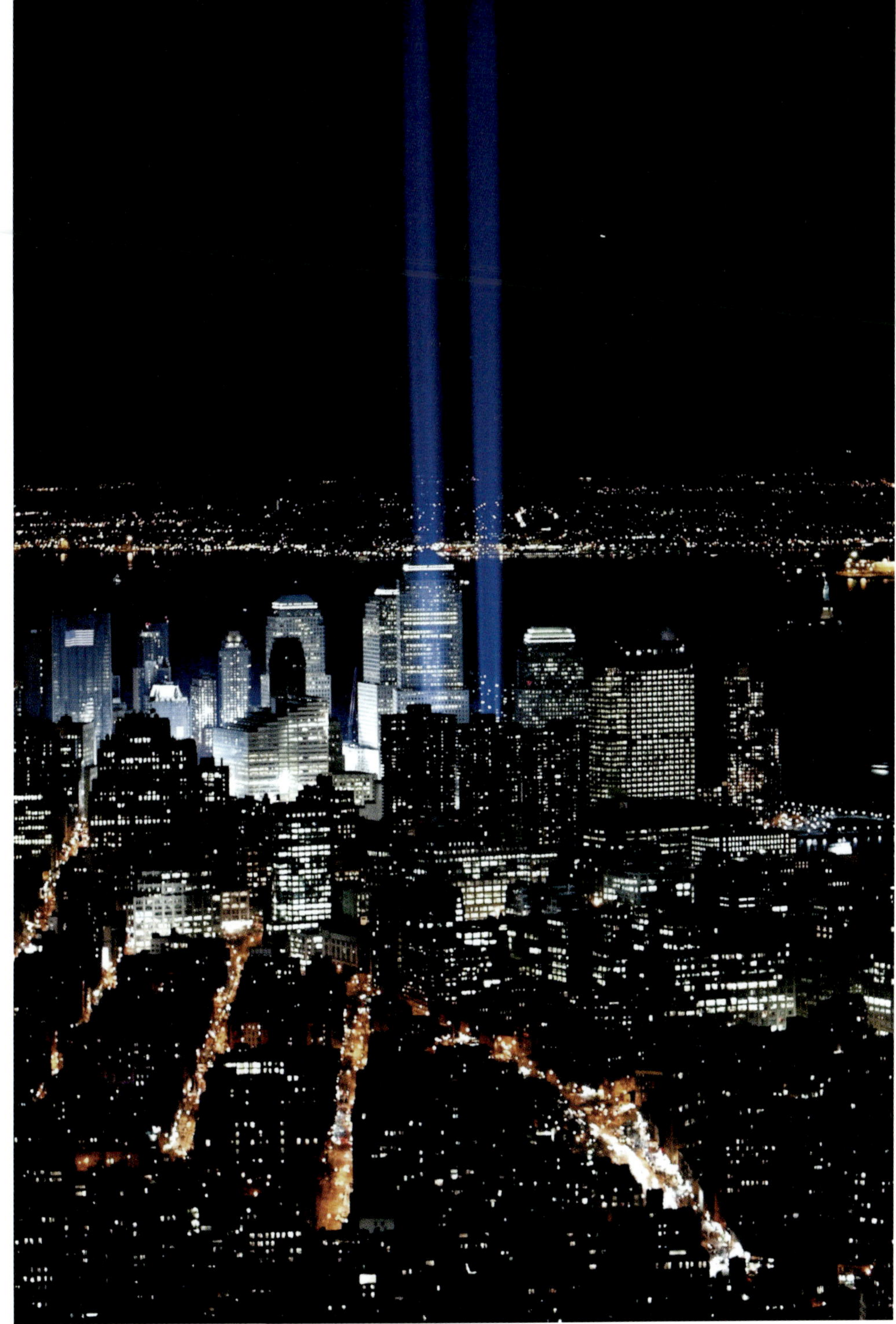

The twin beams of light rise near the World Trade Center site six months after the 9/11 terrorist attacks.

ISO 200 f/2.8 1/15 70-200mm

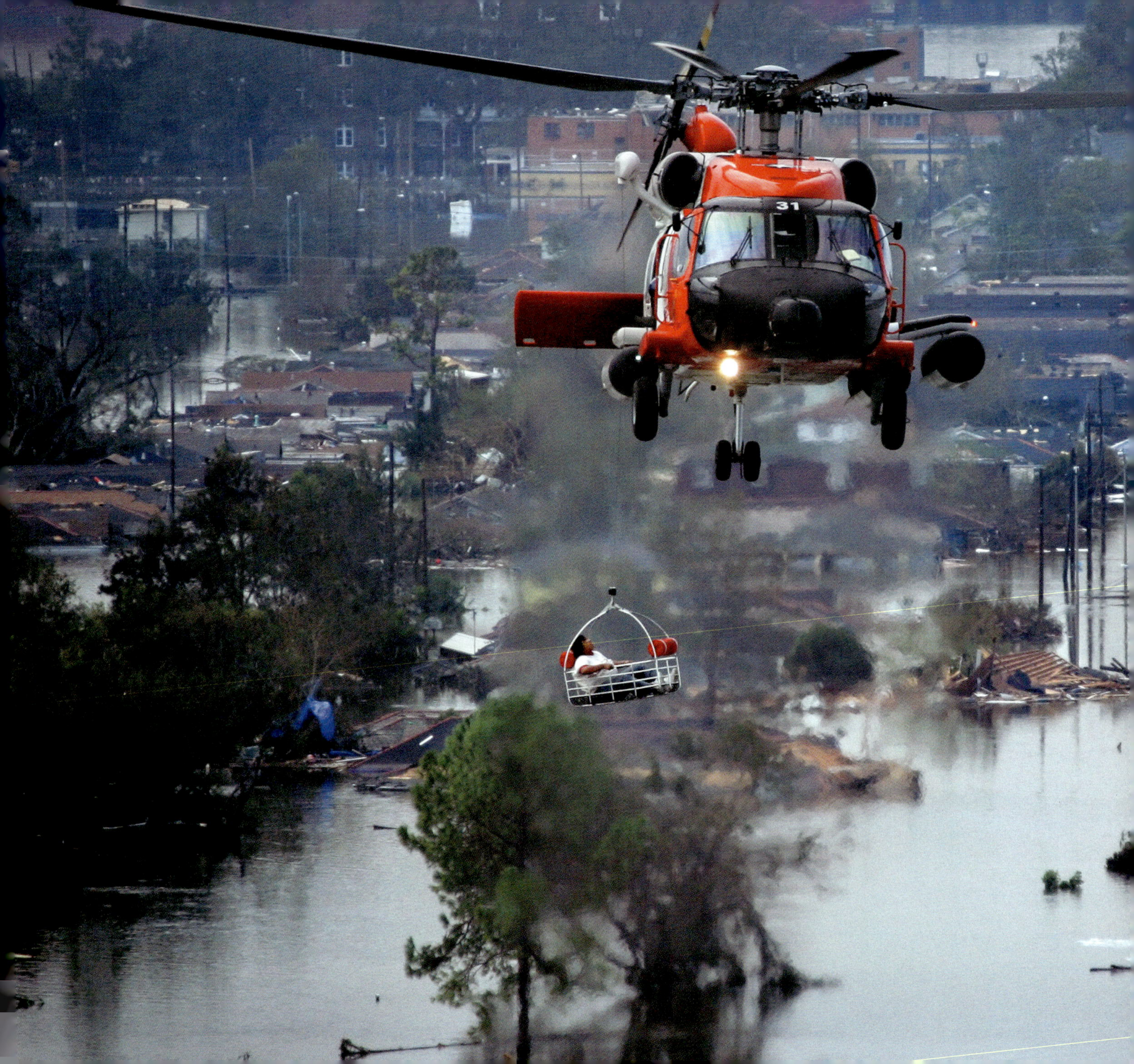
31

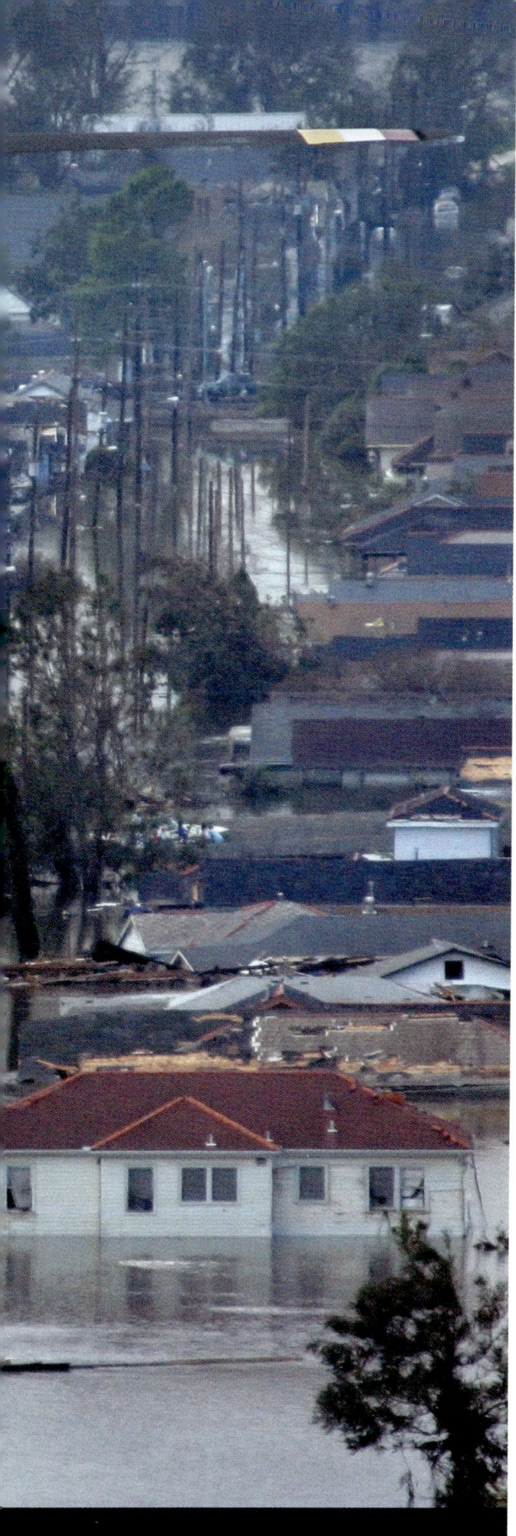

CHAPTER 1

THE VALUE OF AN IMAGE

I was scheduled to cover the U.S. Open in 2005 when I got a call from the *New York Times* asking if I wanted to cover a hurricane.

I'd covered a few hurricanes before, but they were never really a big deal. They were, frankly, kind of fun and involved driving around in 100-mile-per-hour winds, photographing people being stupid. I accepted the new assignment and caught the last flight from Newark, New Jersey, to Houston, Texas, where I met the reporter, Ralph Blumenthal. This was the night before Hurricane Katrina hit.

◀ Helicopter rescue following Hurricane Katrina in 2005.

ISO 800 f/6.3 1/2000 300mm

When you make images like this overseas, you almost always rationalize it. This would never happen in my country. It's a very common thing we say as journalists.

On the way to Baton Rouge, Louisiana we heard on the radio that several Texas-based FEMA groups were headed to New Orleans, so we contacted them and met in Baton Rouge. As part of the FEMA convoy, we were some of the first journalists to arrive in the city. This gave us early access to the Louis Armstrong New Orleans International Airport several days after the storm had hit and the levees had broken.

When we landed in our helicopter, there was a line of helicopters on the tarmac. Their combined sound was thundering. As we walked, the elderly, the sick, and frightened children surrounded us. It's not every day you come off of a jolly green giant with huge rotor wash onto a scene like this.

I saw people being brought in on luggage carts, holding onto garbage bags filled with their life's belongings. I understood that they had to find ways to move people around, but it was so degrading to see that happening on our soil. Eventually, we went into the main terminal and started to see that things were really bad.

We went down to the airport luggage carousel for Delta, in the area being used for triage. This was the location for the extremely sick, the dying, or the dead, and they were just packed side to side. I had to continually step over people to get around. The smell of urine and death was overwhelming. I could hardly breathe. I almost lost it a few times.

I saw people lying on cots and an old woman laying weakly on a conveyer belt. I brought the camera to my eye and made photographs of the scene.

Now, when you make images like this overseas, you almost always rationalize it. You say to yourself that they don't have the infrastructure of America. They are not as modern as we are. This would never happen in my country. It's a very common thing we say as journalists.

Louis Armstrong Airport, New Orleans, September 2, 2005.

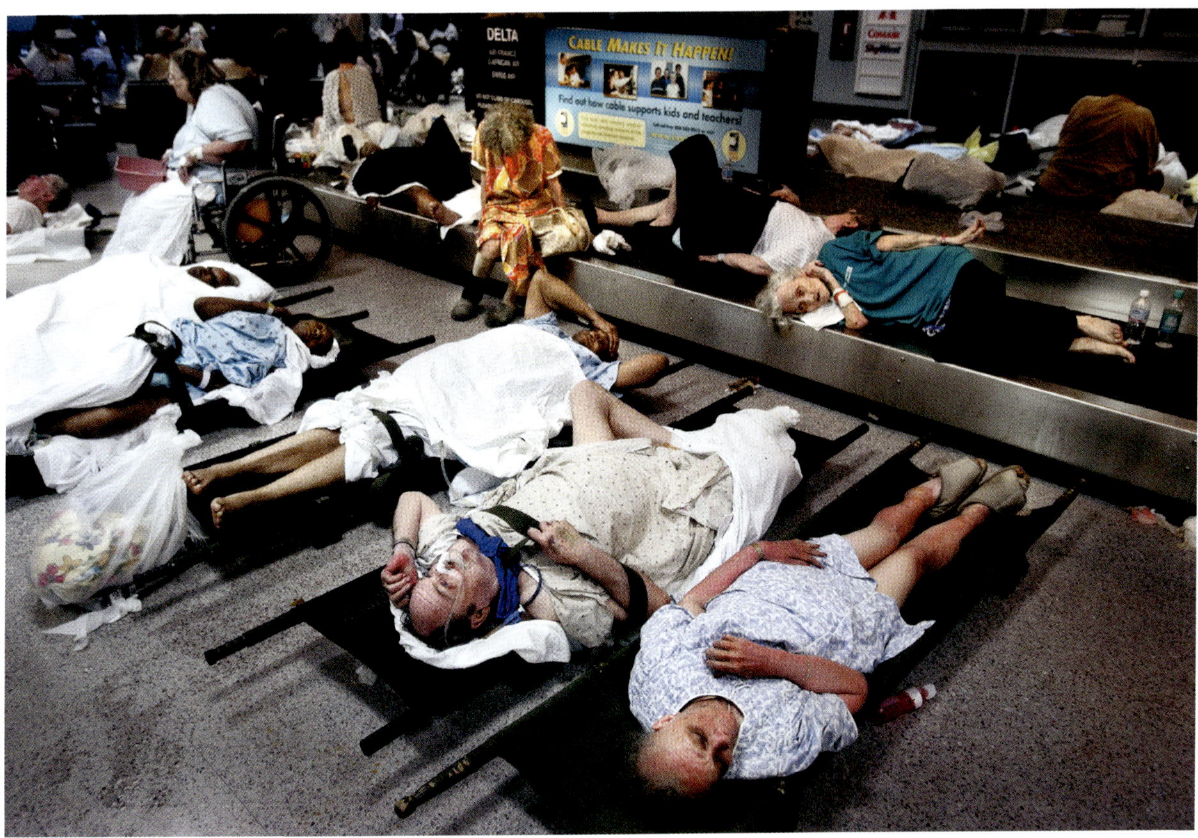

ISO 800 f/4.5 1/60 26mm

Sun shining through rising smoke in New Orleans (August, 2005).

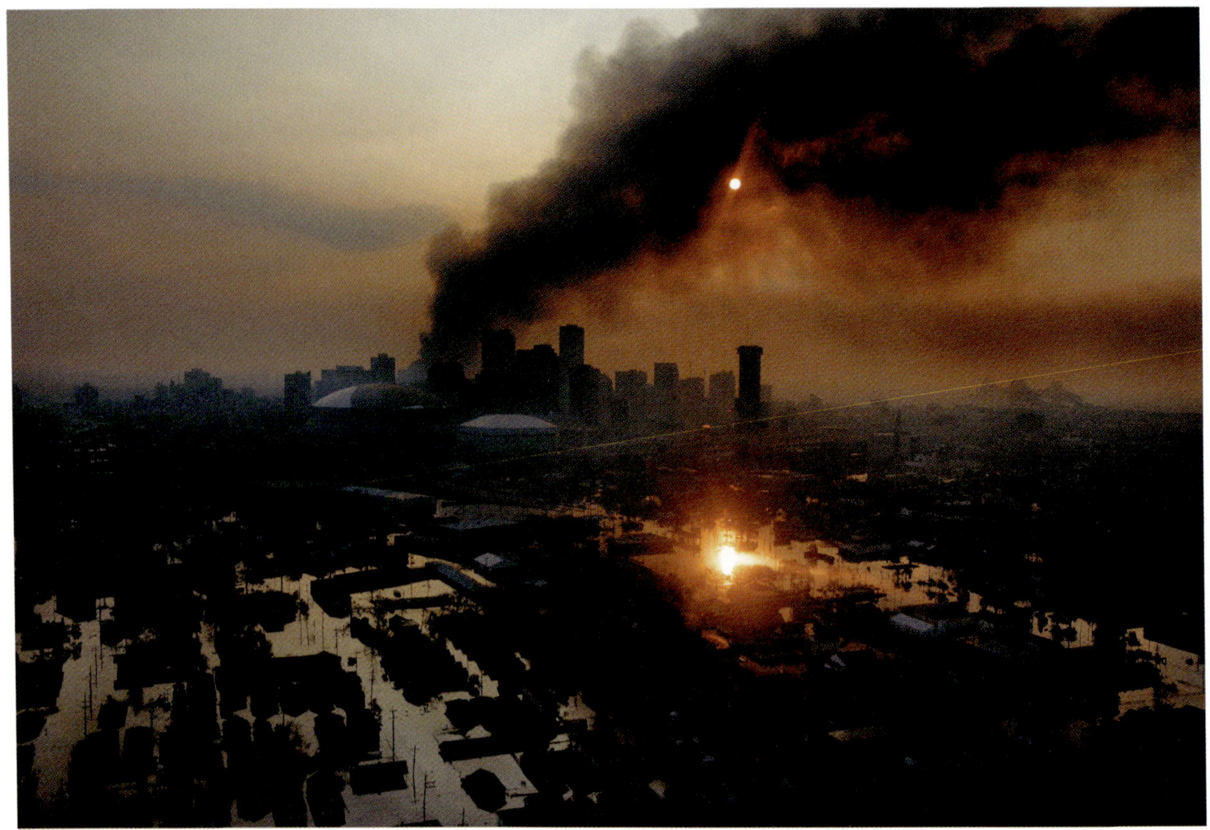

ISO 50 f/4.5 1/500 32mm

But as a journalist you realize that's how you feel about it; how disturbing it is isn't really relevant. You're there to make the pictures. I have to admit, though, I was having a very hard time.

I went straight to the highest-ranking person I could find there and did what any photojournalist who wants to get kicked out would do: I said, "Excuse me, I am Vincent Laforet with the *New York Times.* Am I allowed to be here?" I knew the answer would be "absolutely not." Basically I was begging for her to kick me out.

The woman I addressed started to cry, which startled me even more, and she said, "You're not allowed to be here. I'm probably going to lose my job, but I don't care. I've been calling Washington DC for hours now. I've got 50 volunteers and 900 people per hour coming in, and no one in DC understands how bad it is. You get your damn pictures, and get them in your damn paper. Go!"

I went back and shot more and more, staying very aware of my deadline. I was soon back on a helicopter, making my calls to the office at the *New York Times.*

"I have these images," I said. "They are startling. They are disturbing. I'm not sure you can even publish them, but I think you have to publish them. Make sure that the editors wait for them."

We landed and I transmitted the photographs. The reaction on the other side was very quiet. There wasn't much said. The next day, they showed up on the front page of the *New York Times.*

When you do something like that, there is zero pride in terms of your ego, at least for me. You don't stand up and say that is your image. You say, I did something and I hope it helped people. It's not about you and your experiences as a photojournalist; it's about the photographs you make. It's about the people whose stories need to be told. And that was reinforced more than ever in Katrina.

As a journalist you realize how you feel about it; how disturbing it is isn't really relevant. You're there to make the pictures.

Near Lancaster, Pennsylvania, the Amish and Mennonite horse-drawn buggies share the road with modern vehicles (2008).

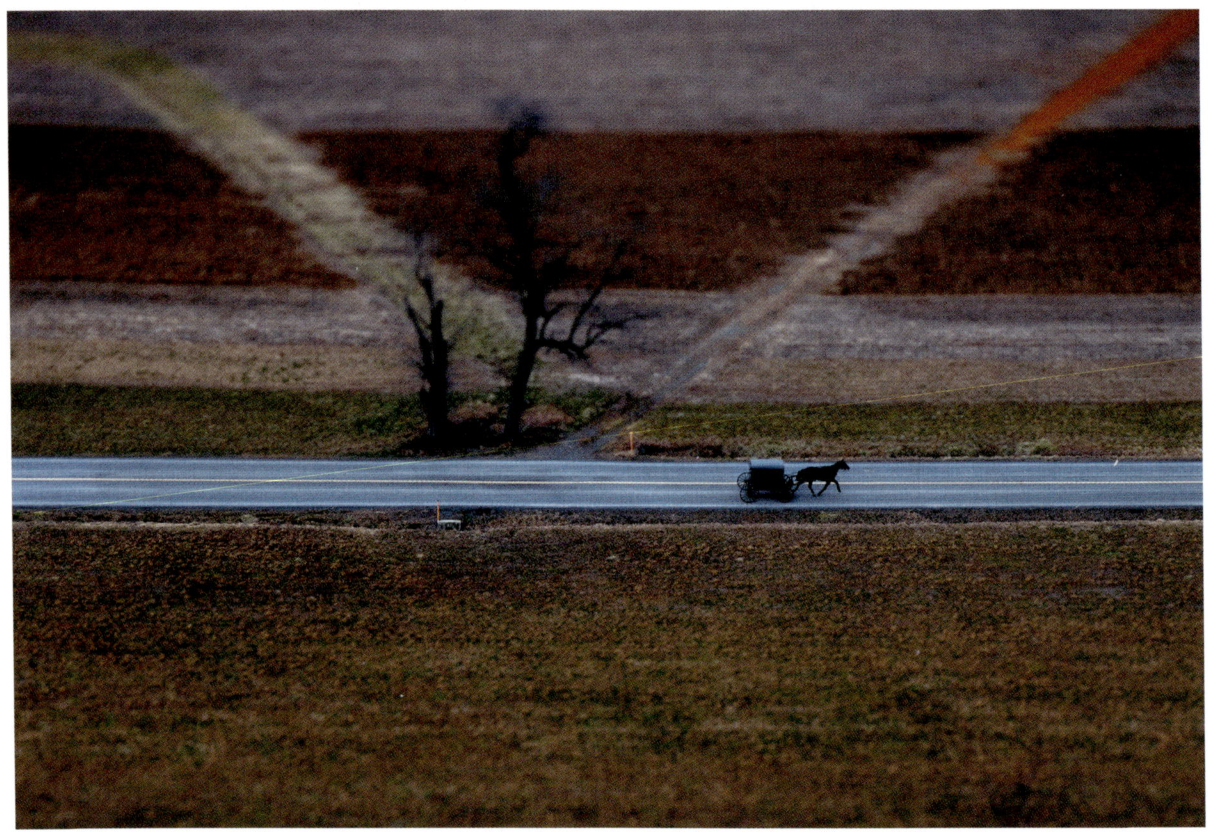

ISO 100 f/4 1/250 90mm

BEGINNINGS

Even in the days before I ever picked up a camera, I recognized the value of an image.

My father was a photojournalist. He worked for an agency called Gamma in Paris, and I grew up looking at the work of the top photojournalists in the world at the time. I was also surrounded by photo books by the likes of Henri Cartier-Bresson, Robert Capa, Raymond Depardon, Brassaï, Helmut Newton, and James Nachtwey. I was surrounded by these images.

And it was many of those classic images that made me wonder what it felt like to be alive that day, to wear those clothes, to walk those streets, to live in those edifices, to drive those first cars, to ride around on bicycles or on horseback. I would just get lost in them.

I would delve into an image and look at it for a few minutes or hours and then come back to it, and I would know intrinsically that the photograph on a very basic level freezes time and immortalizes the moment. Even when there is nothing exceptional happening within it, the record of the moment can become extremely valuable because for the most part, it's true and it's untainted.

I loved and was fascinated by photographs created 30, 50, and 100 years ago. I instinctively understood how Cartier-Bresson's photograph of a family having lunch by the side of a river might be a scene no one at the time would have found remarkable; but with time, that image, and so many like it, would take on an incredible significance.

For me, the photograph was as close as we as human beings could get to an empirical document, and I had a tremendous fascination with that. I have always felt a very close connection to that idea. But a photograph has the potential to be so much more.

Even when there is nothing exceptional happening within a photograph, the record of the moment can become extremely valuable because for the most part, it's true and it's untainted.

Firefighters battle the Zaca Lake wildfire burning north of Santa Barbara, CA, on August 11-12, 2007. The fire burned nearly 250,000 acres, and was California's second-largest fire in recorded history.

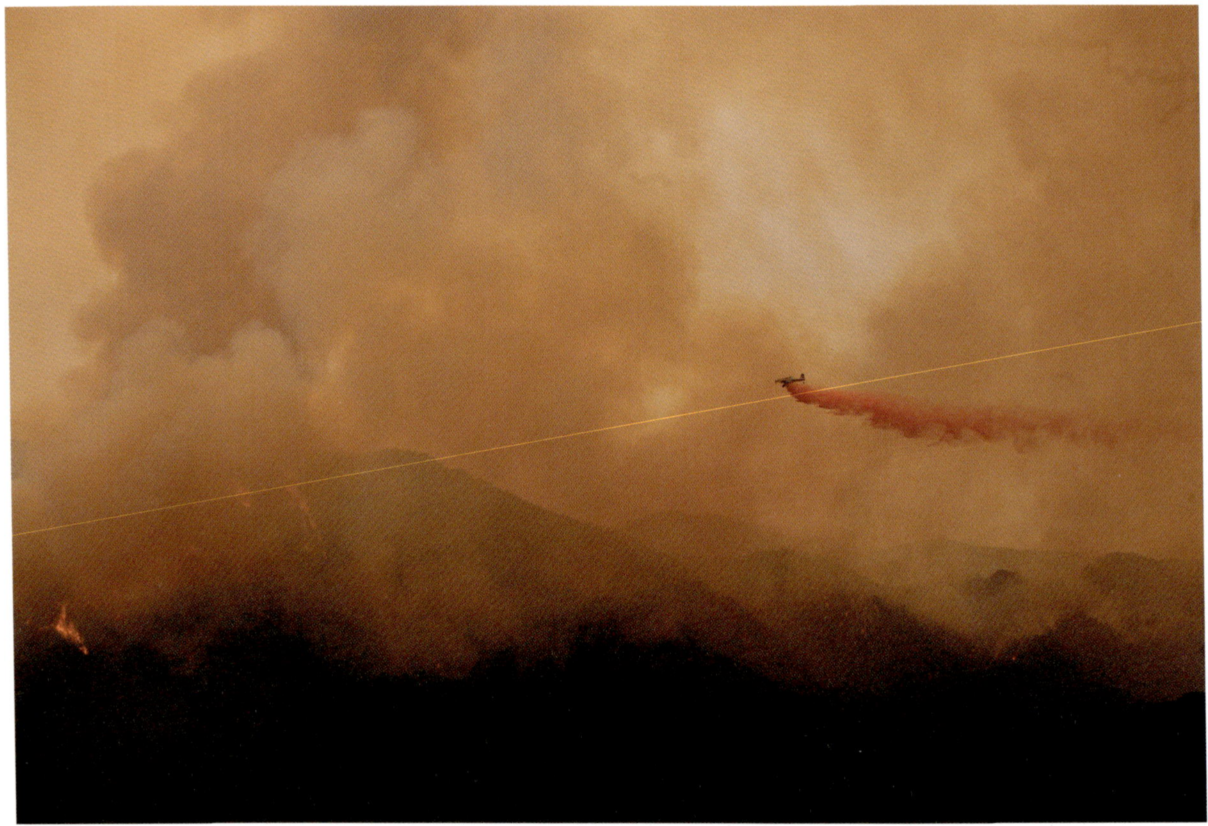

ISO 200 f/5.6 1/1000 70mm

The magic of photography is that every photograph, every piece of art, means something different to someone else, and everyone connects to it differently.

PHOTOGRAPHY FOR OTHERS

A photograph need not always be historic. I consider a photograph of a young girl in her home in upstate New York—with all of her life's belongings on the ground—to be almost as important, if not just as important, as some of the biggest news elements, because it helps to document our lives and where we are today in a very real manner. And that's the real beauty of photography—over time, those images gain incredible value.

I've never been a guy who's been very happy with making an amazing image and putting it in a scrapbook that I put in the closet. I think a photograph needs to be shared.

Admittedly, earlier in my career, it was about ego. It was about getting my image out there and saying millions of people saw it. Later in my career, especially as a photojournalist, I came to learn that a photograph has nothing to do with you. It's about the person being photographed. It's about their story.

The readers who wrote me letters about my images made me feel I was contributing something worthwhile and that I was doing good work. There is nothing better than receiving a letter from a 70-year-old retiree who took the time to write you about a photograph. And the best letters are often not about your best photographs. The best letters I've received were about photographs that I thought were terrible or lacking, and someone wrote me a 10-page letter about it because of how they related to it. You realize that as a photographer, the magic of photography is that every photograph, every piece of art, means something different to someone else, and everyone connects to it differently.

Pakistan refugee (September, 2001).

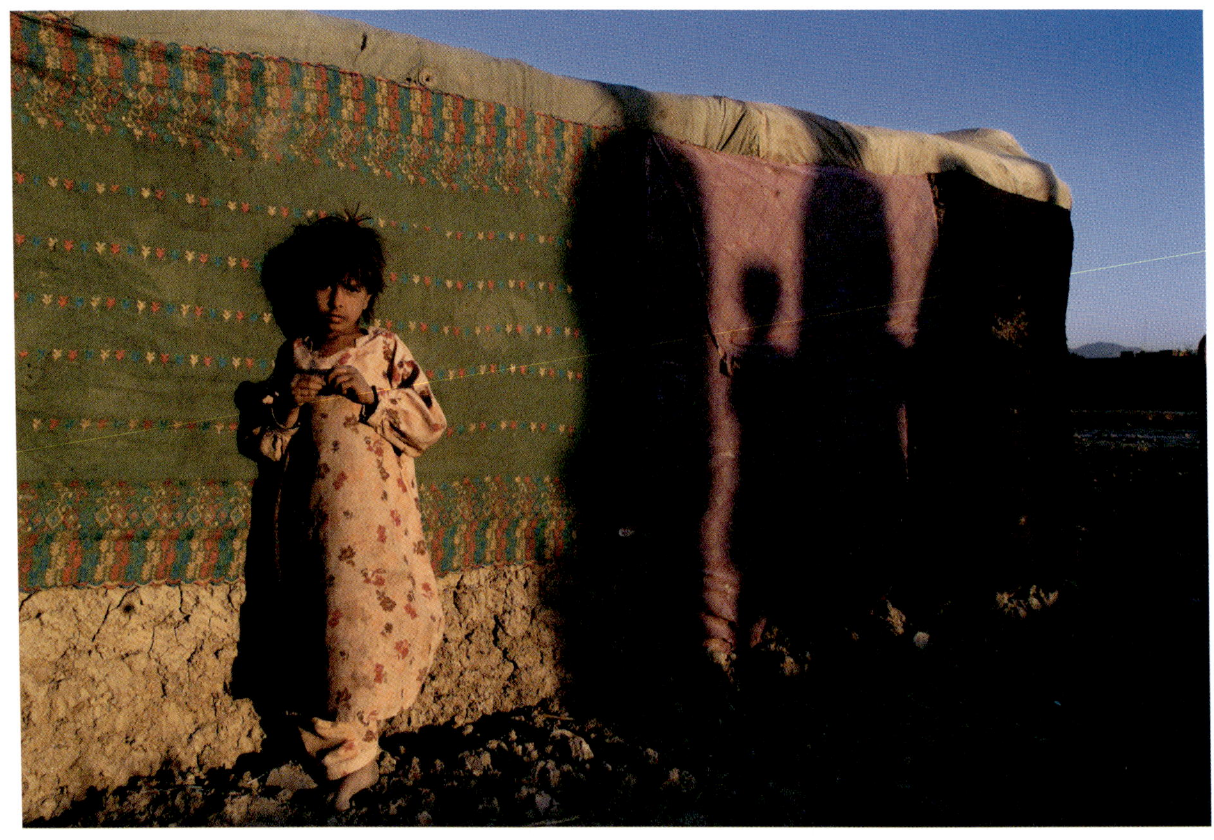

PAKISTAN

Back in 2001 I was in Pakistan, soon after the events of 9/11. I was doing a series of photo essays about just on what I saw. When you are out on the ground, the difficulty is having perspective. I knew the global impact of what was going on, but here I was on the ground, one person documenting normal people in front of me, and it was very hard to understand how to express those global ramifications and the overarching themes with a single photograph.

This was my first foreign assignment in a war zone. I was having a very hard time making sense of where the world was going: It was scary back then and felt like everything had crumbled.

I went back to my roots as a street photographer for the *New York Times* and began photographing Pakistan in the same way I would create images for the newspaper's Metro section. I just took it day by day, story by story, example by example, whatever caught my eye, whatever I saw that was relevant to what I was feeling and thinking.

One day we were in a refugee camp, and as soon as the people, especially the children, saw this Caucasian man with a camera, we were swarmed. It was impossible to make a photograph. But at one moment, a shock of electricity went through me when I saw this young girl by herself. She was standing quietly, barefoot, in front of a mud wall. As soon as she and I made eye contact, everything stopped, and I walked up to her and made a few images. She wasn't participating in all this hoopla. This was not a happy event for her. I never got to engage in a conversation with her, but through her eyes, I felt the confusion and the pain of being uprooted from Afghanistan and ending up in a foreign land, living barefoot in a home made of mud walls. I felt that loss. I felt that confusion.

That photograph is the image that represents the Pulitzer Prize for 2001 for feature photography. I was very flattered that this photograph was chosen to represent that series. I think the value of the image is that it shows, while President Bush was saying, "We'll smoke them out," that there were people who were not the Taliban, who were not Al-Qaeda, who were being affected. These photographs were a reminder that there were real people who were losing their lives and identities when they were referred to as nothing more than "collateral damage."

And that's an important part of the story. It's to remind people that there are always two sides to the story if not many more, and while you can get very gung-ho about chasing the Taliban, you have to understand that there will be unnamed victims who have nothing to do with this, who will be torn apart. The image speaks to that and reminds me that the world is not black and white.

STRIVING FOR THE BEST

The photograph of Chad Hedrick winning the Olympic gold medal in speed skating in 2006 is the antithesis of Katrina and Pakistan. The Olympics are an organized event that is highly publicized, on television, broadcast across the world. You've got 200 photographers to your left and right, trying to make an image. You are basically rolling the dice as to where and how long it's going to take the speed skater to react to his win.

If it's a short race, he's going to react immediately after he's crossed the finish line. But if it's a 1-kilometer or longer race, he is going to be exhausted and maybe fall down, because he is completely out of breath, and then rise up and celebrate once he's recovered. But you have to anticipate and hope that luck is on your side. There are no lives at stake here, but it's nevertheless important for the public to witness people striving to be their best.

The Olympic Games are about athletes dedicating their lives to breaking the world record, against the best of the best from all over the world. When you win a gold medal, you are the best at your sport at that time in history.

It's the ultimate dedication of an athlete to say, I'm going to train for four years for that one race, which lasts less than 10 seconds. And if I breathe at the wrong time, or trip for a millisecond, or someone cuts me off by mistake, my dreams are gone. So you have to respect that will to be the best, to be the fastest person alive, to be the best man or woman on the ice. One mental mistake for a split second can make him go from hero to zero, just like that. From a name in the record books forever to someone no one ever heard of.

For me, great photographers demand that level of commitment. Like most arts, photography is a craft. It needs to be practiced. Before you can skate at the Olympics, you have to learn the basics of how to skate on ice straight, how to brake, how to turn. In photography, you have to learn the basics of what aperture is, what shutter speed is, what exposure is, and what each and every different lens does. You have to respect the technique before you can accomplish what you are aiming for.

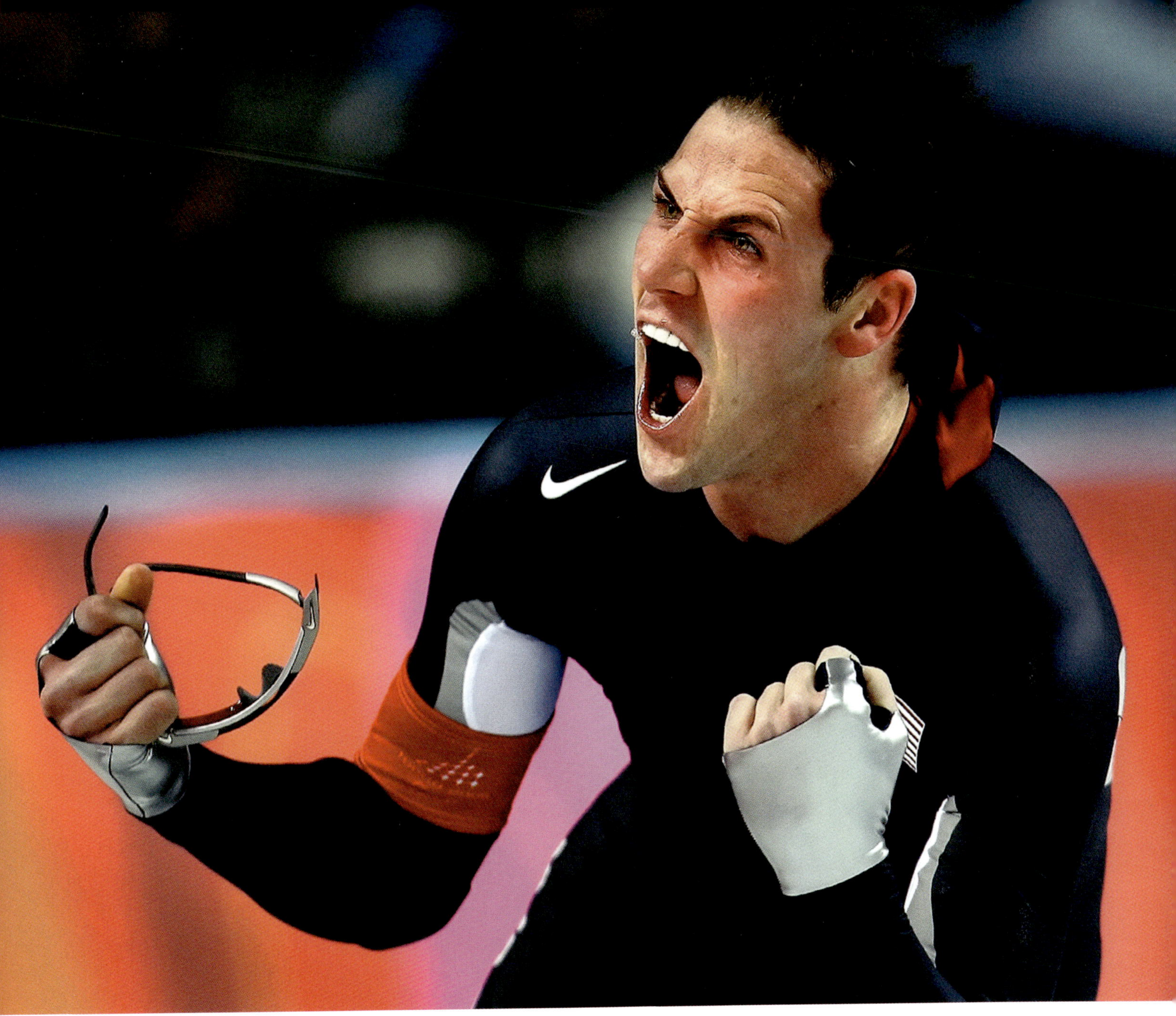

Chad Hedrick wins the gold medal in speed skating in the 2006 Winter Olympics.

ISO 1000 f/3.2 1/800 400mm

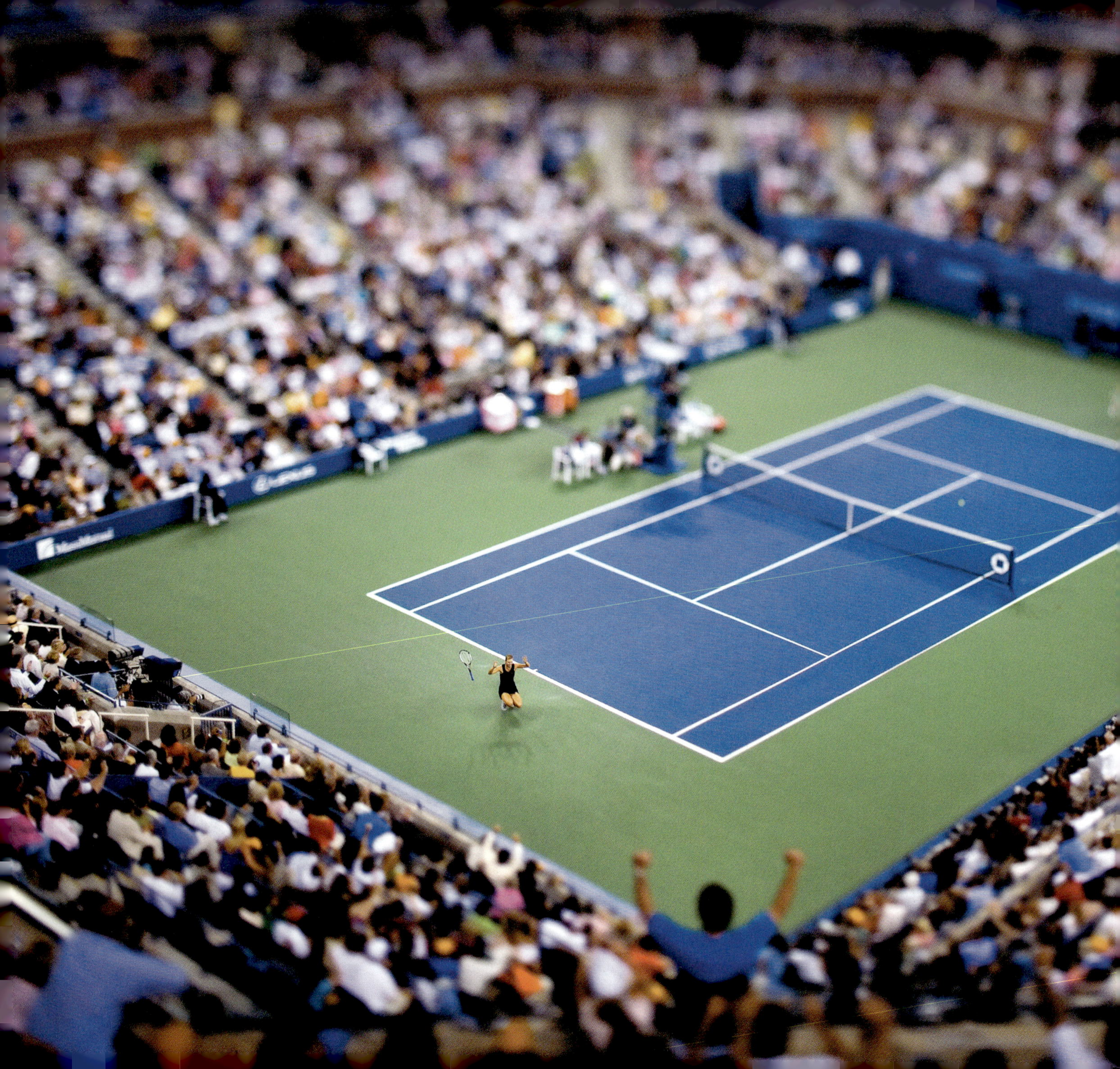

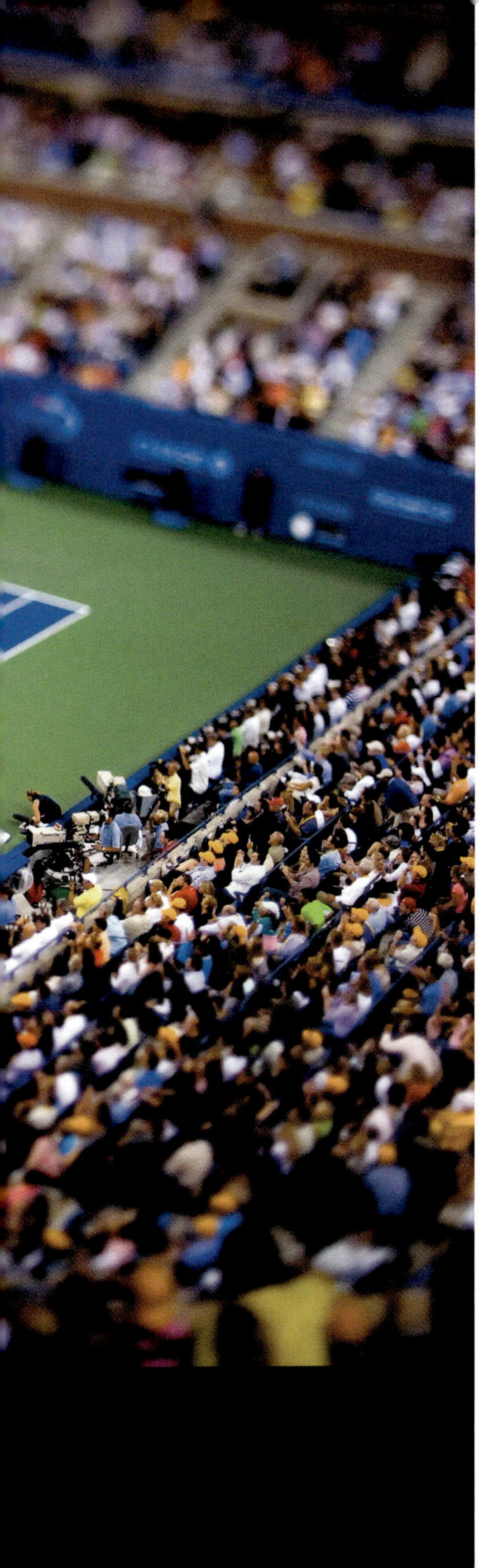

CHAPTER 2

A STORY IN A SINGLE IMAGE

When I was 18 years old, in my first year of college, I managed to get an appointment at the offices of *Newsday*.

With a combination of persistence and naïveté, I charmed the secretary of the assistant editor of photography. She was a notoriously cool gatekeeper and no one could get past her, but somehow I did.

I walked into the offices of a man named Kenneth Irby prepared to show him my work. Even before he opened my book, he looked at me and said, "How did you get in here?"

◀ Maria Sharapova defeats Justine Henin 6-4, 6-4 to win the U.S. Open women's finals match in Arthur Ashe Stadium on September 9, 2006.

ISO 320 f/2.8 1/500 45mm

You are ultimately trying to get an idea or an emotion or the story itself out, all the while trying to balance that with the aesthetic of the photo.

It hadn't been easy; to keep the appointment, I had to convince a friend to drive me from Long Island to Manhattan through a tremendous snowstorm.

I sat there as he looked through my portfolio, which at the time included images of sunsets and my sister. They were pretty pictures, and I had worked for hours in the lab crafting the best fine-art prints I was capable of making.

"I don't know how you managed to get in here," he said, closing my portfolio. "You're no photojournalist. This is not the type of work we do at this newspaper or any newspaper, for that matter."

It was not what I expected to hear.

"You know what, kid, you might have some promise, but get out of here," he said, but then added, "If you are really serious about this, send me some clips in a month. Maybe we'll talk again."

I was sent flying out of his office, feeling angry and destroyed. And now I was left to ride back home through a snowstorm.

I was still angry three months later when I sent Kenneth Irby some clips from my work at Northwestern University's college newspaper. I think I stuffed a foot's worth of prints and clippings into an envelope with a little note, which might not have been as friendly as it should have been.

He wrote me back and we met. My persistence paid off and he became one of my most important mentors.

It also marked the beginning of my understanding of the role of story in photographs.

The garden behind 1 Sutton Place South, atop FDR Drive, between East 56th and 57th Streets in New York City.

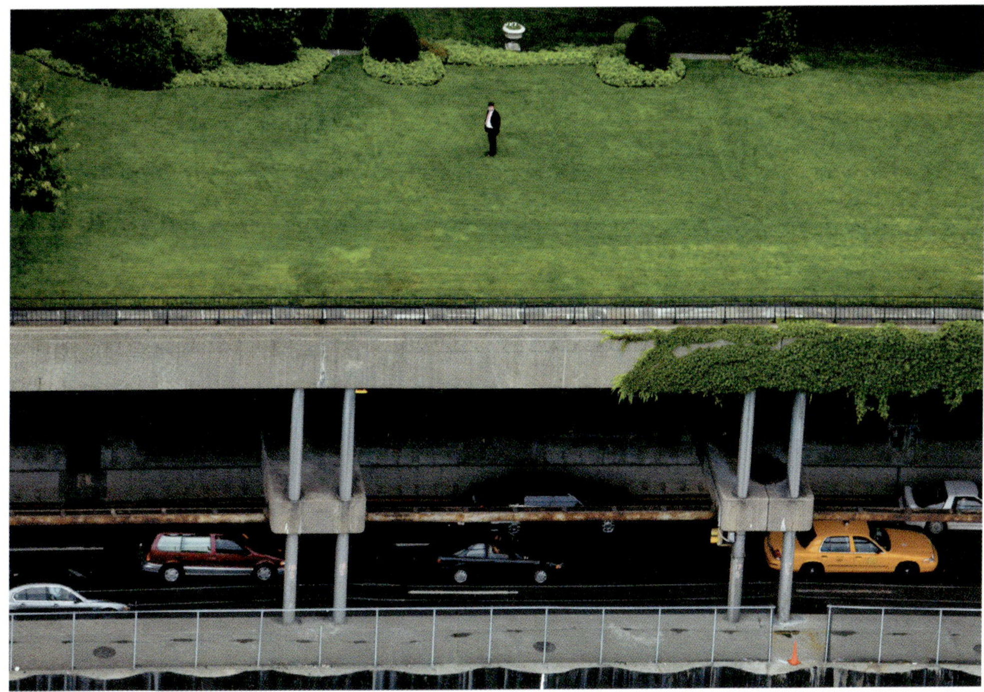

ISO 400 f/5.6 1/1000 70-200mm

THE IMPORTANCE OF STORY

As a photographer, whether a photojournalist or a wedding photographer, your goal is to tell the story of the moment, sometimes the entire event in just one image. It's that one image that a newspaper or magazine is going to use to open the section that communicates what the article is about. It's the ultimate challenge for a photographer.

The ability to tell a story applies to almost everything, whether it's for a newspaper, a commercial job, or a journal, or if you are taking photos of your own family. Even if you're a portrait photographer, story helps to set up everything and touches everything you do.

You are ultimately trying to get an idea or an emotion or the story itself out, all the while trying to balance that with the aesthetic of the photo.

It was explained to me, and I saw it reflected in the photographs that got published at the newspaper: the images that were able to take that 600-, 800-, or 900-word article and visualize it found a home on the page.

The challenge was that you couldn't just veer off and go astray and photograph random stuff. What you took had to be relevant to the event. It comes from the cold fact that there is a limited amount of space on the page, and the photograph either serves the story or it doesn't.

When you are making photographs, the reality is that there are hundreds of images out there. So which is the one image that really captures the essence of the event that day? Which shot expresses the mood, the feeling, and the significance of the moment?

"What's the news value?" is the question you have to ask yourself. What makes this relevant? What makes this worthy of being spoken about or written about, let alone published as a photograph in newspapers around the world? And you have to be mentally on your toes to know that. You can't just passively float through and take random pictures and hope to capture those moments.

That's a real challenge, because it doesn't happen randomly. You've got to be connected emotionally and intellectually to what you are covering. And you need a tremendous sense of perspective. The reality is that usually while an event is happening, most people don't know what the relevance of it is until they've had the opportunity to digest it, but by then it's over.

Aerial photograph of the 2004 New York City Marathon.

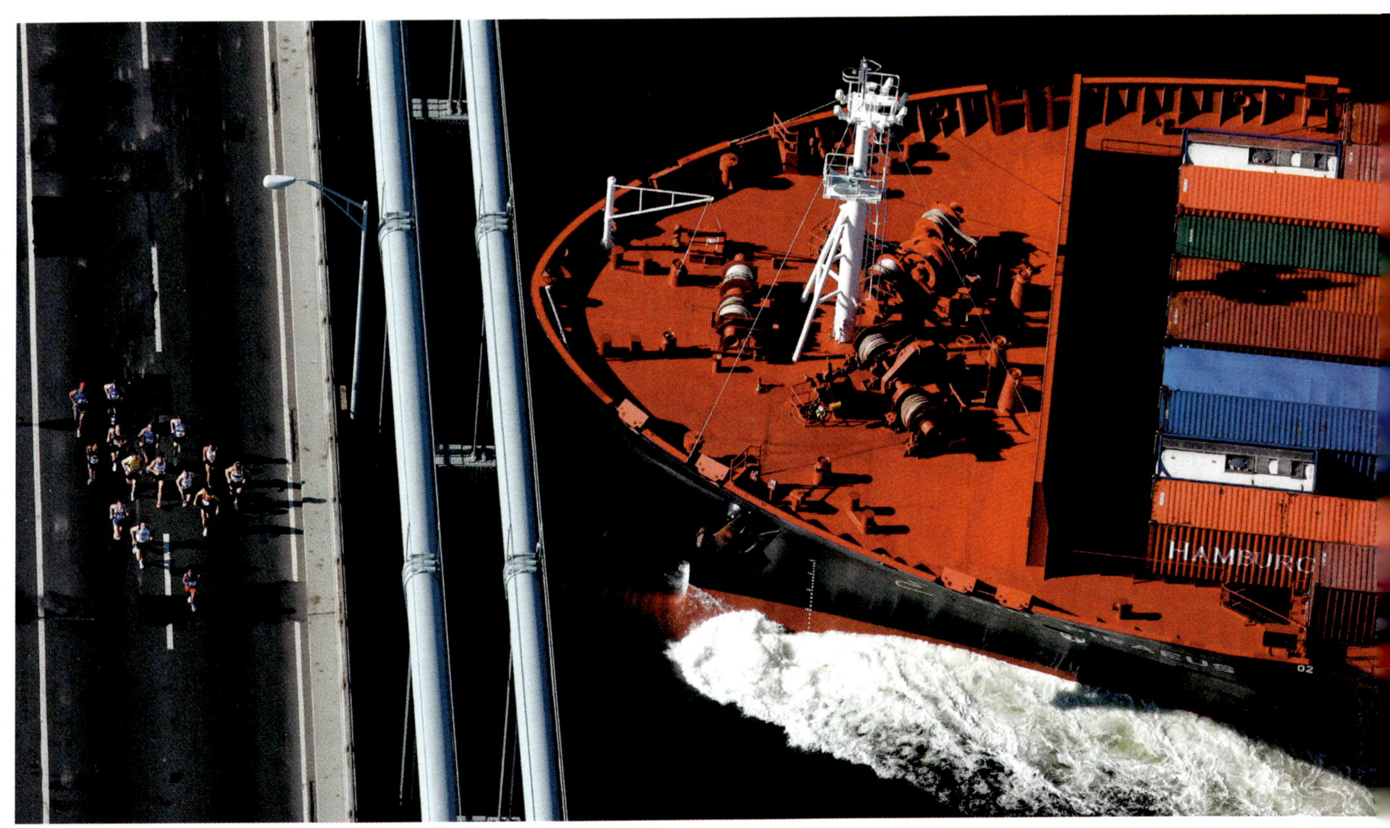

ISO 400 f/6.3 1/2000 250mm

4-year-old Clara Anisha Brown grasped onto volunteer Chad Meaux as they made their way through the flooded streets of New Orleans after she and her family were rescued from St. Bernard, Louisiana, after 3 days without food and water (August, 2005).

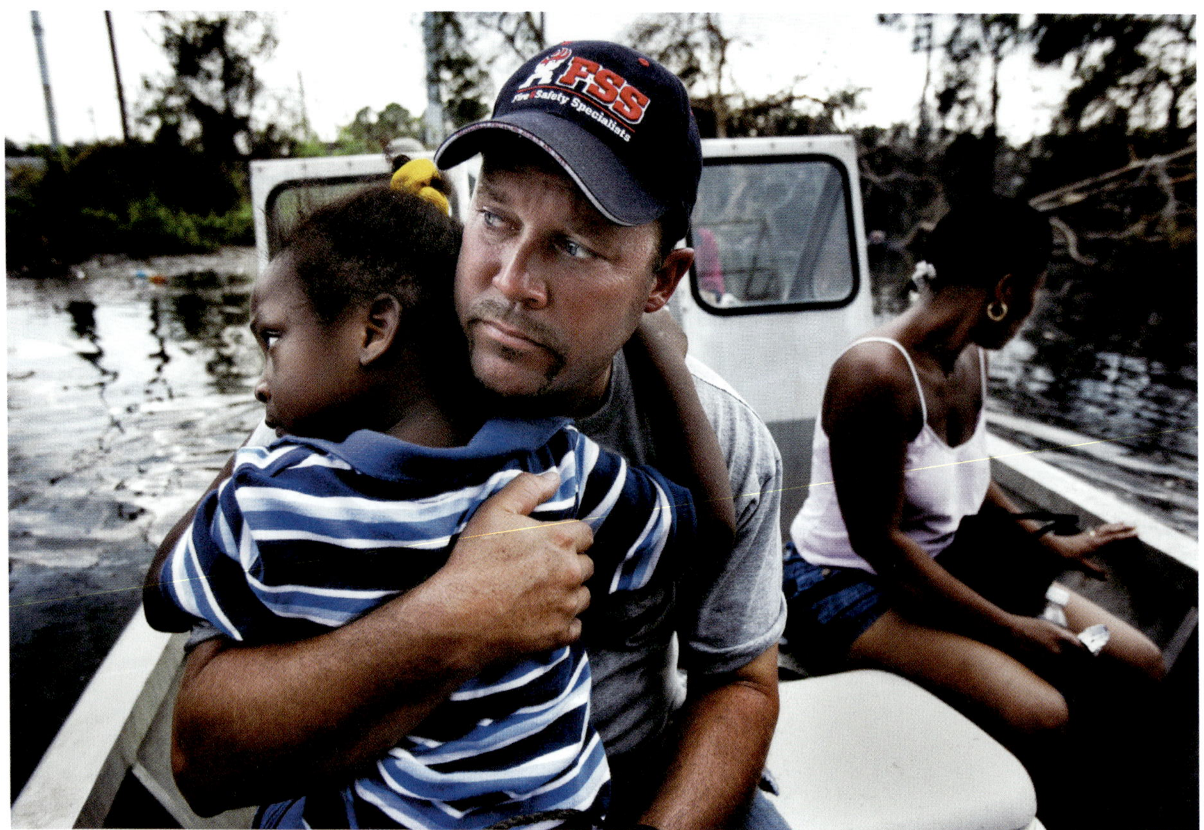

ISO 400 f/4.5 1/250 24mm

The reality is that usually while an event is happening, most people don't know what the relevance of it is until they've had the opportunity to digest it, but by then it's over.

As the photographer, you are live on the scene, and it's very difficult to anticipate what this is going to mean ten years from now or even on a simpler level, in tomorrow's newspaper.

The photograph on the facing page of a volunteer helping rescue a mother and daughter during Katrina helps to illustrate a side of the story of how the disaster helped people overcome, if just for a short period, issues of race.

New Orleans and Louisiana have always been places that have had issues with racism. There has never been a secret about that. If you have ever flown over New Orleans, it's not uncommon to see the Confederate flag on people's roofs. And you hear it in the words people say from both sides.

But here you have this little black girl clinging to this white man in a flooded New Orleans. What you don't see in that shot is that below the waterline are the roofs of this community. This family's neighborhood, their world, no longer existed. The photograph succeeds in telling an important part of the story of this disaster and the people's whose lives were changed by it in dramatic and unexpected ways.

There's a reason why they say that an image is worth a thousand words. It's actually worth a lot more.

Maria Sharapova defeats Justine Henin 6-4, 6-4 to win the U.S. Open women's finals match in Arthur Ashe Stadium on September 9, 2006.

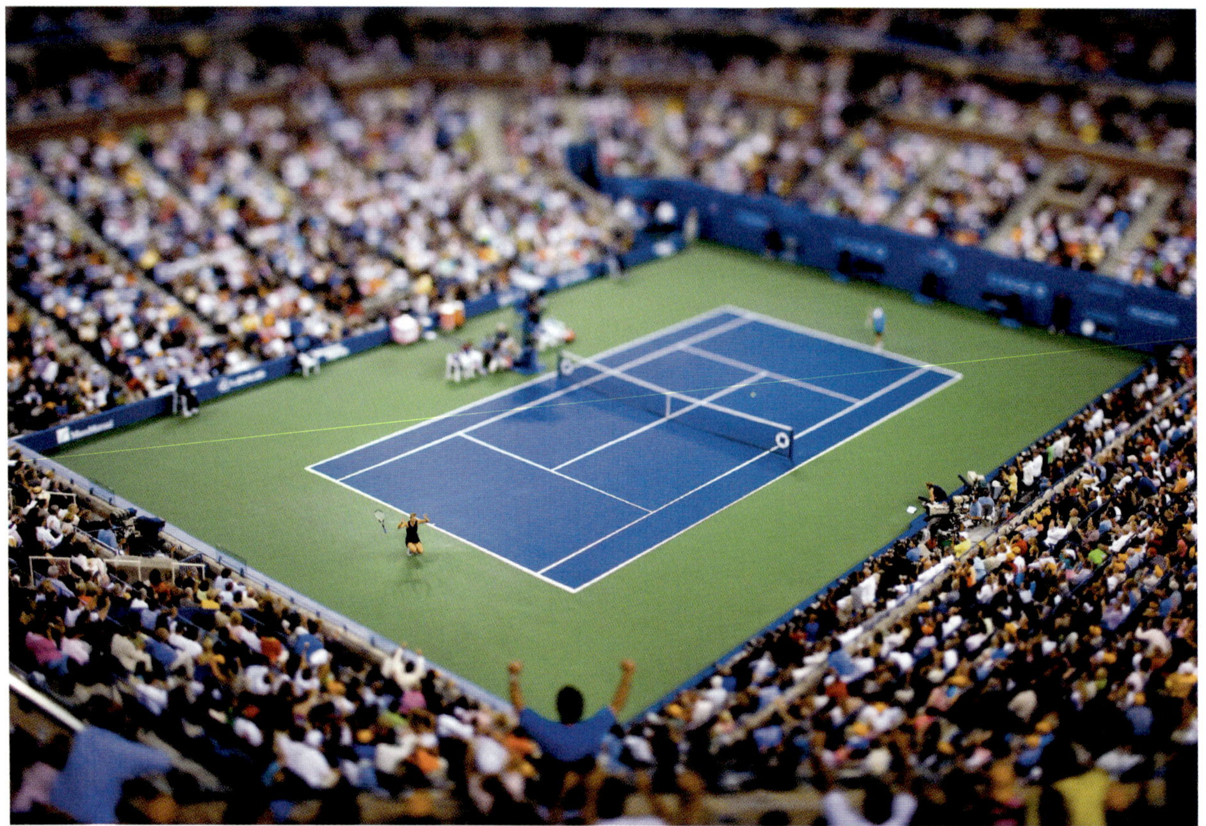

ISO 320 f/2.8 1/500 45mm

STORY WITH CONTEXT

One of the first things I ever photographed in my teens was the U.S. Open. I found an entrance to sneak into the main court at the time, and I would photograph from the cheap seats. I would stare down at the newspaper photographers and dream of being down there with them.

A decade later, in 2006, I found myself in those very seats, on the ground level, surrounded by the best in sports photography. From that level, it's great to capture a very tight moment that shows the incredible emotion of a historic win. While that's an important image to capture, such a photograph can start to look like thousands of other images. Sometimes it's better to see the overall picture.

To achieve this image of Maria Sharapova, I positioned myself at the top level of the stadium where I had shot from as a teenager, and showed the view from the perspective of the spectator.

I was using a 45mm tilt-shift lens, which allowed me to produce something aesthetically different. It shows Sharapova in focus and her opponent, Justine Henin, out of focus. The image tells the story of her victory from the context of the thousands of people who had witnessed the moment. This perspective gives you an appreciation for the scale of the event that you don't necessarily get with a long telephoto lens, where the background is completely blurred out.

This image was a gamble because there was no telling where and when the match was going to end. And predicting which direction she would look when she did win was a combination of experience and luck. I had to make a very big bet that she would turn around and look at the box where her family was sitting. Had she been on the other side of the court, there would be no image with that lens.

On a mental level you are conscious of what the chances are that she'll be on the wrong side of the court, but also how she's going to react and where she's going to point to. And the fact is that you have only one chance to get it. There will be no repeats here. And if you don't get it, no one cares if your battery died or your camera wasn't formatted correctly, or you were soft or out of focus. It's irrelevant.

The other risk I took was with respect to focusing. I was focusing manually, and if you look closely, the top of the racket and the sneakers are out of focus. So you can appreciate how razor-sharp you have to be on the focus during a live and evolving moment.

Despite those challenges, the photograph conveys the story of how Sharapova at this particular moment is at the center of the world, especially at the center of the tennis world, and that Henin is completely irrelevant and out of focus. The front page goes to the winner. The one who loses either never makes the paper or gets buried in history.

STORY OF A MOMENT

This image of a gymnast on the vault is another way to tell the story of sports—in this case, during the 2008 Summer Olympics in Beijing, China.

The practical reality is that there were dozens of cameras in this venue, and the backgrounds I had to choose from were terribly distracting. But after some searching, I finally found one spot, one into which I could barely fit myself to get a decent angle to shoot the event with a 300mm lens wide open at f/2.8.

I chose this angle because the background contained the Olympic colors. It's completely out of focus, but there are no distracting lines. Most important, there are no television cameras in the background, which was the real distraction.

Unlike Sharapova at the U.S. Open, this athlete was not the darling of the Olympics. Few in the crowds knew his name, especially because they were mostly Chinese and there to support their own team. So the choice to photograph the moment tight, without the faces of the crowds, was an editorial as well as an aesthetic decision.

This photograph becomes the story of an individual's pursuit. It's him against the world. It is all about that athlete and his performance. You have enough information to let you know that this is the Olympics, but the moment is all about him. Some events are about individual pursuits, whereas others are more symbolic of what they mean to the country. Those are the kinds of decisions you have to make.

Alexander Artemev of the USA team competes during the Men's individual all-around final at the National Indoor Stadium during the 2008 Olympics.

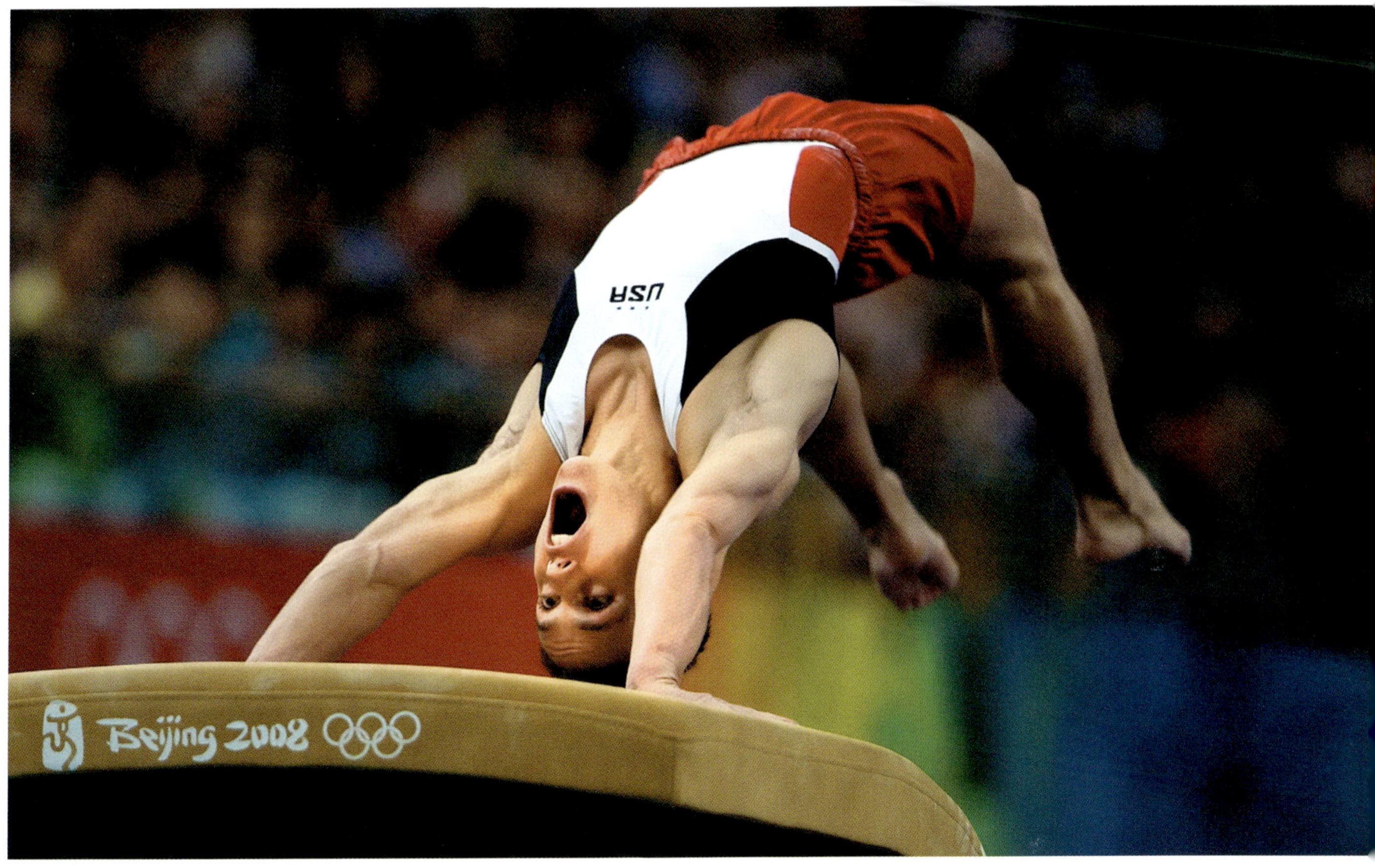

ISO 1250 f/2.8 1/1250 300mm

Department of Transportation bridge painters threw up a wrench to Cesar Pazmino as they rose the flag from half-staff to full-staff on the Brooklyn tower of the Brooklyn Bridge following the 9/11 memorial (April 2002).

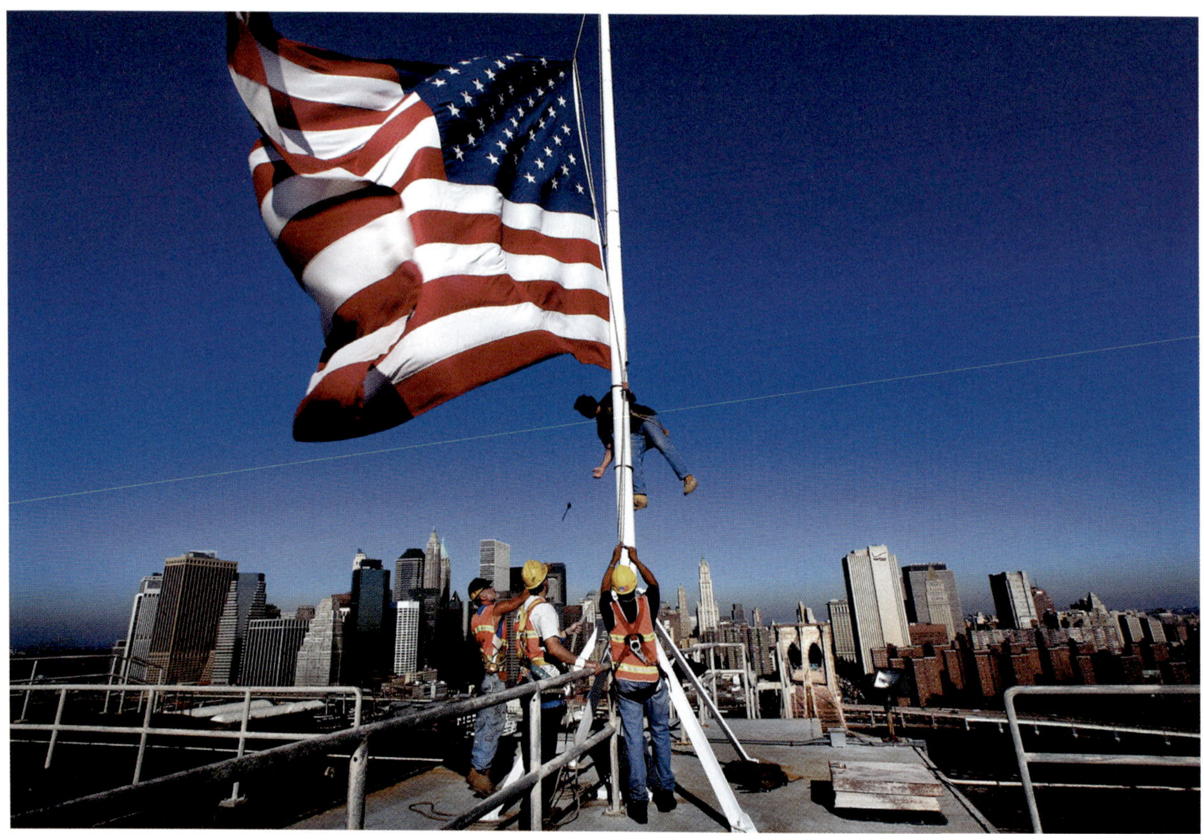

ISO 200 f/18 1/250 14mm

SYMBOLISM AS STORY

Nine months after the 9/11 attacks I was on top of the Brooklyn Bridge, witnessing the flag being raised from half-mast back to full-mast as a sign saying, "Hey, we're back," or at least we're no longer in mourning. We were still mourning, but at least we were moving back toward a normal life.

The reason I chose the wide-angle lens was a practical one. It's a very small physical area on top of the Brooklyn Bridge on the stanchion. You can't back up or you'll fall right off. So you can't use a telephoto lens.

If you made that same shot tighter, you would lose the top of the flag and the skyline of the city. It's not an image about a guy catching a wrench. It's really irrelevant, but it's the element that helps make the moment decisive. It's not about the guys beneath him. There is no context to that. It's not just about a flag. But if you conjoin all these elements—the flag, the men helping him, and the skyline with that one little wrench being thrown up—you have a story that speaks to what happened that day. It becomes a symbol of a city restoring itself.

And though the wrench is not the story, it's the telling gesture, the decisive moment that helps complete the image, because without it there would be something missing.

I remember feeling frustrated making this picture, because the scene itself wasn't particularly dynamic. I chose a shutter speed, which was 1/250 second. 1/125 tends to blur, and 1/500 tends to freeze movement, but at 1/250, the edge of the flag has a little bit of movement to it.

And then you are just waiting, and you have a sense that this is downtown Manhattan at the lower left of the image and the now-empty skyline where the towers once stood. The flag is dead center, and that wrench solidifies this historical moment of New York's history.

What separates a good image from a masterpiece is often found in the details. One inch to the left or to the right can differentiate a great image from a terrible image. The gesture here solidifies it. It's also important that the flag stands above all, and that it appears to be larger than the human being. There is some intrinsic symbolism of the flag representing America, and here it is flying over the city and in many ways carrying it up.

INCLUSION AND EXCLUSION

When you are in the midst of a news story and you are seeing all hell break loose, or you are in a protest surrounded by hundreds of people, you have to exclude everything that is irrelevant to what you think the story is, because if you are busy photographing ancillary stuff or irrelevant stuff, you miss what's important. You almost have to have blinders on to stay focused.

You have to stay focused on what that target is at all times, and it is constantly evolving during a breaking news story. And you have to constantly ask yourself, Am I photographing what's important? Am I at the right place? Am I focusing on the right thing? Am I interpreting this correctly? The challenge becomes finding your target. Just because you know what you need to show, it doesn't mean you can get there or that it will happen. It may have happened 5 minutes ago and you missed it.

You might think the story is clear in this image of the effigy being burned in Pakistan, but if you look carefully, you'll see the man in the center is smiling. This event happened after Friday prayers, where someone decided to put a Yankees T-shirt on an effigy and the crowds decided to play for the cameras.

If you take a careful look at that image, the symbolism of what they are doing is unmistakable, but if you look at a lot of these guys' faces, they are having fun. These are not passionate, rabid, crazy people. Choosing to include those smiling faces helps to tell a part of the story. Excluding it transforms the image into something completely different.

Two weeks after 9/11 I am at a rally surrounded by a mullah's security detail. They are definitely not my friends. The mullah is speaking into a microphone and repeatedly shouting, "Kill America. Kill Bush." And tens of thousands of people are repeating the words after him. And here I am making images literally at his feet, visible to all those people.

I am staring directly at his security detail. This image on page 33 reflects a 30- or 40-second exchange. He didn't flinch. I didn't flinch. This wasn't an ego battle. I wasn't there to confront the man. I wasn't looking to make a point. I was there to try to capture this kind of look. I was a journalist and relatively safe, but under any other context if someone were to look at me like that, there wouldn't be any doubt that this man was possessed by tremendous hatred for who I was and what I represented.

Self-proclaimed supporters of Osama bin Laden burned an effigy of President Bush as thousands gathered in the streets of Peshawar following morning prayers at the Qasim Ali Khan Mosque (September 2001).

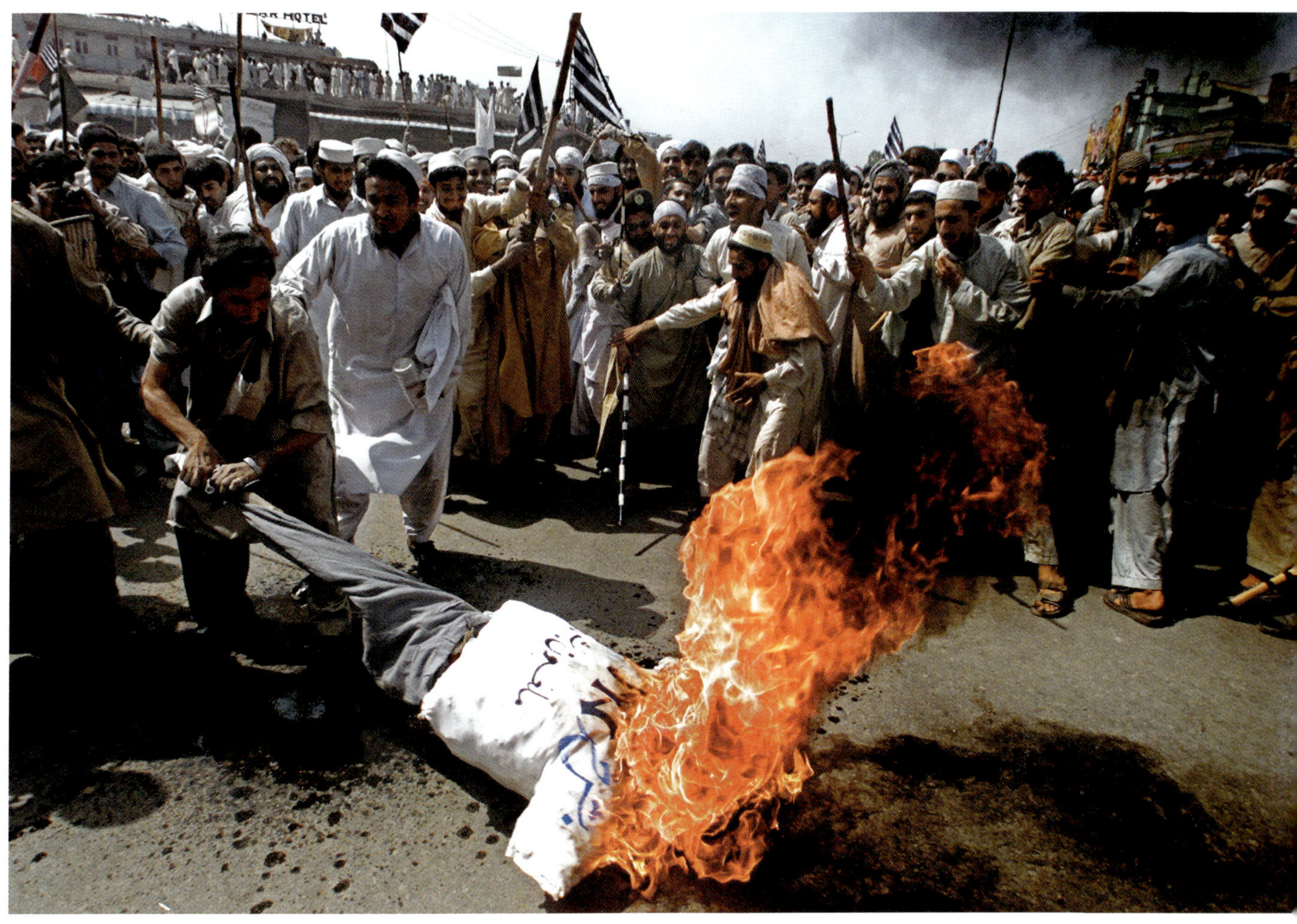

You have to stay focused on what that target is at all times, and it is constantly evolving during a breaking news story. And you have to constantly ask yourself, Am I photographing what's important? Am I at the right place? Am I focusing on the right thing?

What I read in his eyes was, "You are not welcome here, and if this were any other circumstances I would cut your throat. You are not our friends. We are at war." And that is the storytelling element of this image, because in the photograph this man is looking at the viewer.

If this were created vertically as a portrait, the same image would have lost its context. This is not a portrait. This is not meant to go on the *National Geographic* cover. I shot this with a 24mm lens, and I purposely included the two guys right behind him. The story of this image, which was important to express, was that he wasn't alone. He had people around him, men who were of the same spirit.

Although there's an intrinsic beauty to this man's face, there is no doubt that he is a warrior. He is a disciplined, serious guy. At a basic level, this man has one goal in life: he's on the security detail to protect the mullah and anyone who's a threat to him. However, on another level you could reasonably assume, given what the mullah was preaching, that he was part of an effort to kill the enemies of Islam. I represented that, and the readers of this newspaper, looking at this image, could definitely feel that.

Guard to one of the local clerics join a crowd of more than 15,000 pro-Taliban supporters as they listen to speeches given by religious leaders during an anti-American rally (September 2001).

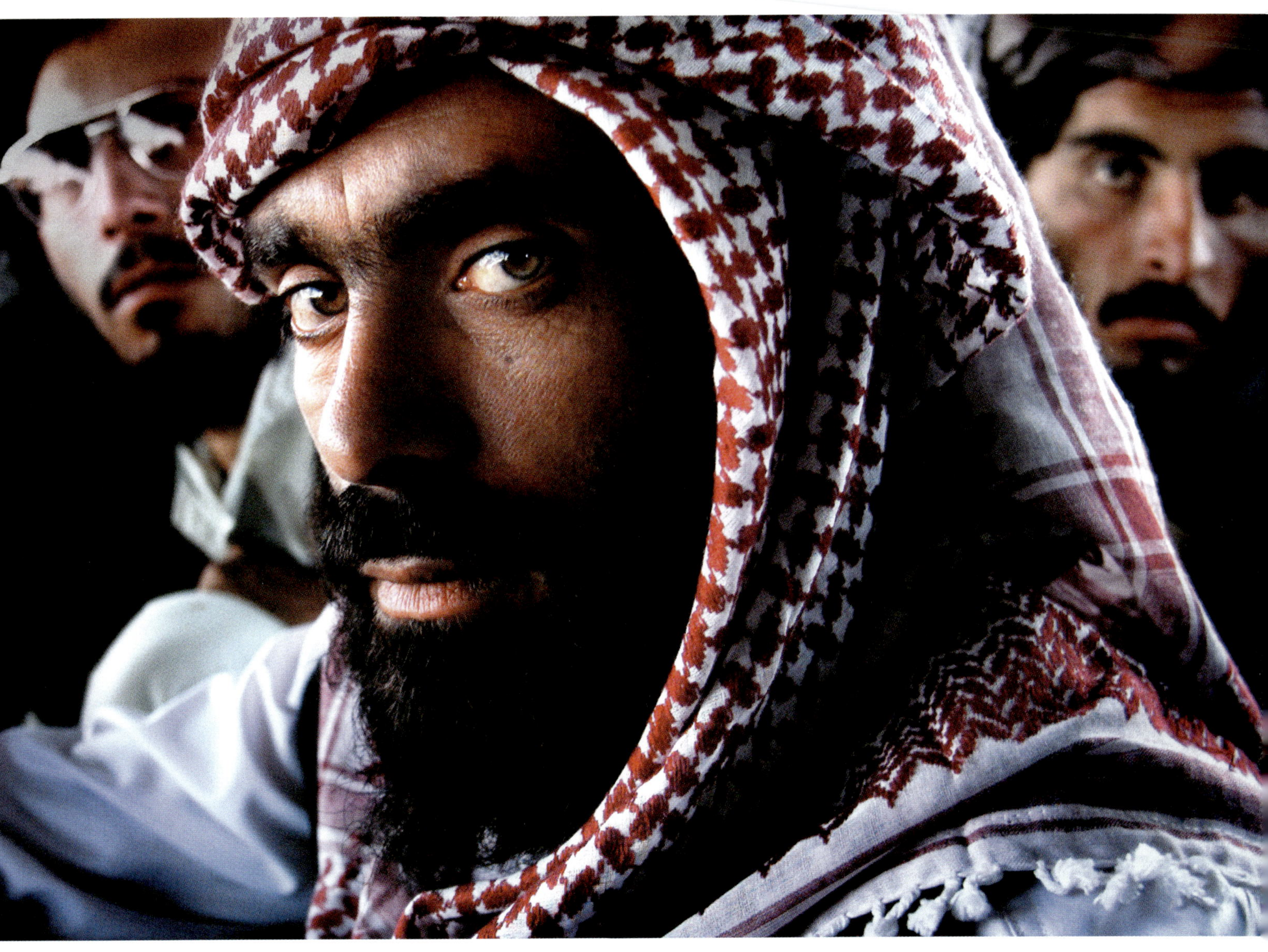

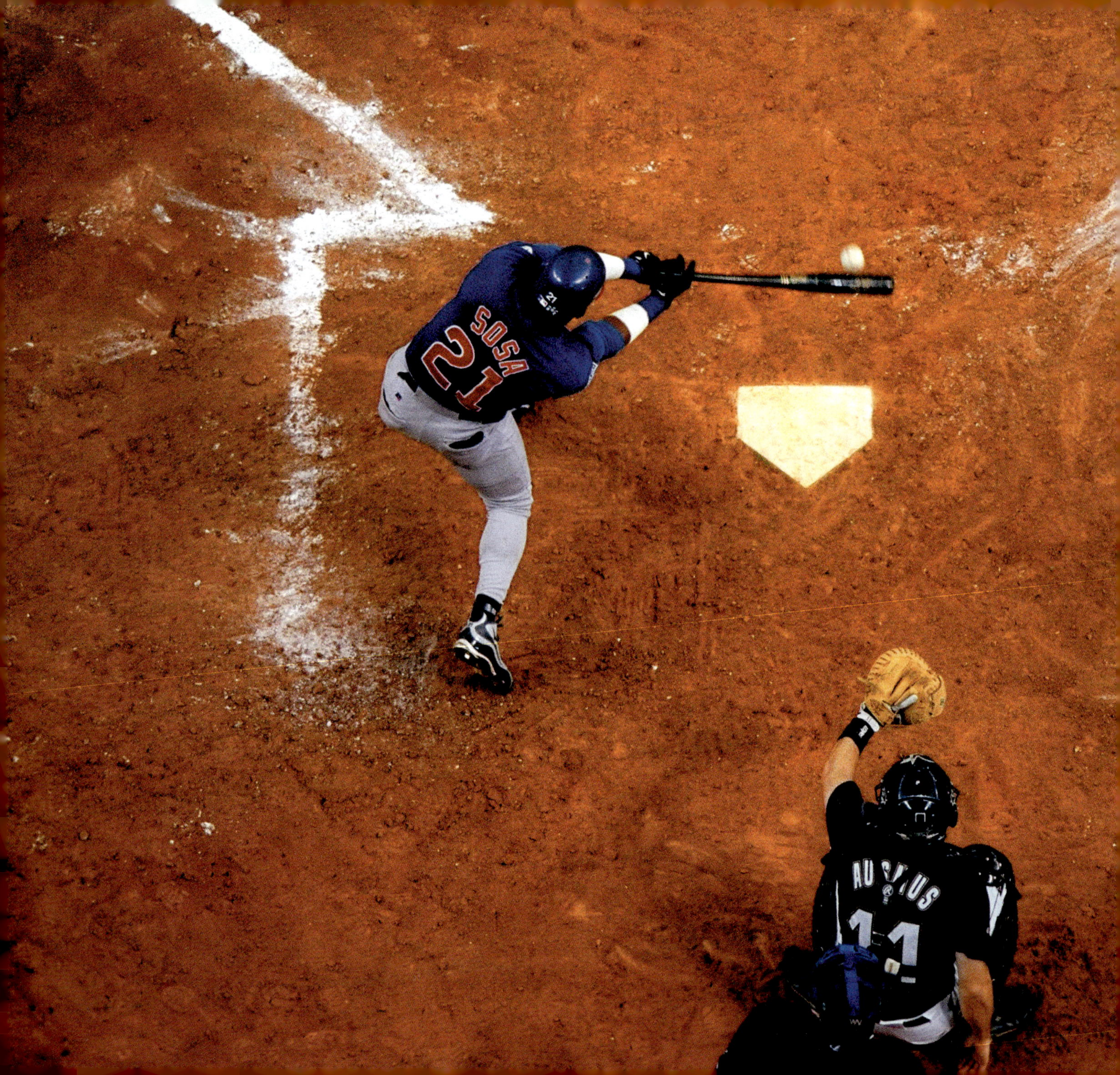
SOSA
21

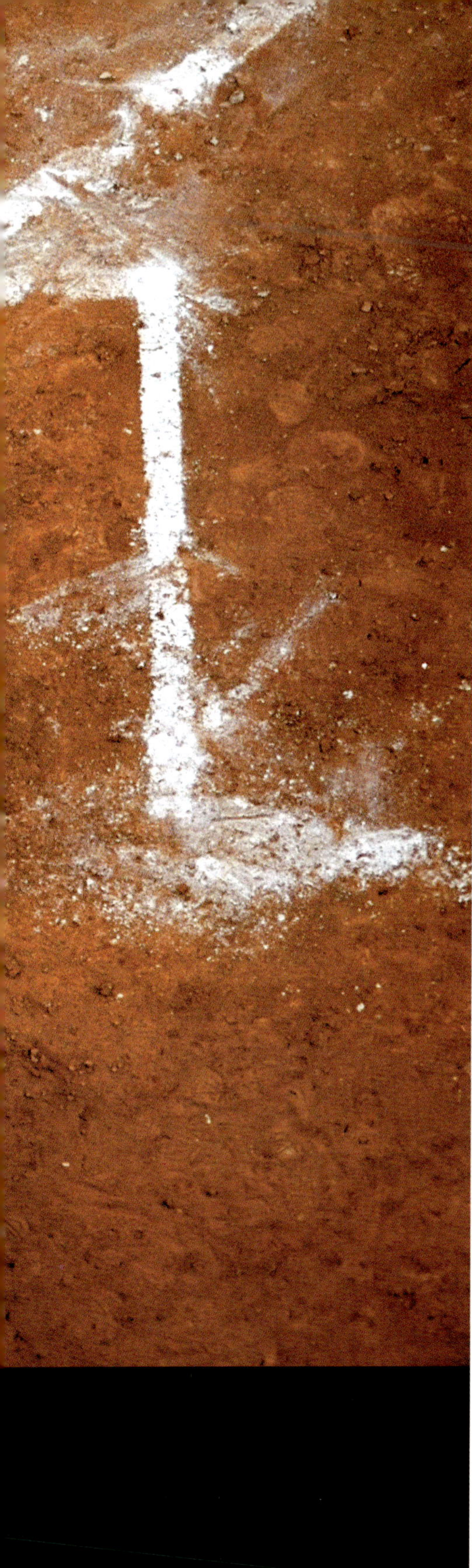

CHAPTER 3

MARRYING THE STORY WITH THE AESTHETIC

There were a lot of things happening in 1998, but during the summer of that year, it was all about baseball and the home run competition between Sammy Sosa and Mark McGwire. Along with dozens of other photographers, I was at the Houston Astrodome in anticipation of Sosa hitting his 66th single-season home run.

And though the event promised to be historic, the venue was horrible.

◀ Right fielder Sammy Sosa of the Chicago Cubs swings at a pitch during a game against the Houston Astros at the Astrodome in Houston, Texas (1998).

f/28 1/800 400mm

Photographers were relegated to two wells, our only options for photographing home plate. Our creative choices were thus limited to shooting either tighter or looser. And the background offered nothing but two big television cameras hulking behind Sosa. I was stuck.

I had photographed in venues across the country, and this was by far the ugliest stadium, from the ground perspective, that I had seen. This was one of the first domes in baseball. Fluorescents, which didn't help the aesthetics, illuminated the field. So it was easy to justify the potentially bad results by thinking I had 65 other home run pictures that were just beautiful. This photograph was destined to be a total dud.

But then I looked up and saw there were catwalks just above home plate, so I started to negotiate access to it. I did so by striking a deal with the photographers from the *Chicago Tribune* and the *Houston Chronicle* to replace a roll of film in each of their remote cameras on the catwalk.

This decision to shoot from the catwalk rose not from my desire to want to make an overhead shot, but rather from my refusal to make terrible pictures.

This photograph for me is not just about the historic moment, but also about careful composition and geometry. Perspective lines lead almost perfectly out of the corners of the image directly into the batting zone. The home plate repeats those patterns. And there's a right angle formed by the batter. It's a very geometrical image.

The fact that Sosa's arm is positioned almost perfectly parallel to that rectangle helps create a sense of balance. You also have this pristine uniform and all this mess of chalk and dirt. And of course, the pinnacle of it is that the only circular element is the big white ball. The perfect combination of ball and bat meet over home plate, and becomes Sammy Sosa's historic 66th home run.

The action and the name and number on the back of Sosa's uniform tell the story, but it's also a beautiful photograph. This is how I would paint it if I could.

This was a very big turning point in my career, where I stopped following the press pool and accepting where I was going to shoot from and making the best of it. The image was going to be terrible.

Instead I looked to create my own solution, to make a better image.

An aerial view of the wasteland that used to be Owens Lake, California (August 2007).

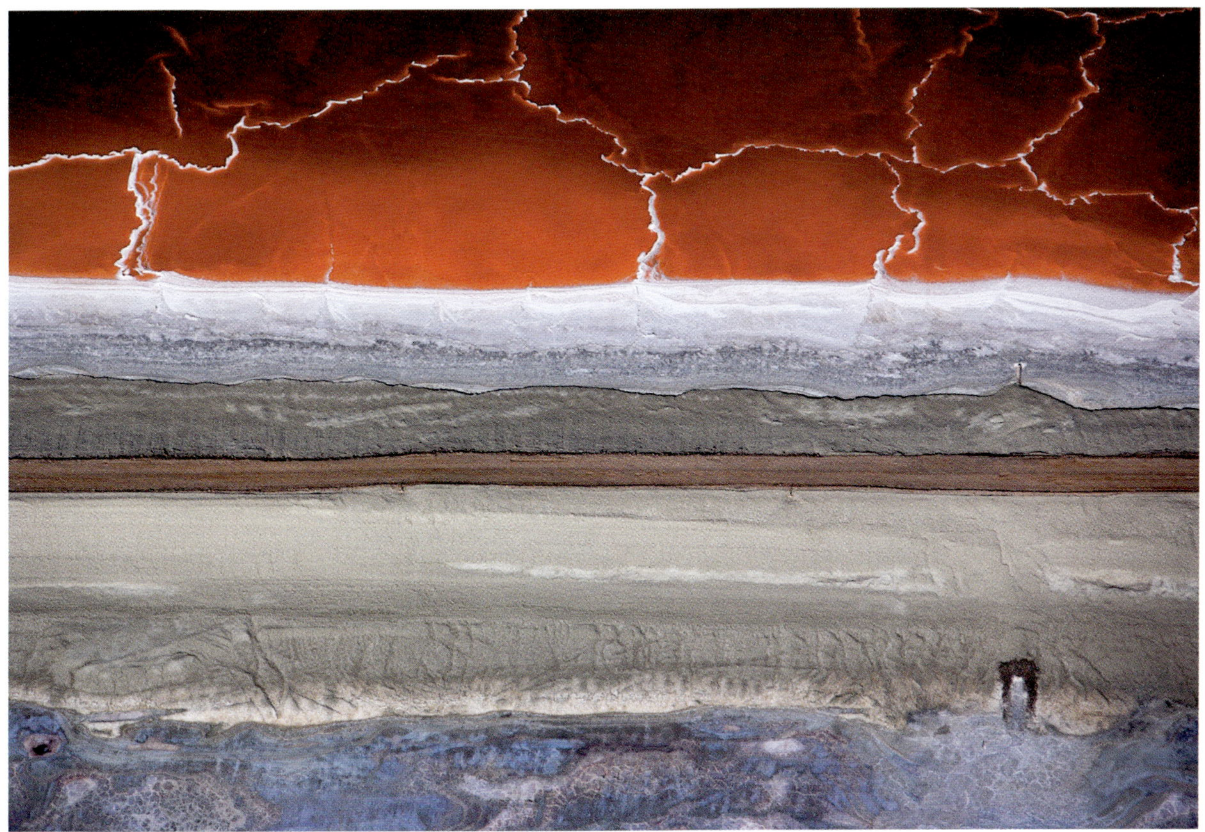

ISO 100 f/5.6 1/600 200mm

Underwater at the Women's 10m synchronized diving competition (2008).

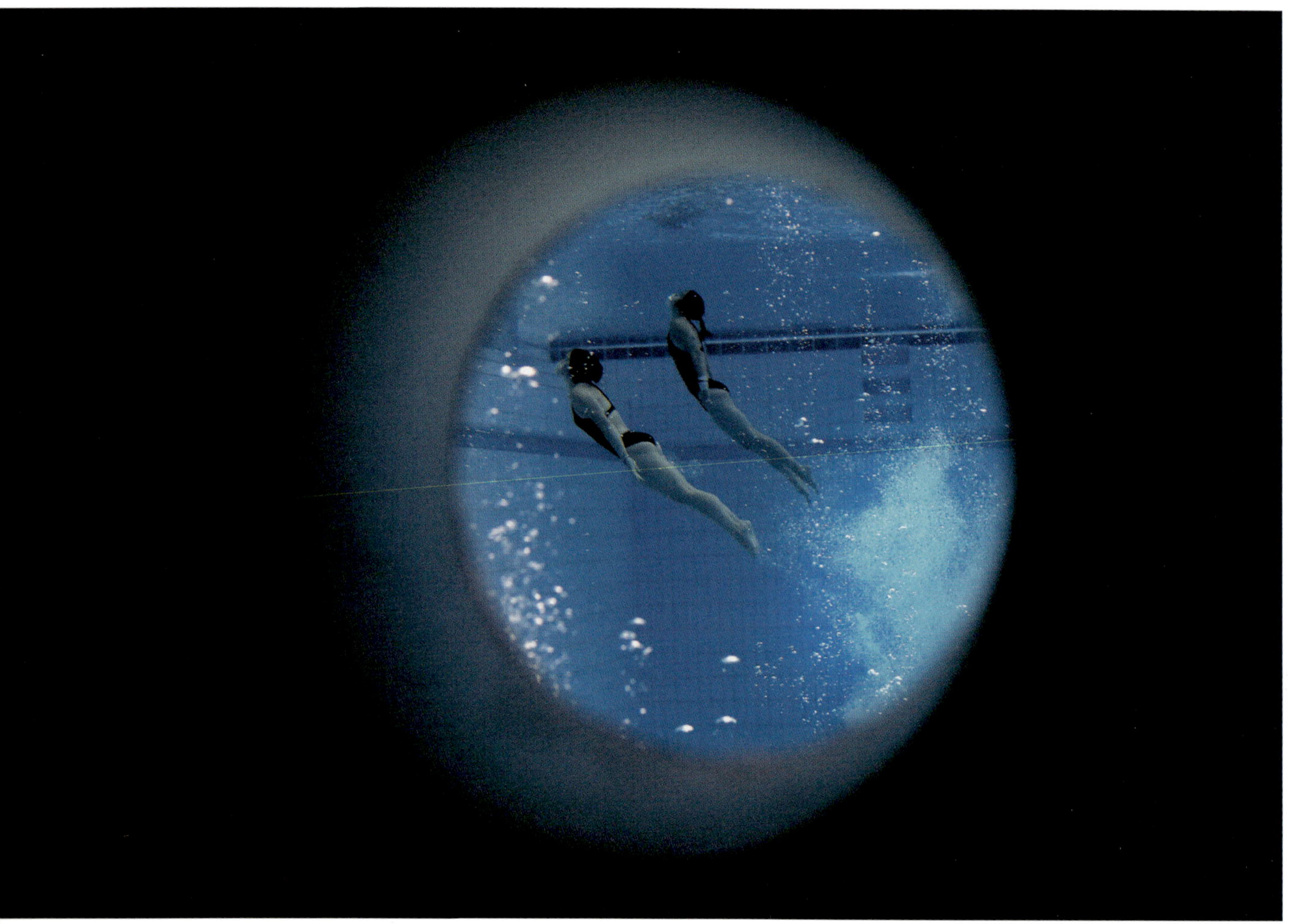

ISO 500 f/2 1/1600 50mm

The way to make great photographs demands more than just aiming for the best.

THE REAL SECRETS

I developed my skills as a photographer shooting sports, but when you are shooting at the professional level, the reality is you are in competition with hundreds of the world's best sports shooters, all of whom are jockeying for position and trying to outperform one another. They are creating amazing images as well as playing a high mental game, a game that you can't possibly win.

The secret is to stop competing with them; you can't win playing their game. You've got to play your own game, but it's not an easy thing to do.

The newspaper just wants the picture that tells the story, and it's something you can often deliver if you play it safe.

For a while I did just that and the paper was happy. They were in hog heaven, because most of the images going into the paper were being shot by their staff photographers. These weren't photographs taken by a competitor or the wire service. They were mine.

But I found myself not feeling happy with those photographs. I didn't want to look at them again. It just wasn't enough to me that I'd gotten an image and it had run in the paper. So what? There were hundreds of other photographers shooting the same event, and they all had similar versions of what I had captured.

So the challenge for me was to tell the story but also to look at the frame as if it were a painting, to look at each photograph as if it were something that could be framed and displayed at a museum.

If I have any secrets, it is that the way to make great photographs demands more than just aiming for the best. It's actually about being able to say no to all the mediocre or good pictures that are out there. It's the ability to persist in the pursuit of the best photograph. That is the real secret.

From the air, you appreciate your world in a very, very different way, and you have a very different relationship to your three-dimensional environment.

A PROUD MOMENT

Though I'm often recognized for the many aerial images that I made while at the *New York Times,* I have to say that the paper never had the resources to send me up on a helicopter to take pretty images.

I generally had what I called my laundry list—I had to shoot stadiums, I had to shoot for real estate assignments, you name it, but I always tried to shave off 10, 15 minutes at the end of the one-hour flight and find an image that might just make it into the Metro section or, best, onto the front page. One such time, as we were flying back from an hour-long flight in a helicopter, I asked the pilot to take a quick detour through Central Park on the way to West 30th Street to the heliport where we landed. That's when I saw the skating rink.

What I first saw were shadows of people. From the air, you appreciate your world in a very, very different way, and you have a different relationship to your three-dimensional environment. I remember seeing these shadows kind of swimming around, and we were turning around in circles seemingly forever, for a good two to three minutes, waiting for that one moment. It happened when that one skater did a pirouette and just kind of solidified the image.

This photograph wasn't associated with any particular story or historic event, but it's one of the images I'm most proud of from when I worked at the *New York Times.* Photo editor Karen Getinkaya and I convinced them to put it on the front page.

The *New York Times's* front page is the most expensive real estate in the news business, and they generally only put newsworthy images there. There is no news value whatsoever in this image. It's just a photograph documenting everyday life, but it's a very beautiful graphic image, and it showed up huge on the front page. I was proud of it because it made the *New York Times* respect the value of an image even when the emphasis was on aesthetics rather than just news value.

Skaters at the Lasker Rink in Central Park are dwarfed by their shadows in this aerial view taken February 22, 2004.

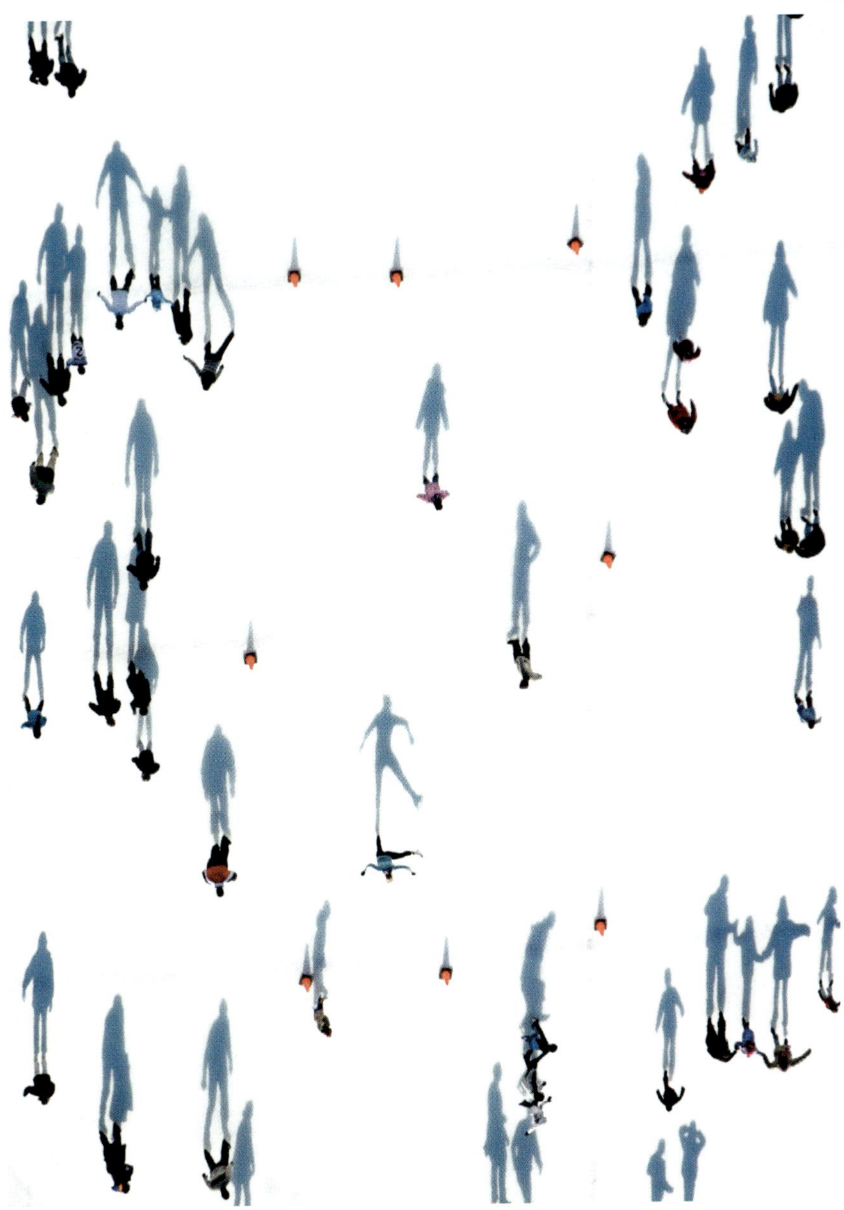

ISO 400 f/4 1/1000 70-200mm

Three cowboys share drinks and conversations by a fire at the end of the day's work in Waimea on the Big Island of Hawaii for an essay on the Hawaiian cowboy, or paniolo, in January of 2006.

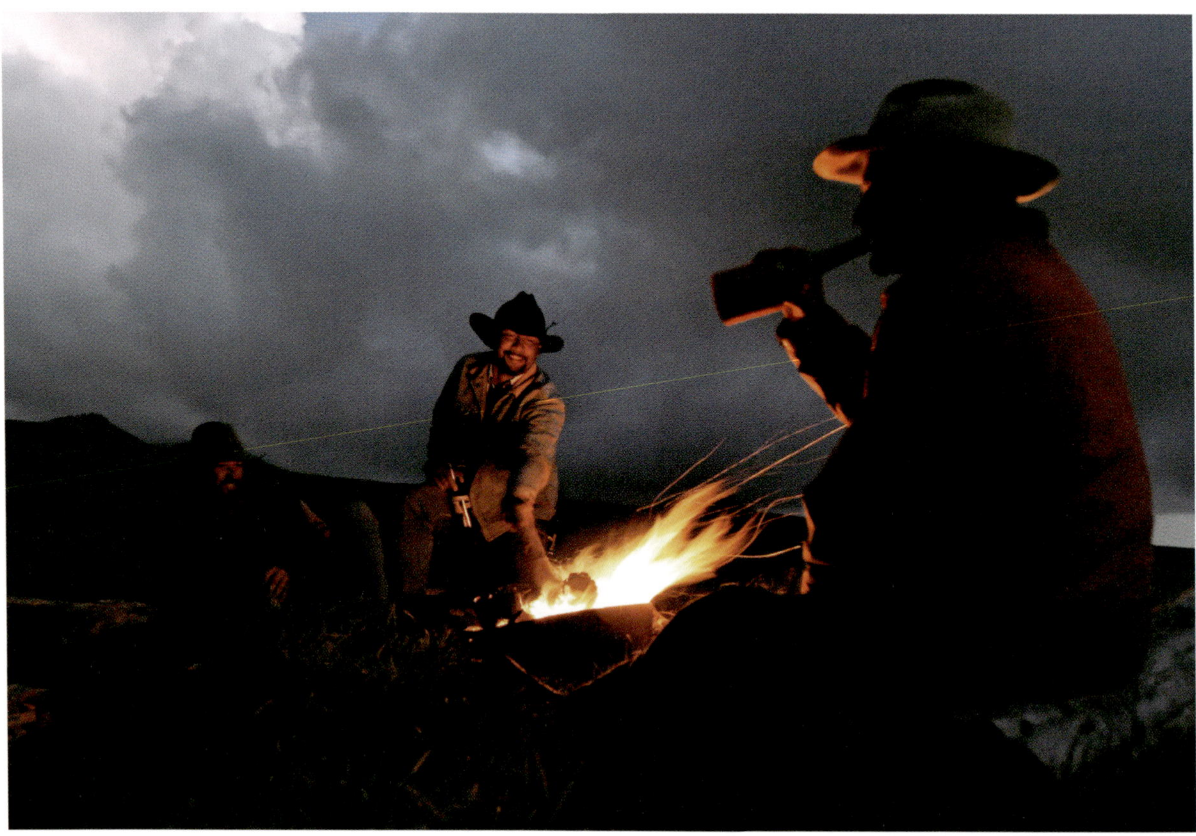

ISO 400 f/2 1/2 24mm

TAKING RISKS

Near the end of an exhausting two-week shoot for a commercial client on the *paniolo,* or Hawaiian cowboys, I casually asked the paniolo shown here if they ever got together when they were not actually at work. They said they often get together over bonfires at the end of the week. I asked them if they'd mind if I photographed them, and they agreed.

So they started their fire and they had their drinks. My goal was to find an angle where the geometry felt right. So, there's that diagonal line falling through the image. There's the classic silhouette of the cowboy in the foreground. There's the cowboy resting on the left and the other one stoking the fire.

On a technical level this photo was shot at ½ second at f/2. So only the person at the center is sharp, and I shot at this slow shutter speed so you could see the embers flying off the edge of the flames. There was very little light, but to me this represents what if felt like after a demanding two-week shoot. They were tired and I was exhausted. It was time to let go and relax.

I thought this was a very important image as part of the series to show that these paniolo who work very hard during the week yet have a very blessed job, also have this camaraderie among them. It's not easy work, but it easily beats a lot of jobs out there. There's a sense of freedom that you feel when you look at that image, and I think that the long exposure adds to that.

There was a risk in shooting the image this way, especially by making the choice not to use flash. The reality was that most of the shots I made that night were out of focus or soft due to motion blur. But I wouldn't have gotten the image that you see now, if I hadn't risked failure.

To me, this image represents a pure moment of Americana. It's a nostalgic look at the cowboy that we all have imagined. So adding artificial light is somewhat counterintuitive to me. Having the scene lit by nothing but the fire is appropriate and lends to the purity of the moment. That's why I shot it that way. There is nothing better than beautiful natural light.

This image isn't technically perfect, but I think we can pursue perfection to a fault. We photographers pay attention to the rule of thirds and technical directives. We try to get the highest pixel count and the most dynamic range. Yet at the end of the day all that perfection can lead to failure, more times than not.

You have to have a healthy respect for this desire for perfection, yet it has a very good chance of sucking the life out of your photographs.

As a photographer, particularly a photojournalist, you are constantly reminded that though life can be devastating and terrible, for the most part it is beautiful, and that beauty can be found in the familiar and the ordinary.

BEAUTY IN ACTION

Sports imagery often revolves around the action, the key play, but there's also a potential for strong, graphic beauty even in the midst of a photographing a challenging, even dangerous, sport.

This image speaks strongly to the power of an aerial photograph's ability to capture the beauty of nature. People see surfers all the time from the ground, but when you shoot directly down, you can see how absolutely gorgeous that water is and the relationship between the human being to the size of those waves. You can clearly see how small those surfers are relative to the power of nature, and how dangerous and beautiful it all is at the same time.

The photograph marries the liveliness of the white foam with the contrasting calm of the dark water. It also marries the beauty of that water with the danger of what they are doing. So in many ways the aesthetic and the content are playing against each other. It's a graphically pleasing image, but it also gives you a clear idea of what these guys are engaged in.

Beauty can be found in the familiar and the ordinary. It's just a matter of opening your eyes. There are few things more satisfying than capturing that beautiful moment, when things line up just right, and making an image that reveals the beauty of the everyday.

Surfers practice in the days leading up to the Rip Curl Pipeline Masters in 2006.

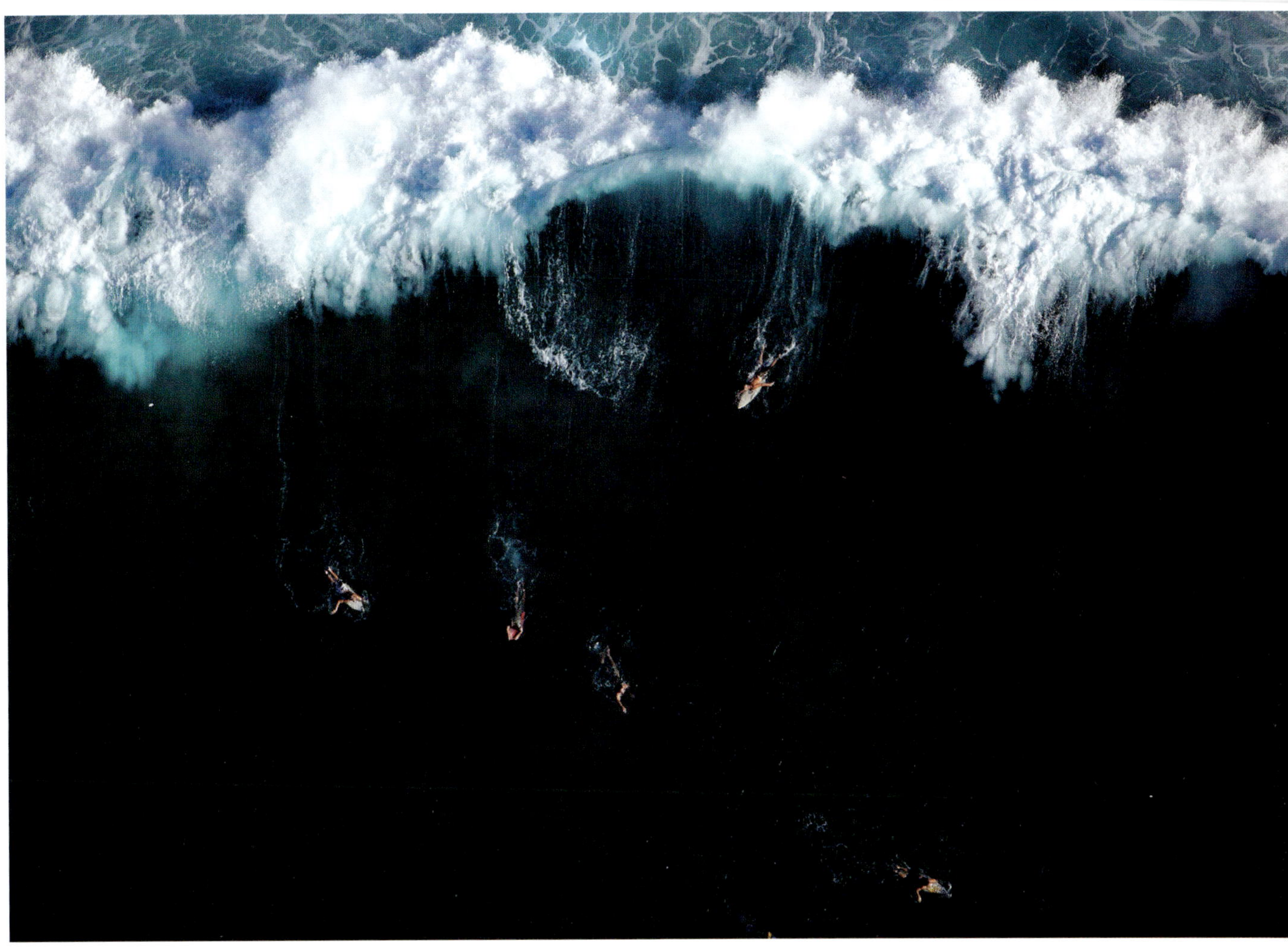

ISO 200 f/5.6 1/2500 700mm

PHOTOGRAPHING WHAT ISN'T THERE

When I was offered the assignment to return to New Orleans a year after Katrina had hit, I didn't want to go. In fact, I was so reluctant to go back that I told my editor that I would rather be sent to Iraq than go back to New Orleans.

I was so afraid of what I would find there. The initial story had been so emotionally draining that I was worried that going back a year later and seeing a tremendous lack of progress would throw me into a tailspin. But I did go, and took this shot, an image I wouldn't have made when I was younger.

One of the hardest things to do as a photographer is shoot emptiness, or shoot something that's not there but which conveys what is beneath the surface. As a younger photographer, I was always looking for that moment, that thing. This is a subtle image that's actually packed with information.

What this particular image says is, here we are a year later. The vegetation has grown back. There are the remnants of two homes on the back left, but there is nothing rebuilt, and these concrete stairs and stoop are the only things left of the house that once existed here.

You can see the brand-new levee behind, in the background, and new electrical poles. So the infrastructure has been rebuilt. It shows that the 9th Ward region is virtually a ghost town: it's really speaking to the remnants and the lack of progress. When I look at this image, I feel a tremendous amount of emptiness at the thought that that whole neighborhood is gone. The people are gone and the houses are gone. There is still news value there, because again it's about the levee.

Concrete steps are all that remain of a house in this tilt-shift photograph made in the Lower 9th Ward on August 24, 2006—one full year after Katrina devastated the area.

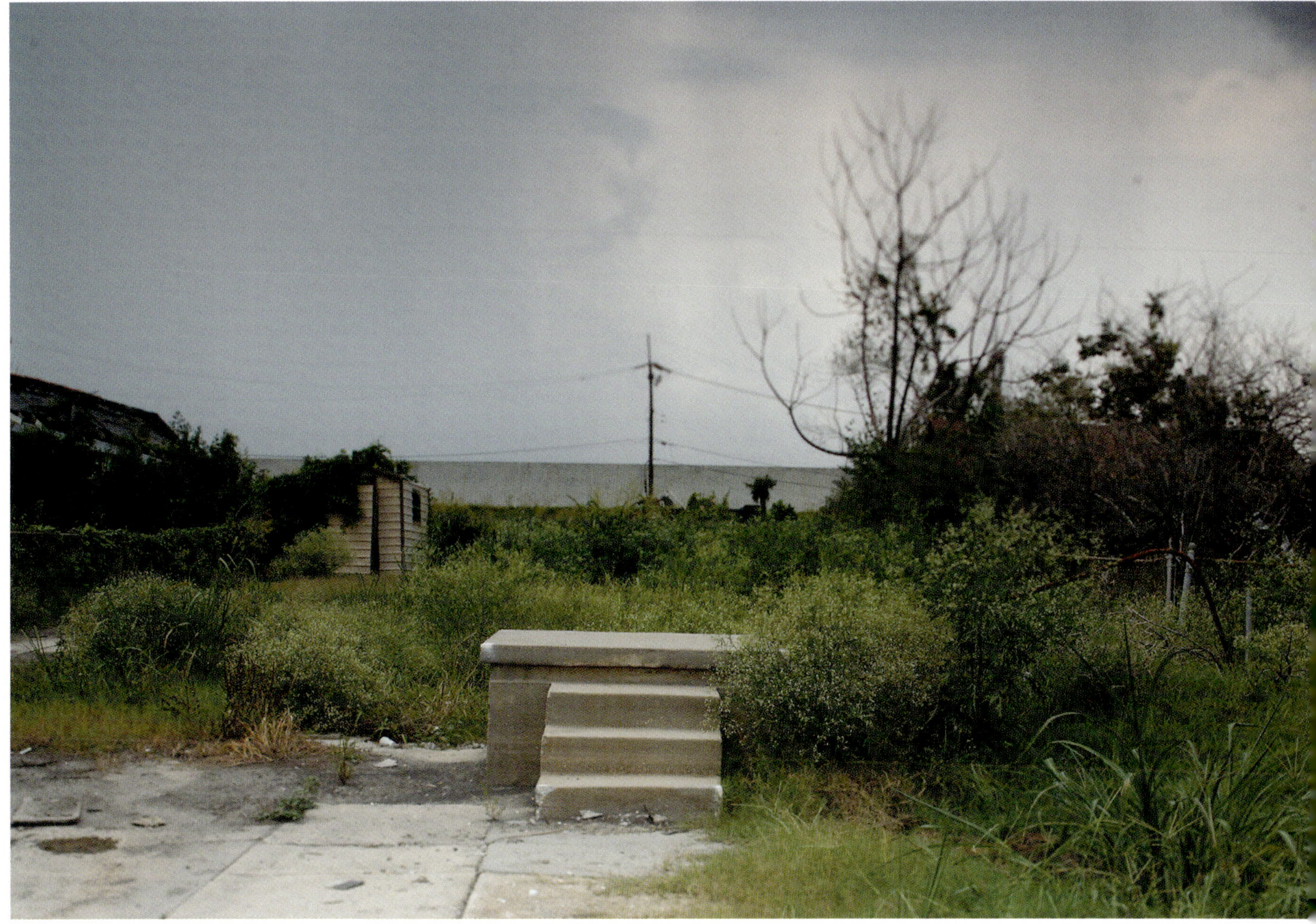

ISO 100 f/5.6 1/160 45mm

It takes a lot of guts to take a picture of nothing and expect people to feel what I was feeling. It brings the image to a whole new level. Often I tried to make images that popped off of the page. This is more of a style of image that you might see shot with large format for a museum. It's not so much a newspaper or magazine photograph, but it speaks to my evolution as a photographer. After years and years of making what could be called "banger" images, I was striving to make something more poetic and subtle.

Try as you might to ignore that lower 9th Ward, it's still there. Politicians might not want tourists to go down there, not allow residence to go there. That loss of that community is still there. Sadly, it's represented by that stoop.

Your approach to an image should speak to what you are trying to see and what's there, and in this case, 99 percent of the photographers are going to walk right past it and not even notice it's there. It's a very unspectacular image. It's not meant to pop off the page, and it's an image that you are only going to get if you study it and think about it.

Besides the choice to shoot that image with a tilt-shift lens, which helped throw the tree out of focus, the image doesn't involve any major technical feats.

It's unspectacular in the way it was shot, but it's an image that welcomes risk because it invites the viewer to completely miss it or to actually study it or ponder it a little bit more.

Images are happening around you every second. You can photograph anything in a million different ways, but what I always try to remember is to photograph something as if I've discovered it for the first time. And if I have photographed it before, I find a way to see it as I've never seen it before.

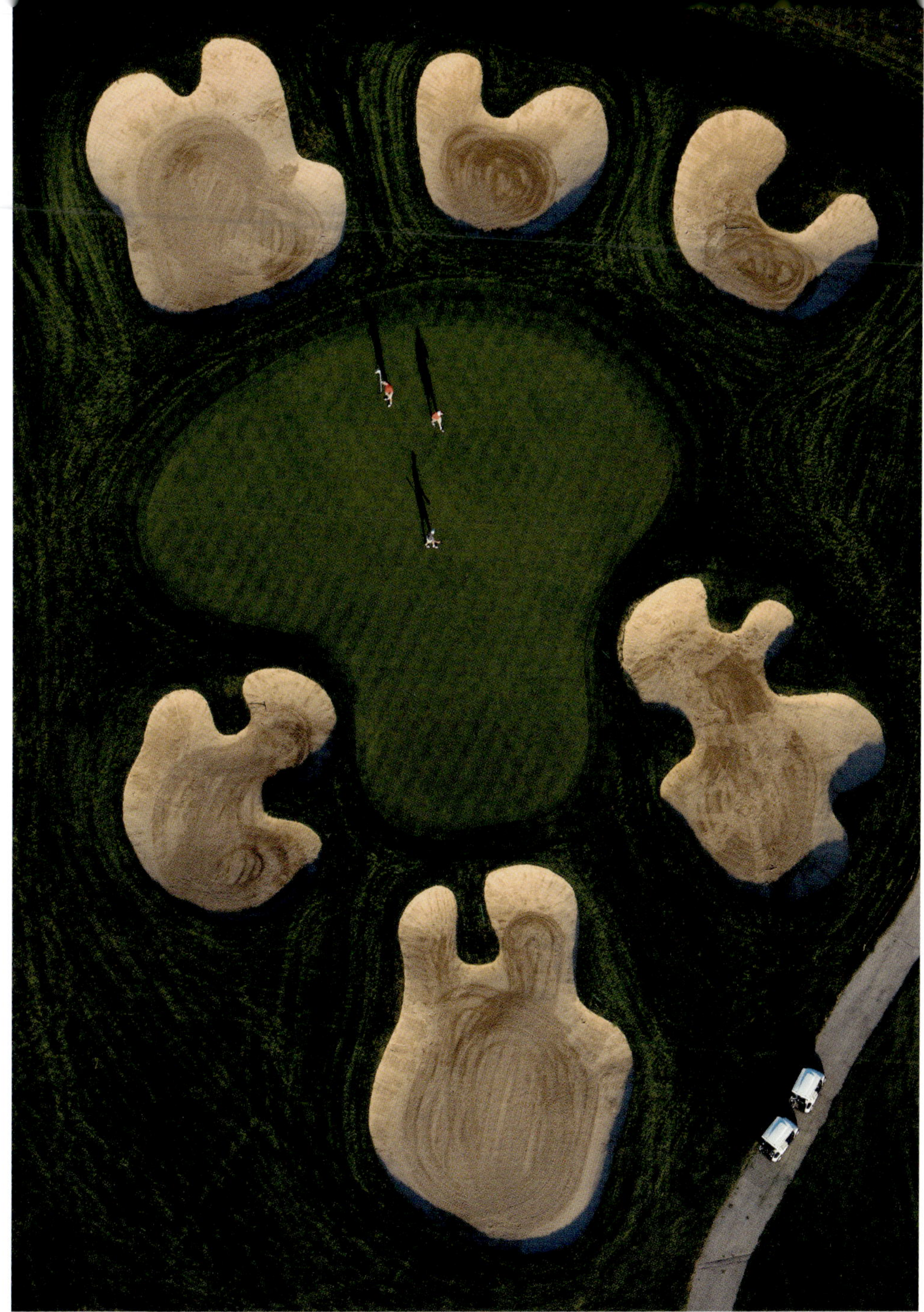

A trio of golfers completes their round of golf at the Cog Hill Country Club in Lemont Illinois, just south of Chicago on August 7, 2007.

ISO 320 f/3.5 1/1250 110mm

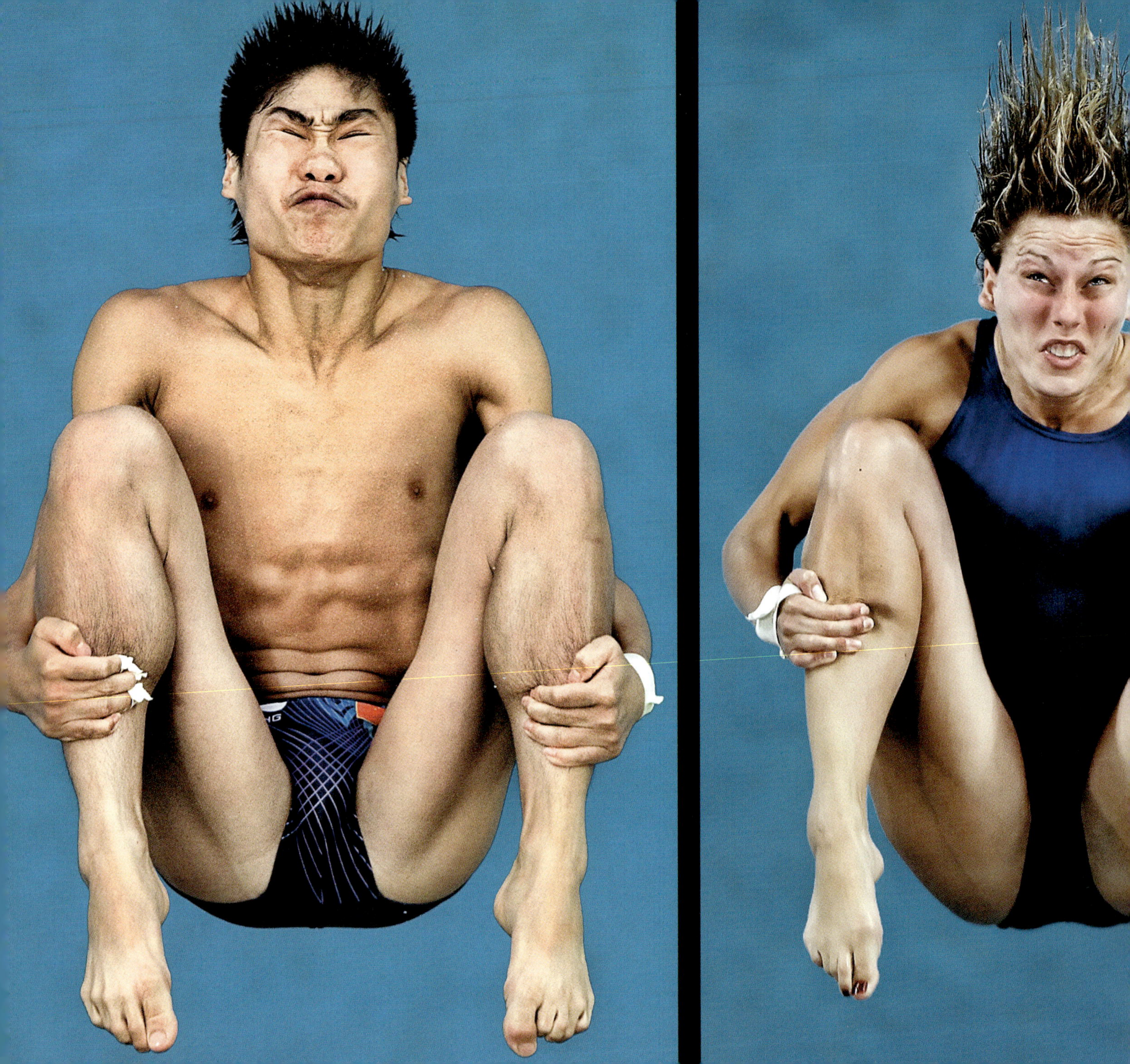

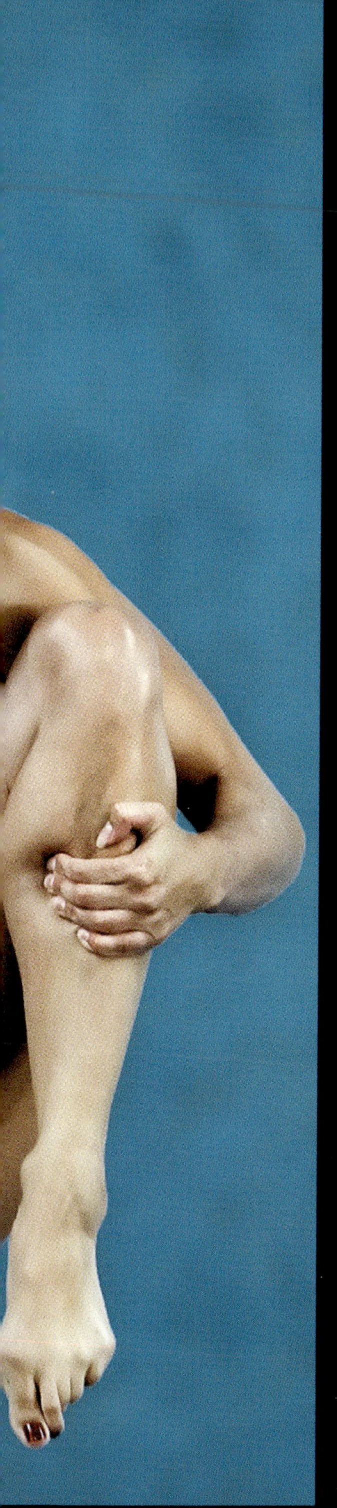

CHAPTER 4

THE ART OF SPORTS

One thing that can really help make an exceptional sports photograph is research. And in the case of the Olympics, it includes looking at the work of other photographers.

It's kind of an unspoken thing that we all do. We look at what everyone else is shooting, and we find the good angles because we don't have time to find them ourselves sometimes.

So, over the weeks before shooting a sports event, you would examine the venue through others' images and you would think, "Oh, that's a great angle, let me try to find one when I get there."

◀ Divers in the 2008 Summer Olympics.

ISO 1600 f/2.8 1/1600 300mm

The idea is not to go and duplicate their image. If you do, you're not really doing anyone any service. It's kind of dishonest on your part, and you're not contributing to the photography world.

I was scheduled to photograph volleyball on the last day of the Games, which included the final between China and the United States. I knew that there was one spot in the entire stadium that was dead center that had the Beijing logo. I'm not a big logo fan, but in this case I thought it would work. Trying to use words in photography is seldom very effective.

I got on the very first bus out to the venue and it was pouring rain, a real downpour. I just dashed to this location, and it is one of the times I brought only the equipment I needed. I had three lenses, including a 15mm fisheye in a small camera bag. I didn't bring a laptop; I didn't bring a long lens. I knew I wanted this image, and this image alone.

I also knew that if I had to drop off my stuff, someone could beat me to this one spot—the only spot in the stadium like this. I also knew that in the Olympics, once you leave your spot, you lose it. So I knew that once I sat there, I was going to live there for the next four to five hours.

It rained nonstop for the entire time. It just wouldn't stop. And although initially I kept wiping the water off my camera and lenses, at one point I recognized that sometimes the greatest photographs happen by mistake, or when you accept the adverse conditions.

So I allowed water to accumulate on my 15mm fisheye lens. I set the aperture to f/16 and calculated the hyper focal distance to ensure that both the foreground and background were rendered acceptably sharp. So, I didn't focus on the girls; I instead focused on this barrier itself, and used the depth of field to render the overall image sharp, especially the water droplets that were collecting on the front element of the lens. I patiently waited to use those droplets as part of my composition during the final.

Five minutes before the match, a Russian photographer walked up to me, looked at the water on my lens, picked up a wet sandy towel, and said, "Oh, no good, no good," and started to wipe these perfectly accumulated water droplets off of my lens. We nearly had an international incident right then and there.

I let it go. I wiped it clean, and waited almost the entire match for the water to accumulate again in that way, then shot a few frames, getting the shot I'd waited all those hours to capture.

This image is all about layers. You've got a foreground, middle ground, and background layer, ideally. You know where you are: you're in Beijing in 2008. You can see it's a volleyball court. You can see the players. And what makes this image special is that the unexpected foreground element. How often do you see water droplets in a photograph? It's pretty rare. But the droplets also convey that the entire match was played in the rain—it's both factual and visual.

It's an image that goes right back to marrying the aesthetic with the content.

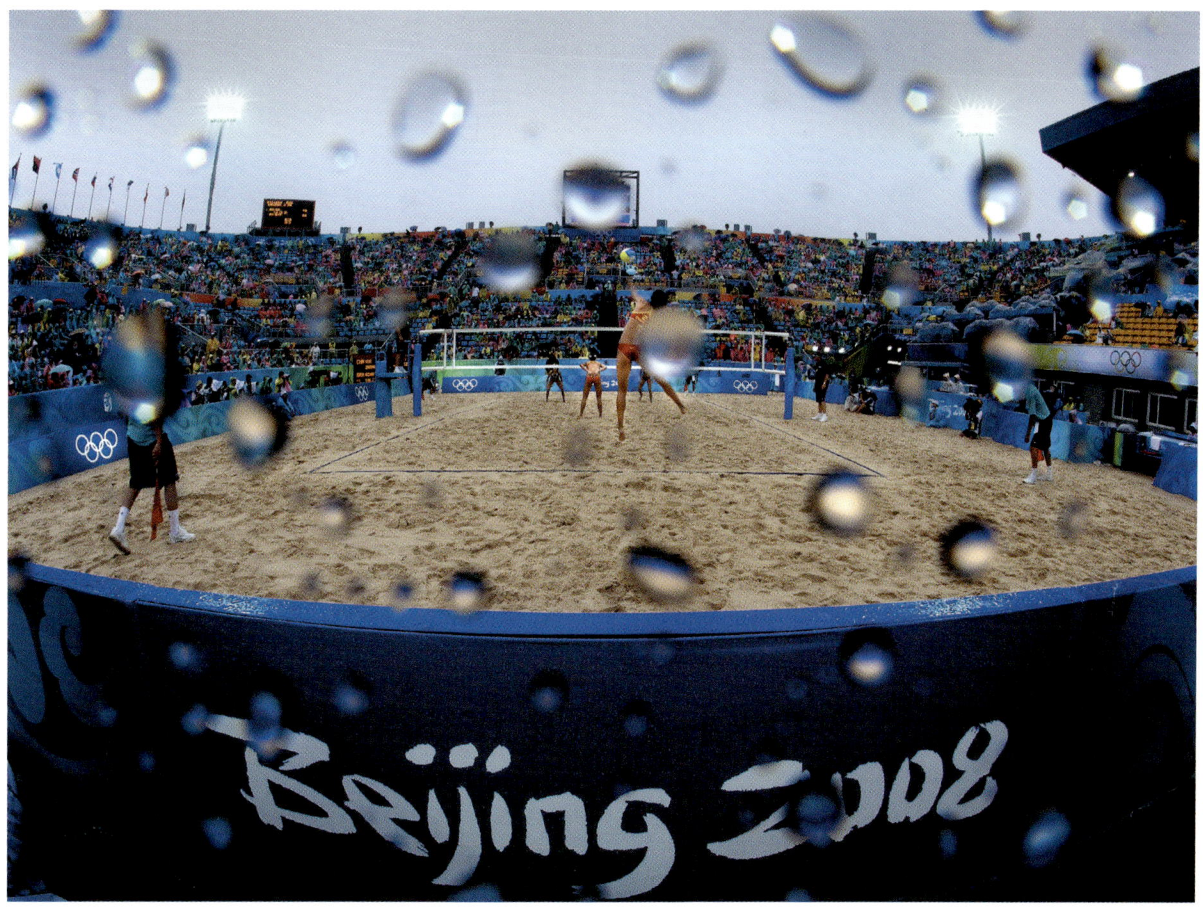

USA's Kerri Walsh and Misty May-Treanor win the gold medal in the Women's Beach Volleyball game against China. The game was played in the middle of a downpour, but not delayed.

ISO 640 f/22 1/50 15mm

SPORTS BEGINNINGS

I got into sports photography pretty haphazardly by working at my college newspaper, the *Daily Northwestern.* The biggest thing at Northwestern, as at most college campuses, is football. I started photographing football my freshman year. But the reality was I didn't even know what a first down was. I was a European kid. I had no clue about football. But I had the ability to manually wrack focus and keep the player sharp better than most people. This was before autofocus, so that skill was invaluable.

This was when being a sports photographer was a really sought-after skill because not many people could follow an entire action sequence and get sharp, well-exposed frames. Keeping someone in frame, let alone in focus at f/2.8 using a 400mm lens was no easy feat. I don't know where the ability came from for me, but it was there.

Though I knew nothing about the game, I watched people around me. I looked at the photographs in the *Chicago Tribune* and the *Sun Times'* every week because those photographers went to the same games I did. I saw how they shot versus how I was shooting, and tried to narrow the gap. I studied them like a hawk and learned that your position relative to the action and your lens choice were critical. I learned to anticipate, and recognized how invaluable that ability was for photographing sports.

Creating great sports photographs is ultimately all about anticipation. You come to realize that for every single moment for every single play in football, there are four likely outcomes for the quarterback. There is a chance of a fumble, which leads to a turnover; a sack, which is a big moment in the game; a simple hand-off to the running back; or a long throw for a 10-yard gain or a touchdown.

So you generally start with the quarterback. Watch his eyes. Figure out where he's leaning, and then you have to decide whether you're going to stay on the quarterback or the football. It's very formulaic. You can start a game and spend the first 15 minutes with the quarterback. Once you have enough stock of him, you then go to the running back and the wide receivers. You have to feel the game and have a sense of how it's going.

If the team isn't making any forward progress, you stay close to the quarterback, because it probably means defense is doing well, or the offense is doing poorly. If this is a team that's known for throwing 20-, 40-, or 50-yard touchdown passes, you stay farther away from the quarterback and get those amazing catches.

Super Bowl XLI

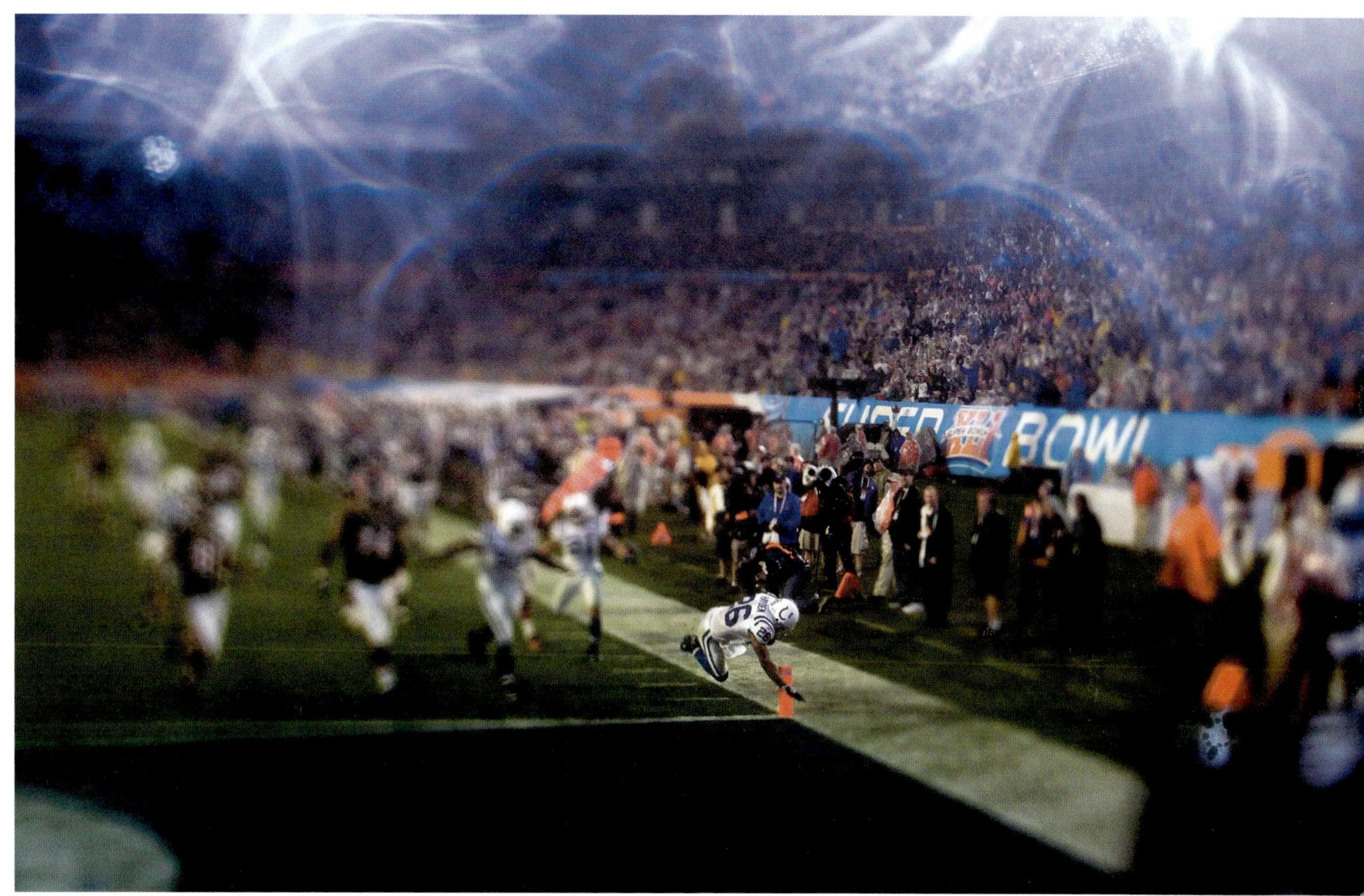

ISO 800 f/2.8 1/640 45mm

Sprinter Usain Bolt of Jamaica sets a new world record and clinches his second gold medal in the Men's 200M final in the 2008 Summer Olympics.

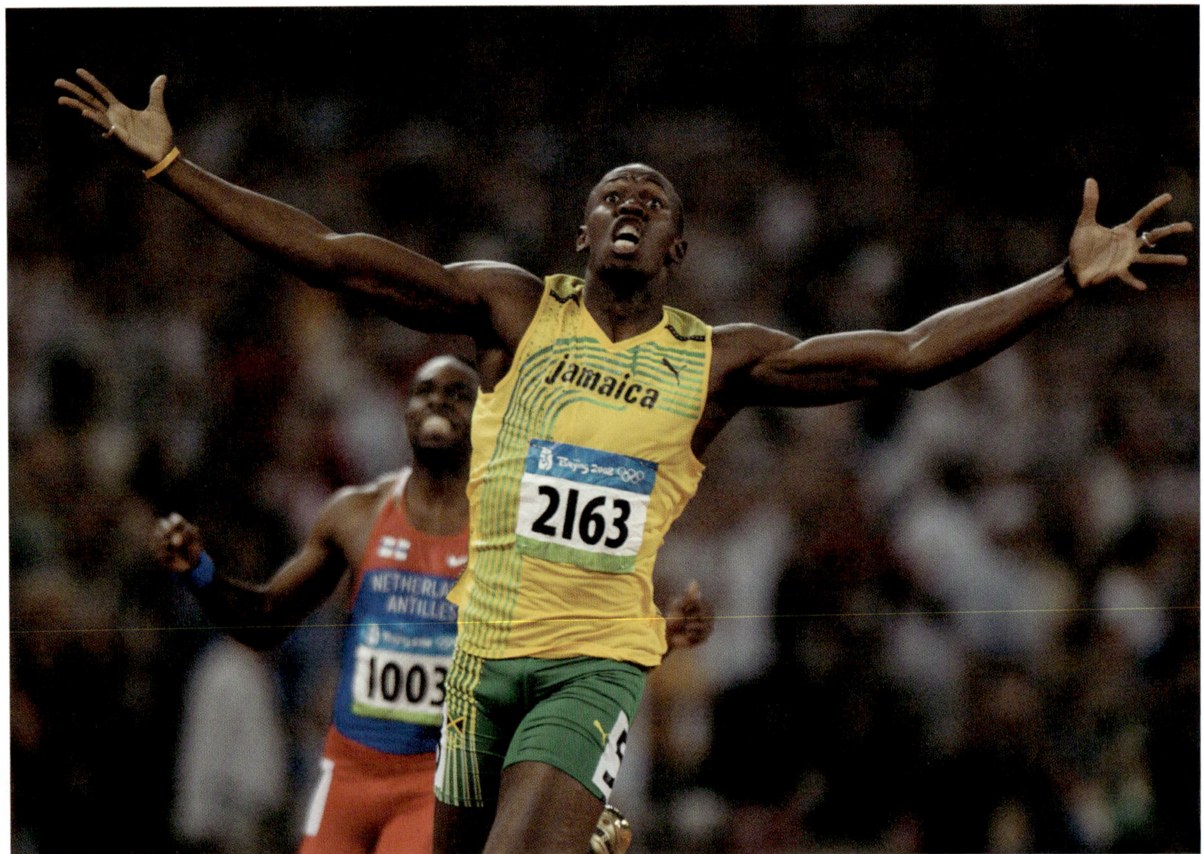

ISO 1000 f/2.8 1/000 400mm

THE APEX OF EMOTION

This is Usain Bolt winning the 100-meter final in the Beijing Olympics. It's a race that lasts less than 10 seconds, and I got there 12 hours ahead, which is insane.

What I was looking for in this image, which was shot with a 400mm lens wide open at f/2.8, was just Bolt and his pure joy at winning. The challenge as a photographer is capturing that spirit without cutting off his limbs and or having a distracting background.

To his left was a gang of photographers, and to his right was a big space-telescope–looking television camera. So I was composing as tight as possible to isolate him and make him pop right off the page.

The tricky part was I was using a fixed focal length, so I was calculating the best possible spot where he would likely react to winning. In a 100-meter final, an athlete often reacts a quarter of a second after they've crossed the finish line because they take a quick glimpse at the scoreboard to see their time. They might see that they've broken a world record, and *boom,* they instantly react.

On the other hand, after a 10-kilometer race they might collapse immediately or walk a few hundred feet past the finish line. And so again, you make a choice and you make a gamble, and you hope it pays off. In this case, he slowed down and started celebrating immediately.

So, that's what you always have to be ready for—the unpredictable. Here he's at the height of his reaction. I like the fact that the guy who is clearly 5 yards behind him is out of focus and not distracting, but you still see a big smile on his face because he has won the silver or bronze. It gives the photograph a little more context, that even winning second or third place is a momentous occasion.

Tsuboi Bustavo of Brazil (bottom) and Peter-Paul Pradeeban of Canada play table tennis in the 2008 Summer Olympics as seen in this long-exposure photograph.

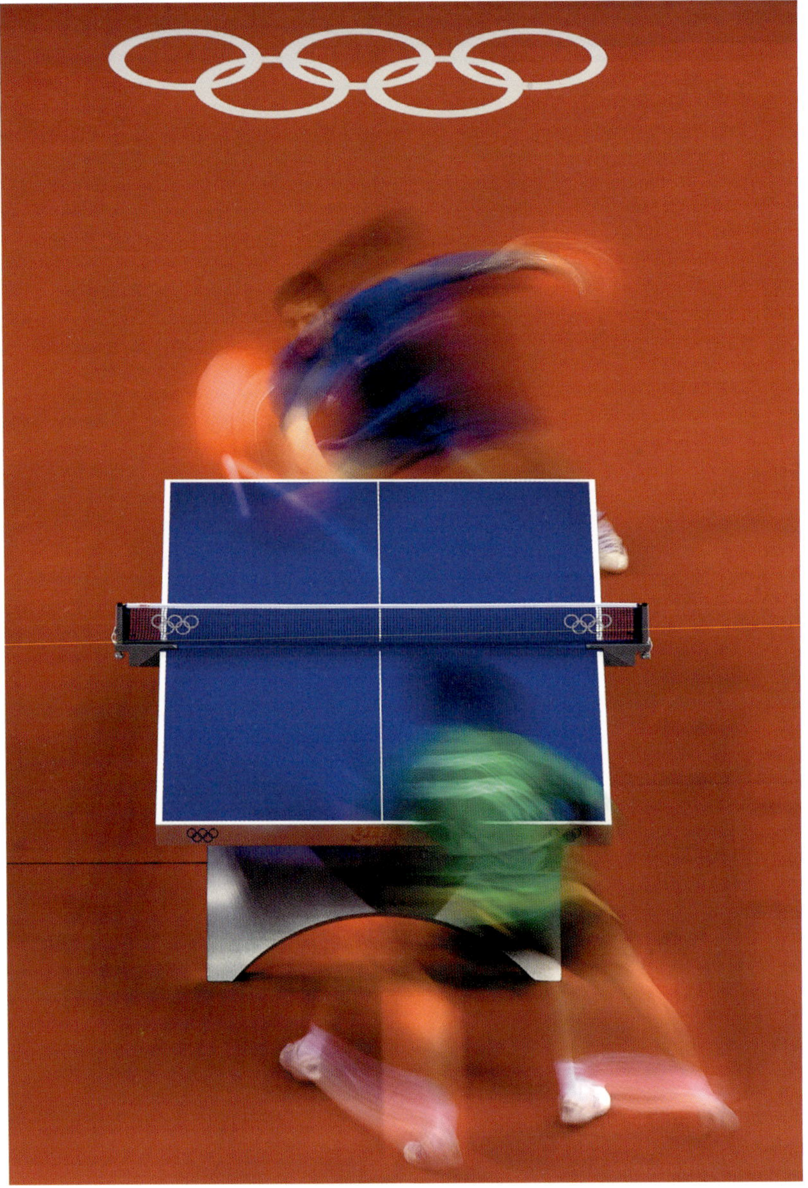

ISO 50 f/10 0.300000s 300mm

FINDING ORDER IN CHAOS

Sports are incredibly chaotic and unpredictable to the average person. The reason we go see a sporting event is that no one knows who's going to win, or when the game-winning touchdown or decisive turnover is going to be. That's what makes it exciting.

As a sports photographer, though, you need to break sports down in very formulaic ways, and know what all the options are. What can happen? You have to dissect every single sporting event you photograph very methodically, whether it's a batter's swing in baseball or a serve in tennis.

Tennis is an especially good example, because it's a sport that is maddening to shoot with a fixed lens. The players move around the court like crazy. But you learn to study the athletes and see that they have a very characteristic serve, or forehand, or backhand. And you need to figure out the best position and what the best lens is for these shots.

When photographing tennis players, you know they're always going to serve on that line on the right side of the court. There's not going to be much variation there, and you find the perfect angle. And you can shoot the entire game just trying to follow the action.

You can refine your choices by deciding that you're not going to spend much time on a forehand shot if this guy's known for a great backhand. You're not going to spend much time on her serving if she's not known for her power in serving. You'll spend more time waiting near the net if you know that these two athletes like to come in very close, as was often the case with John McEnroe and Björn Borg.

You have to study the sport and know it. What makes a great photographer of tennis is someone who gets great images of the initial serve as well as the backhand and forehand within five minutes of the competition, and who can sit back for the rest of the match and wait for the special moments that are unpredictable.

HANDLING THE STRESS

Photographing sports forced me to study things and dissect them like never before. And I learned from some of the best sports photographers at Allsport, which has now become part of Getty Images.

We would go to the track or the field the day before and study the light. We wouldn't take a single picture, but just observe how the light changed around the course the entire day, from sunrise to sunset. This allowed me to plan the specific spots where I would position myself during certain times of the day, to take advantage of a certain quality of light.

Sports also made me very comfortable with long lenses, and with shooting extremely tight. Any mistake and you're out, whether it's focus or framing. Any wrong move, you're done. That approach really influenced my aerial photography and most of my photography in general. So when I have a 500mm in my hand, I'm as comfortable as most people are with a 50mm.

It also helped to accept the fact that I would often have only one chance. It's probably the biggest factor in photography, across all fields, more so in sports, but especially in photojournalism. There's a tremendous amount of pressure that comes with that reality and it can lock you up mentally. It can completely destroy you.

Your heart starts to beat like you're running a marathon. You become faint and you can start to shake, given the amount of pressure on you. At a certain point in your career, you realize that you're cooked if you're feeling that way. But what you need to remind yourself is that this is one of 10,000 swings you've already shot this year. Don't worry about the significance of it right now.

Keep your emotions cool and collected, as well as your mental state, and treat it as if it's just another swing. Just shoot it, get your picture, and block out all of the emotion.

The danger for me was I became so good at this, that I would equate it to being a sniper or a hired killer. I learned to utterly block out every emotion.

But the result was that it removed all emotion from my photographs. It made me a very effective sports photographer because I rarely missed the shot that would be prominently published in the paper. I could capture all these photographs, but emotionally I was dead, and I learned that I had to be careful about that. You can't go too far in that direction. You've got to have a little bit of life left in your images.

Michael Jordan flies underneath a basket as a group of Atlanta Hawks looks on during Jordan's last season with the Chicago Bulls.

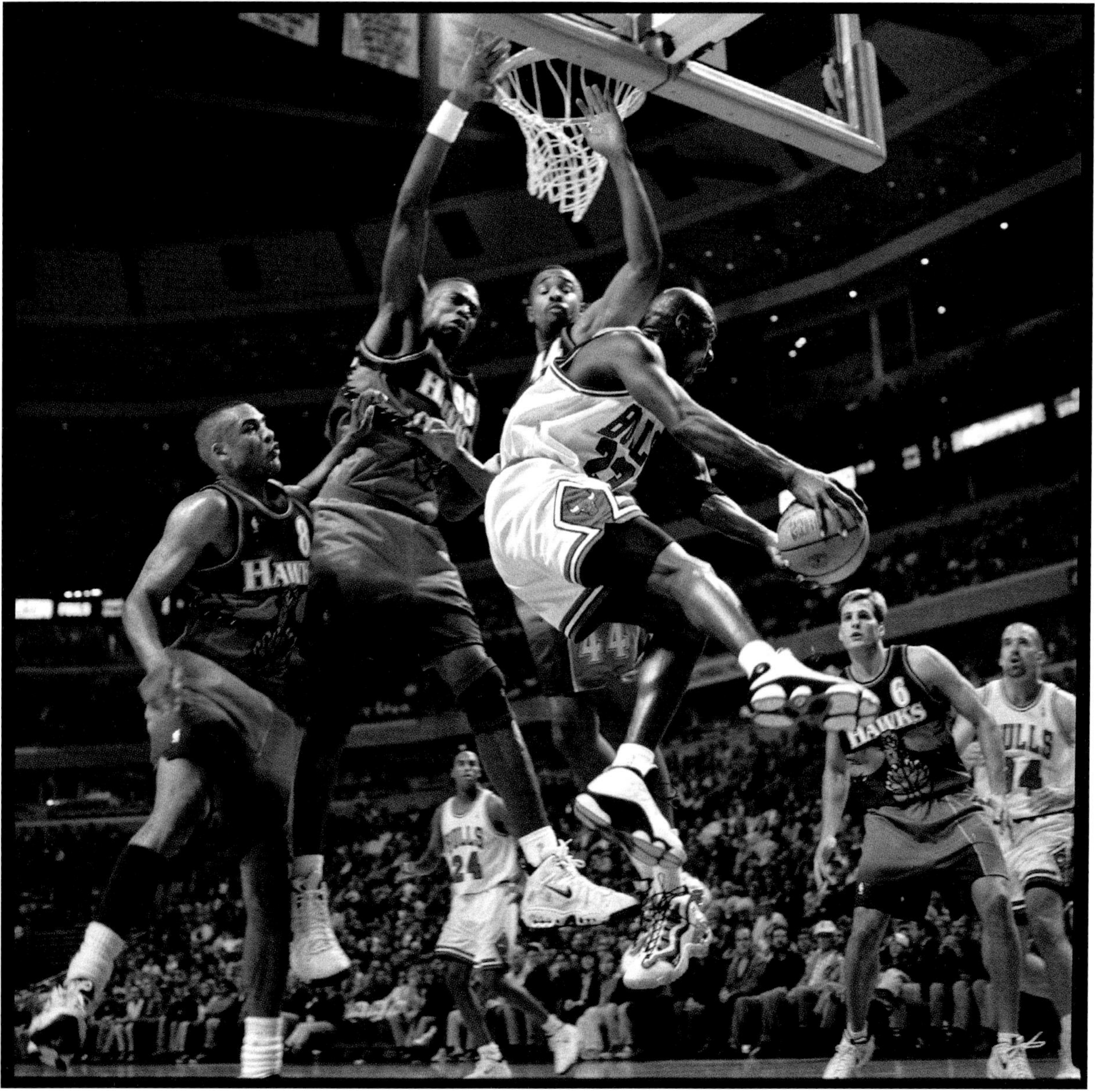

f/2.8 1/500 80mm

BACKGROUND AWARENESS

Background is incredibly important for a great sports photograph, perhaps more so than with any other genre of photography.

This is because the actions in any sport are pretty repetitive. It's a batter at the plate; it's a tennis player hitting a serve. These are actions that happen over and over and over again. You've likely seen them a thousand times.

So, what you want to do is isolate that action and consider the choice of the background. You often have three things that you can do with the background.

The first choice is to shoot wide and embrace the background because it is either beautiful or informative. You might make this choice because the fans are booing the player or jumping in the air. The background might include the scoreboard, or the lights that make it look grandiose.

Another option is to go the polar opposite and shoot extremely tight because the background is distracting and you need to blur it out. This was the case with the old Shea Stadium, where they had orange seats that made for a horrible background.

The third option is somewhere in between. It's kind of a no man's land, and harder to pull off. But, just as you would include or exclude anything in your framing of any subject, you can make choices for depth of field in shooting sports. The single most common approach is to go as tight as you can without risking cutting out part of the player's body or part of any crucial element, such as a bat. The tighter you go, the harder it is to focus, the harder it is to find all action, and the harder it is to capture.

It's very unpredictable. If you go too tight and something incredible happens, such as a bat breaking, the broken bat is out of the frame. But if it's just a regular everyday swing in very bad light, it pays off to go super, super tight, because literally, things start to look different.

Weightlifter Andrei Rybakou of Belarus wins the silver medal and breaks the world record with an 185 Kg snatch in the Men's 85kg Weightlifting competition.

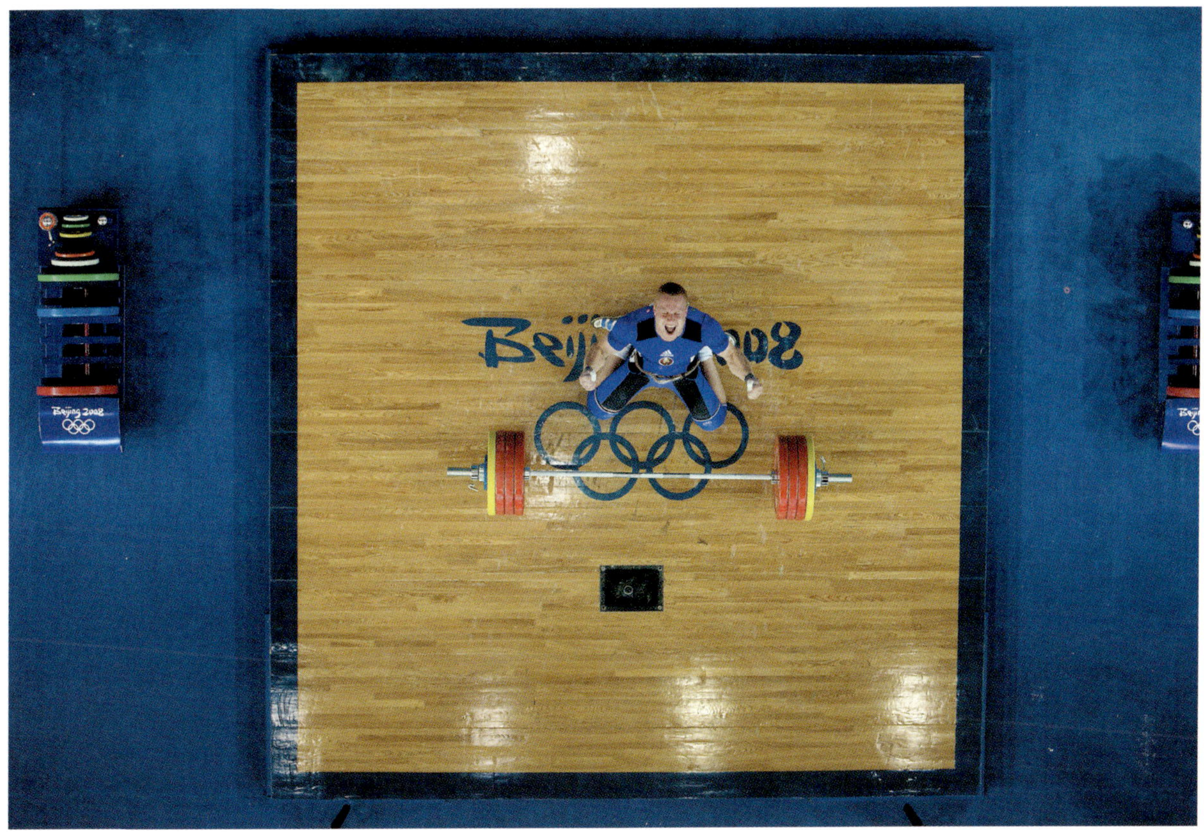

ISO 640 f/4 1/320 73mm

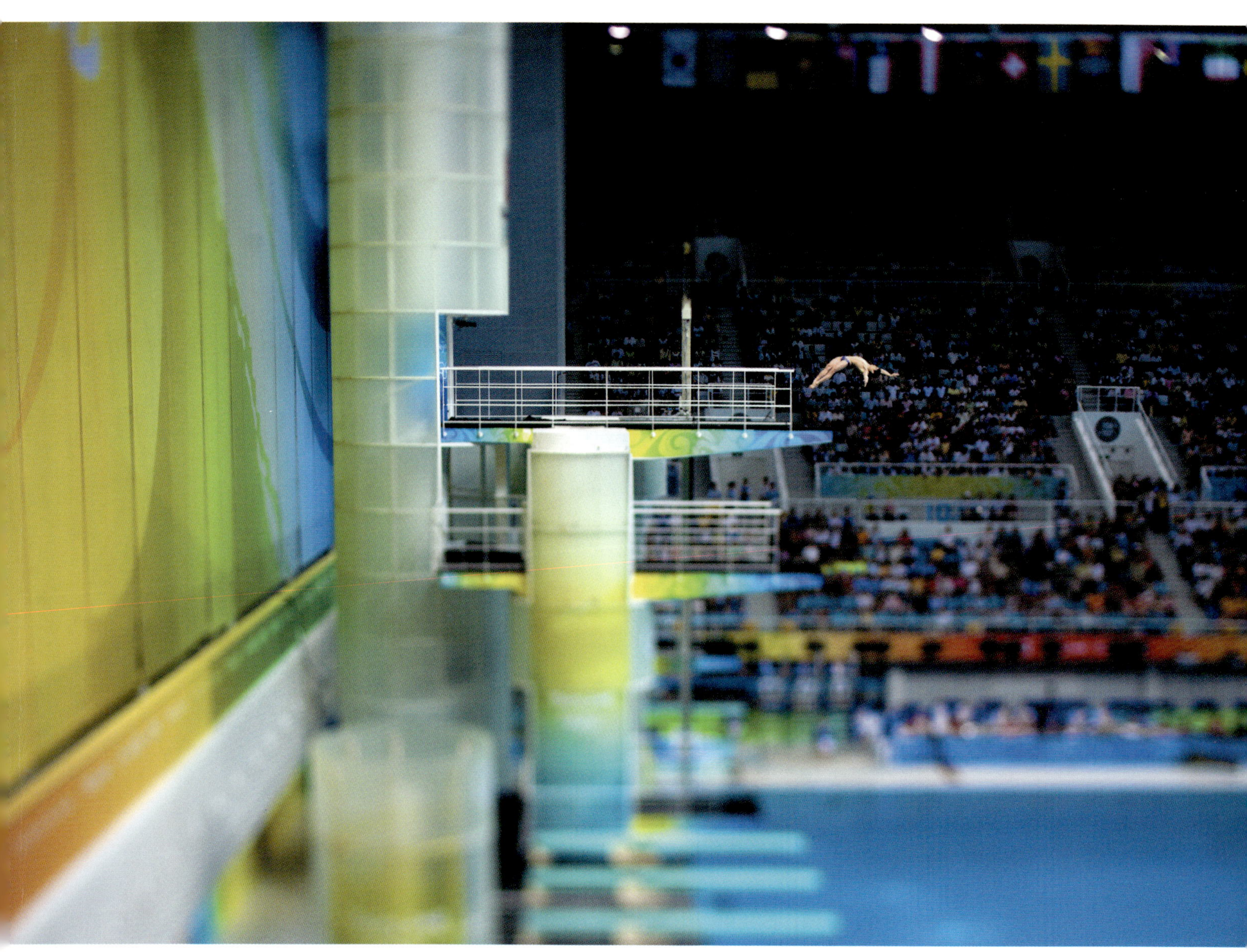

The Men's final of the 10 meter diving competition in the Summer 2008 Olympics.

ISO 400 f/2.8 1/400 45mm

A TELLING MOMENT

This is an example of when the best choice was to go wide. Though you can't really see it, the background was full of reporters wearing different colored shirts and typing on laptops. With a telephoto lens, the background would have looked ugly.

Fluorescent lighting illuminated the venue, so most people were shooting pans at slow shutter speeds. The background was too ugly to freeze the athlete mid-air and still make the image work.

I went to the extreme and used what most people would have considered dead space in the composition. I used a tilt-shift lens and maximized the tilt so that only the center focal plane was in focus. Everything at the top and bottom went out of focus. It's pretty carefully composed, in that the flags are at the top of the frame with the three lights. The rule of thirds absolutely applies here.

Then I just waited for the diver, who would go on to win the gold medal, to dive off the board. It's a very balanced picture, and the decisive moment is him arching his back as he leapt off the diving board. This photograph helps provide a sense of scale and reveals what a very dangerous feat this is. You don't appreciate that with a 400mm-lens shot.

You appreciate how small he is, given the size of the venue, and you start to calculate the distance from his body to the water. It gets you thinking a little bit. It also gets you to think about him just releasing—letting go. It's like the ultimate leap of faith.

Making the choice of how to handle the background frees me to capture the key moment, the "sustentation moment," in a single frame.

This photograph helps provide a sense of scale and reveals what a very dangerous feat this is. You don't appreciate that with a 400mm-lens shot.

THE SUSTENTATION MOMENT

The sustentation moment is an apex, or top, of a curve. When you throw a tennis ball up, it stops at a certain point on the curve before it reverses direction. This is a fantastic illustration for shooting sports at slow shutter speeds, where you don't have enough shutter speeds, because it's at that moment at the apex of the curve where things freeze.

It's actually very easy to judge, as you're shooting, where an athlete leaps up, stops momentarily, and comes down; you're basically waiting for that moment. And that's what that frame is. It's just studying the motion.

The image of the diver on the previous page was made using a single frame, because I learned that when shooting in the continuous-burst mode, this peak moment would sometimes happen between frames, even when firing at 10 frames per second. When you are shooting continually, you can't pay attention to your composition, and you can't really anticipate the moment. And there's really only going to be that one moment.

It's actually very easy to judge, as you're shooting, where an athlete leaps up, stops momentarily, and comes down; you're basically waiting for that moment.

USA's Michael Phelps wins his 8th gold medal in the 4 X 100 meter relay race (2008).

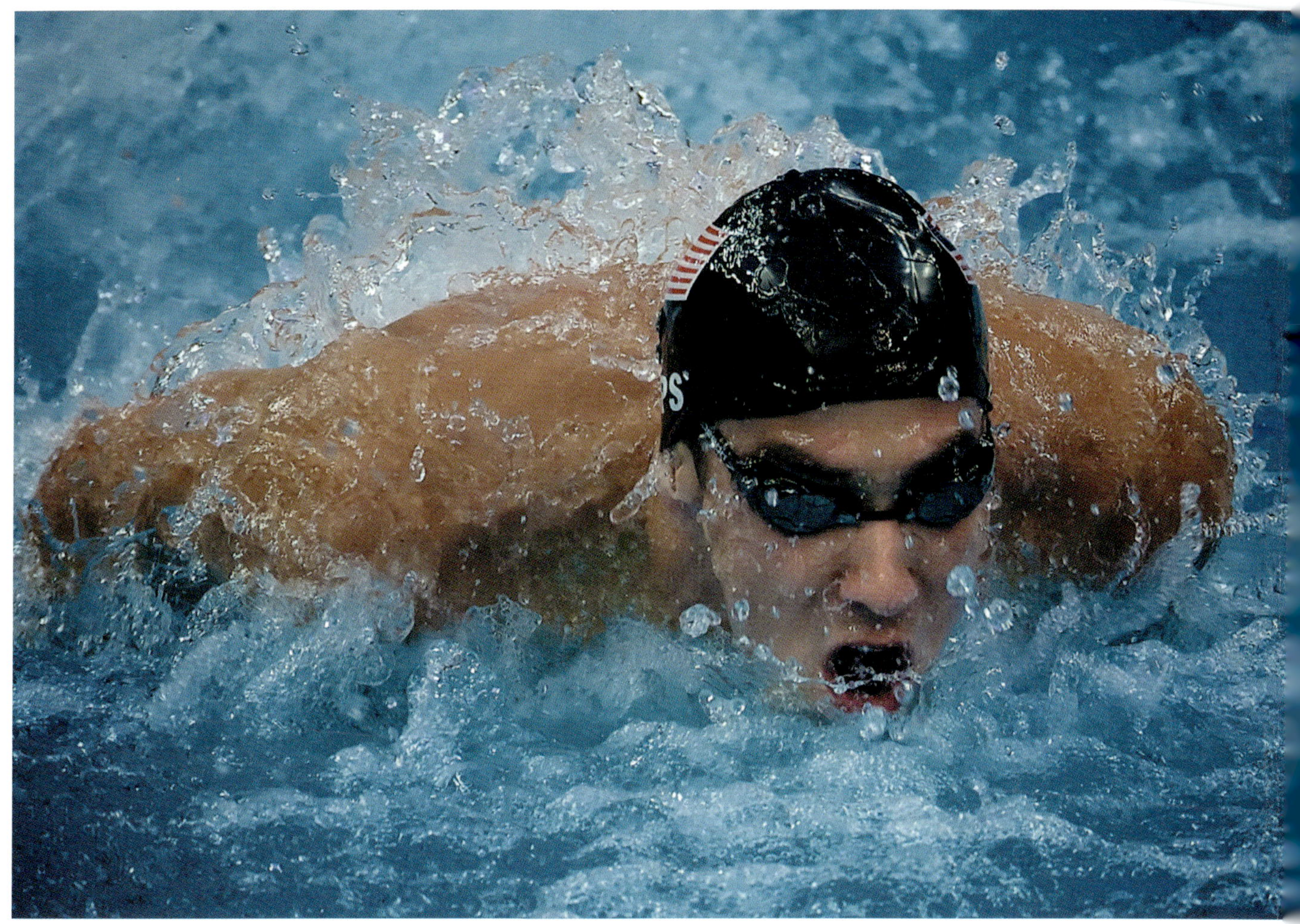

ISO 2000 f/5.6 1/640 800mm

China's Liang Huo competes in the Men's semifinal of the 10 meter diving competition in the 2008 Summer Olympics.

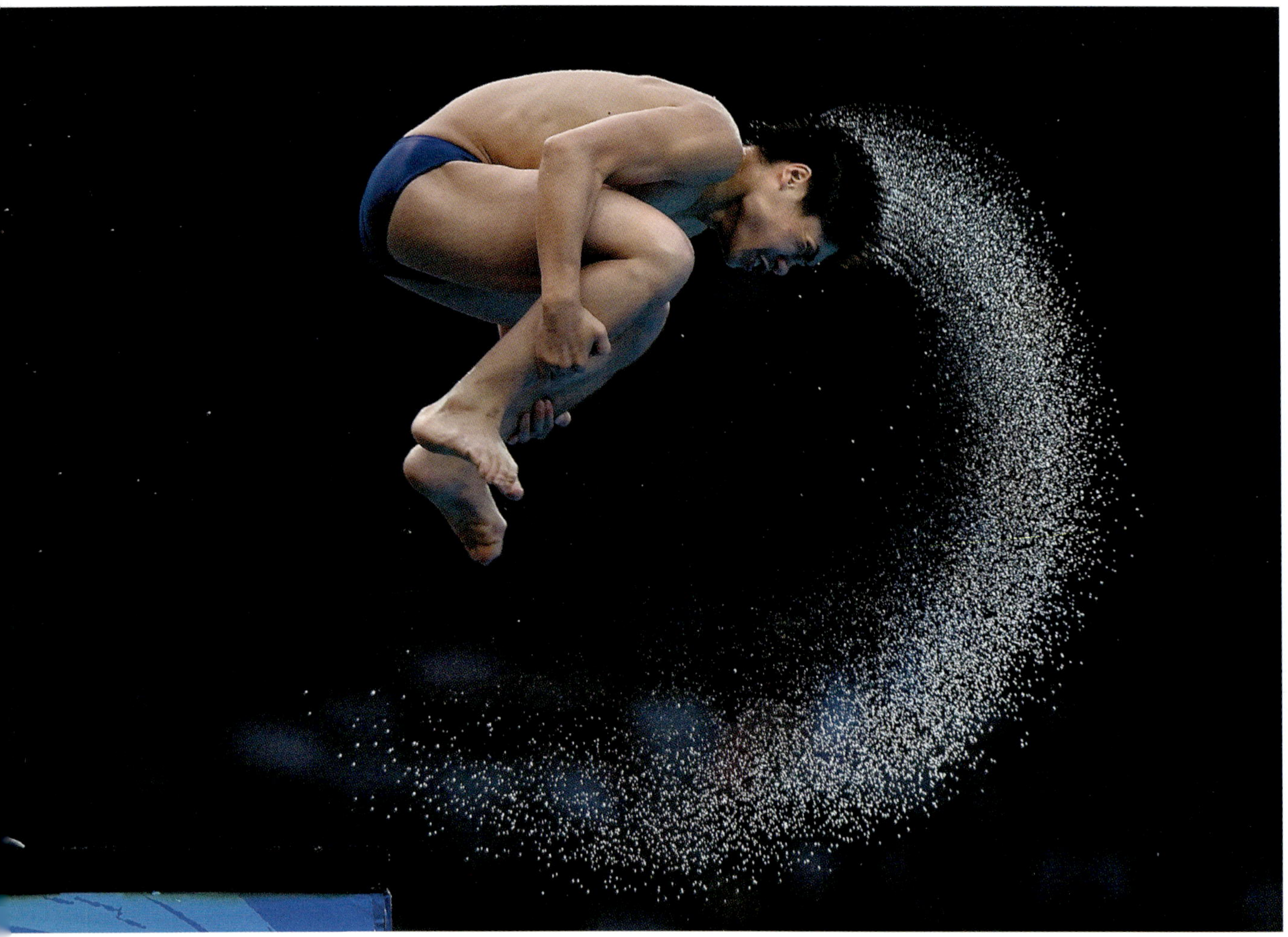

ISO 1250 f/2.8 1/2000 300mm

I knew I wanted to completely isolate that background and blur it out. I shot it wide open on a 400mm lens, which also allowed me to use the fastest shutter speed possible to freeze the image of those water droplets.

PAYING ATTENTION

During the Olympics in Beijing, it had been overcast for over two straight weeks. Day in, day out. During that entire time, I carefully evaluated different venues and how they might look differently should sunlight decide to make an appearance.

So when the first day of sunlight came, I already knew the kind of image I intended to make. I knew I wanted to completely isolate that background and blur it out. I shot it wide open on a 300mm lens, which also allowed me to use the fastest shutter speed possible to freeze the image of those water droplets.

This image was shot uncomfortably tight, because that's just the way I wanted to do it at that time, and I was bored with loose images. My assistant, who was to my right, shot the same image with a 200mm lens, composing with more room around the athlete. He also nailed the moment and won the award for college photographer of the year that year. His images captured the same moment but it wasn't the same image. It does make a difference when you go uncomfortably tight and really blur out that background.

THE UNUSUAL BACKGROUND

This is the winning point for the gold medal in wrestling. On the ground level, the background was made of television cameras, referees, and fans in stands. It was ugly.

So I had to go overhead, which gave me this gift of yellow, blue, and red concentric circles. These are also storytelling elements in that once a wrestler drags his opponent out of the circles, that's how he scores. The match and the image would be pretty boring if it all happened in the yellow area.

What's really interesting about this image is you don't know whose legs belong to whom and you're not sure who's who. Most important, you certainly don't want to be the guy who's on the bottom with his head down.

It is a beautiful geometry with the colors and the curves, and the repetition of those patterns and their shoes. It's red and blue uniforms, it's red and blue lines, and it so happens to be the gold medal–winning move. It's an incredible dichotomy between beautiful, quiet lines and colors, and the chaotic spaghetti of limbs that captures a key moment, which happens in a split second.

For the athletes in that second, either they've lost the gold medal or they've won it. This photograph speaks to how everything is so beautifully set up, from the venue to the uniforms, but in the end the reality is that there is only going to be one gold medal winner. To these guys, it's chaos; one wrong move and there goes the medal.

As the photographer, I only had two athletes to work with, but what I was really aiming for was the right geometry and color palette. I had to find that right elevation, so I wasn't so low that I caught a distracting element in the background, or so high I couldn't see their faces. I had to find the perfect balance between being too high or too low, and too tight or too loose.

It feels electric to witness a moment that is so dramatic and even historic. As a photographer, you are going to see 20 or 100 moments like that in your career. The majority of people experience that excitement through a television, but as a photographer you get to feel the thrill in person.

When you physically feel the vibration of the cheers and pure joy of 20,000 people or more around you, it's hard not to get emotional about it. There is nothing in the world like it. It's something you never forget.

Andrea Minguzzi from Italiy wins the gold medal during the sixth session of the Men's Greco Roman Wrestling competition in the 2008 Olympics.

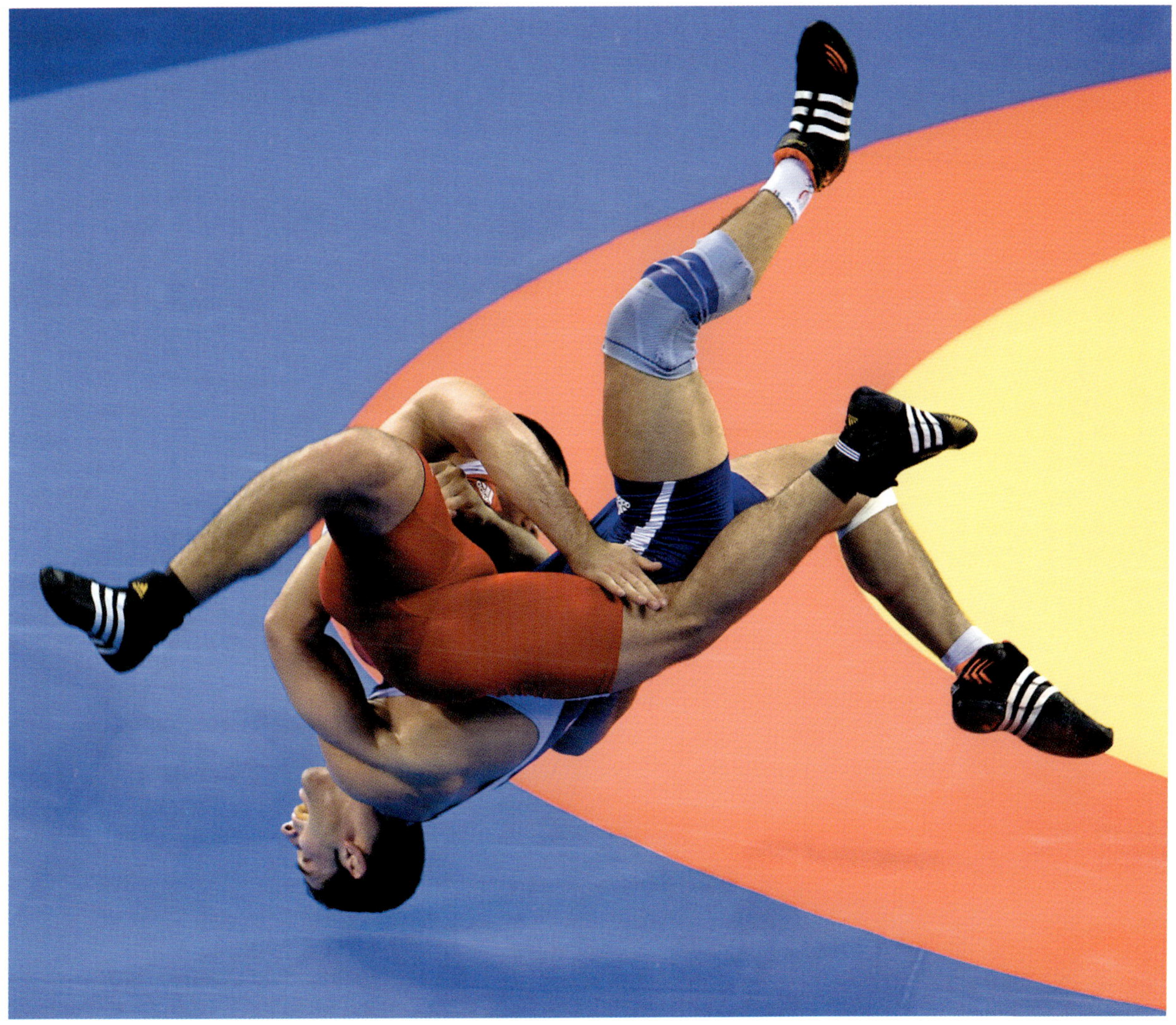

ISO 1000 f/3.5 1/1000 300mm

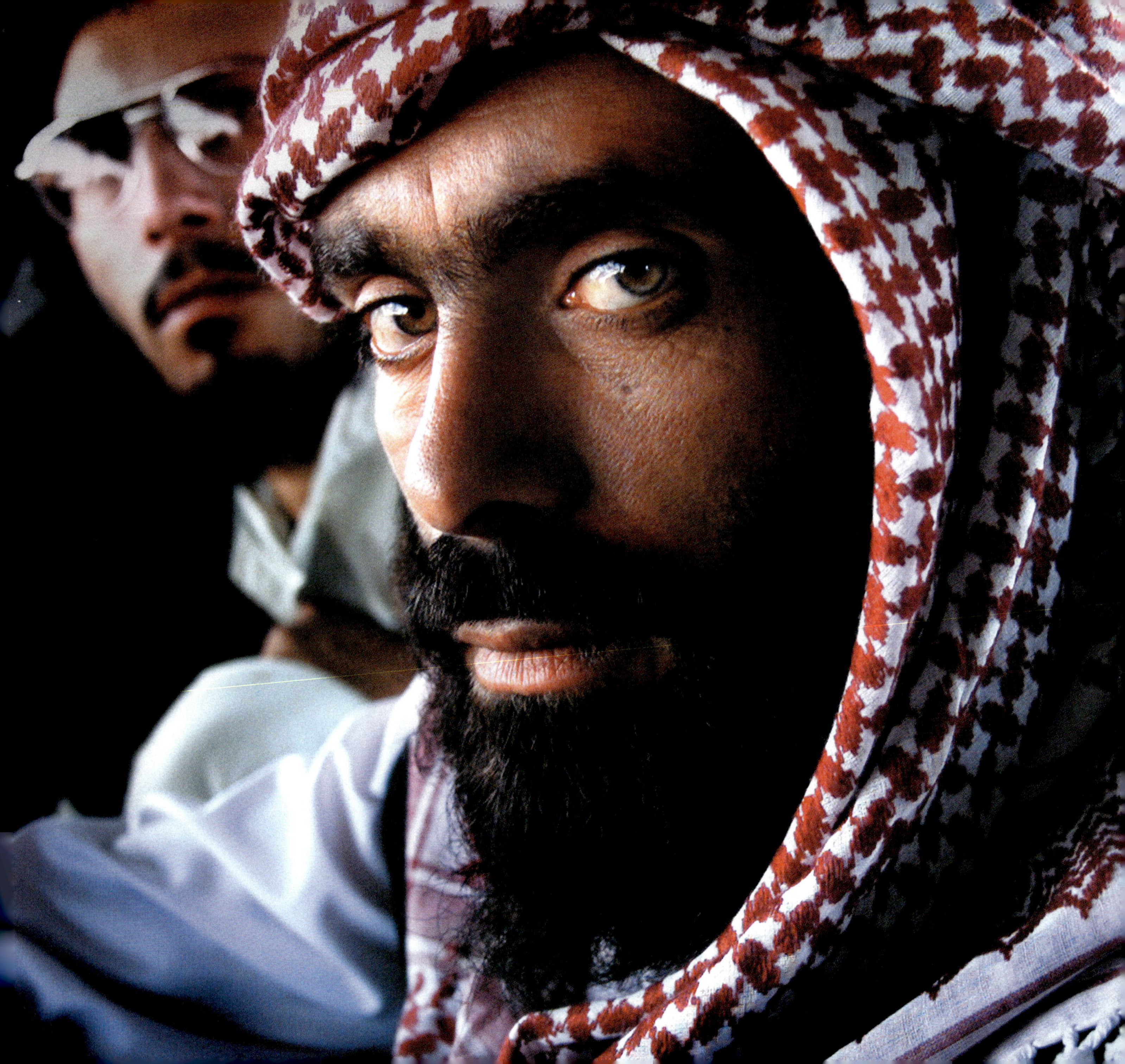

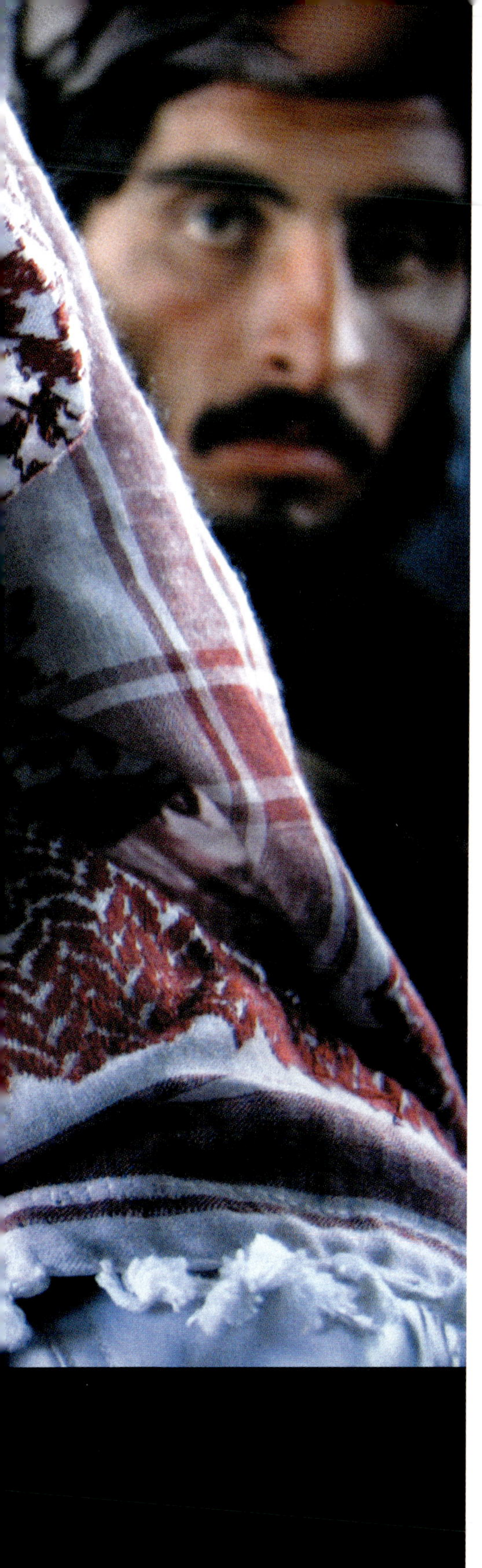

CHAPTER 5

DOCUMENTING WAR AND TRAGEDY

Any illusion that you are somehow protected or invulnerable because you have a camera and press credentials completely dissolves in a war zone.

I came close to death after photographing in a refugee camp in Pakistan in 2001. It was an organized trip coordinated by the Pakistani government. We rode for approximately three hours in a 13-car convoy, and we had to pass through 13 checkpoints before eventually arriving at a bevy of tents and refugees near Kandahar, Afghanistan. It might as well have been the middle of nowhere.

◄ Guard to one of the local clerics join a crowd of more than 15,000 pro-Taliban supporters as they listen to speeches given by religious leaders during an anti-American rally.

We were an incredibly disruptive force, media personnel from all over the world making photographs and trying to interview people with the aid of interpreters. The hard part was trying to find moments that looked somewhat authentic and genuine amid this gaggle of photographers and reporters.

In this image, two women are walking away from the press. The bright colors of their traditional garb clashed dramatically against the plainness of the sand. The way the monochromatic backdrop and sparse environment contrasted with their colorful clothing expressed the sense that they were facing a very empty future.

It was sad to see people leave all their belongings and end up in a situation where they didn't have much more than tents and some water coming from the United Nations.

At some point, one of the guards became unhappy that I had photographed something. I noticed his irritation, but I just kept doing my job. As we returned to our vehicle, I could see that he was following us. We were in the last car in the convoy, and I could see him riding parallel to us, pointing an M60 machine gun in our direction.

We had made a big mistake being the last car in the convoy.

The gates that secured the camp closed, and we were separated from the rest of the convoy. We suddenly found ourselves surrounded by about 30 military men with AK-47s.

I pulled out my cell phone only to discover that I had no signal. And if I'd had a signal, George Bush wasn't going to answer; and even if he did, the Delta forces would never come to save us.

Thirty guys with guns surrounded us. It's at moments like these that you immediately lose the illusion of being invulnerable. The fact that you might see yourself as some unarmed idealist or objective observer doesn't mean much of anything. These men with guns just don't care.

I never felt more alone than at this moment in my life.

Thankfully, a female reporter from the *Chicago Tribune* started screaming at them in their dialect. She spoke Pashto!

They were not used to being screamed at by a woman, let alone a Westerner, and they certainly didn't expect to hear her speaking in their own language. They were completely disarmed.

Refugees in Pakistan (2001).

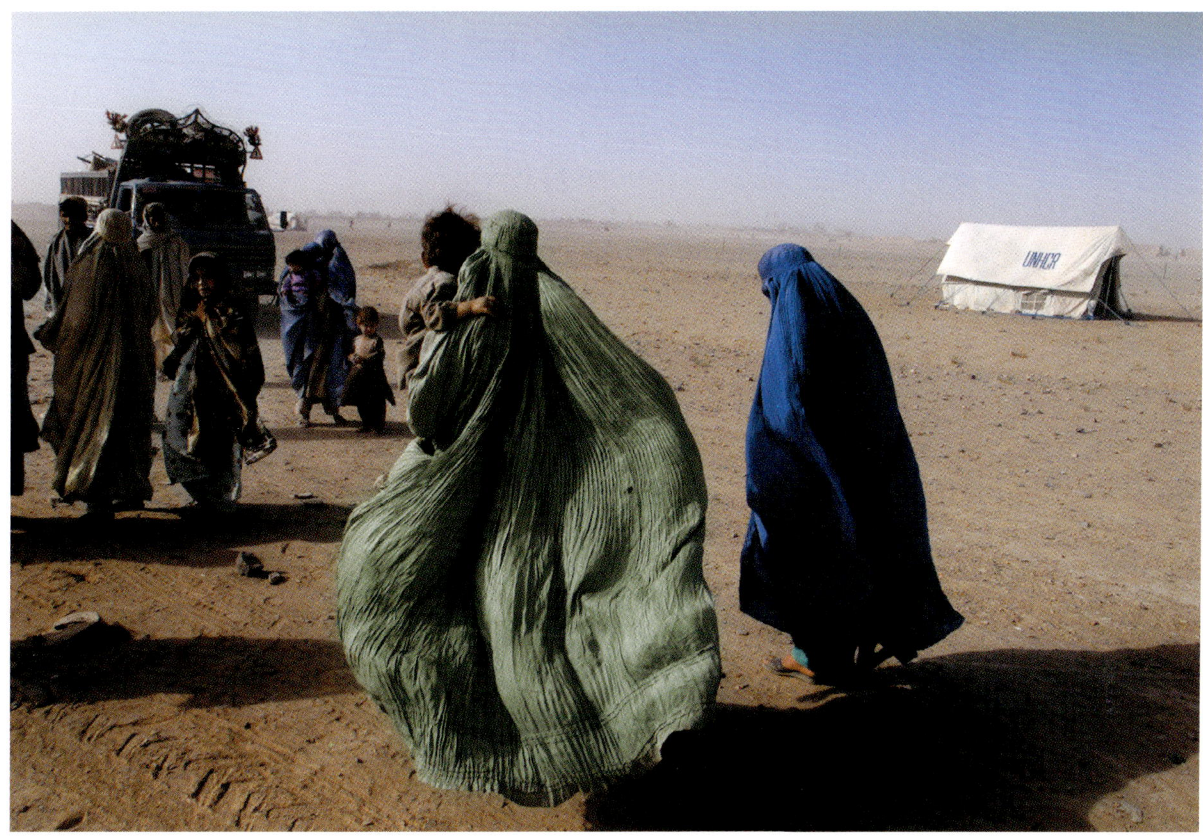

She convinced them that my fancy digital camera had already transmitted the photographs back to Washington, and that at this point they were only getting themselves in more trouble. We explained they should have let the armed man who had fixated on me get in trouble, because now all of them were putting themselves in deep water. After a very tense 25 minutes, they let us go.

It was the longest 25 minutes of my life.

HARSH REALITY

As a photojournalist, you try to do your job with honor, and you try to stay as objective as you can. You come to the table with the purest of intentions. But ultimately, you're on your own as a journalist; you're no different than the people you're covering, and not only can you become endangered as easily and as quickly as your subjects, but also you can in fact become a burden to others by becoming yet another victim, especially if you're irresponsible.

There used to be this unspoken rule that journalists were off-limits. That has been chiseled away, as was painfully demonstrated with the untimely deaths of two great photojournalists, Chris Hondros and Tim Hetherington, who were both killed in Libya in 2011. Prior to that, my friend Tyler Hicks and other journalists were captured and imprisoned by the Libyan government.

You have to be constantly aware that you're walking around in a country or a community with cash and $5,000 to $20,000 worth of camera equipment on your body. You're basically a walking ATM that represents the per capita yearly income of the entire town you're walking into. And you're completely unarmed.

TAKING RISKS

I nearly got myself killed again after making these images of two corpses in a hospital morgue.

Another journalist and I had heard that there had been some sort of uprising, and that the police had violently squashed it—by shooting a 12-year-old boy and an elderly man in the head. We confirmed that when we arrived at the morgue. It was clear to us that they had been executed, each with a bullet wound straight in the middle of their foreheads. I made my photographs, which, with the starkness of that room, spoke to the extreme severity of what had happened.

We were the first people to get that image. These were some of the first dead bodies we knew of. I'm sure there were others who had died before, but these were the first documented victims of the war in Pakistan.

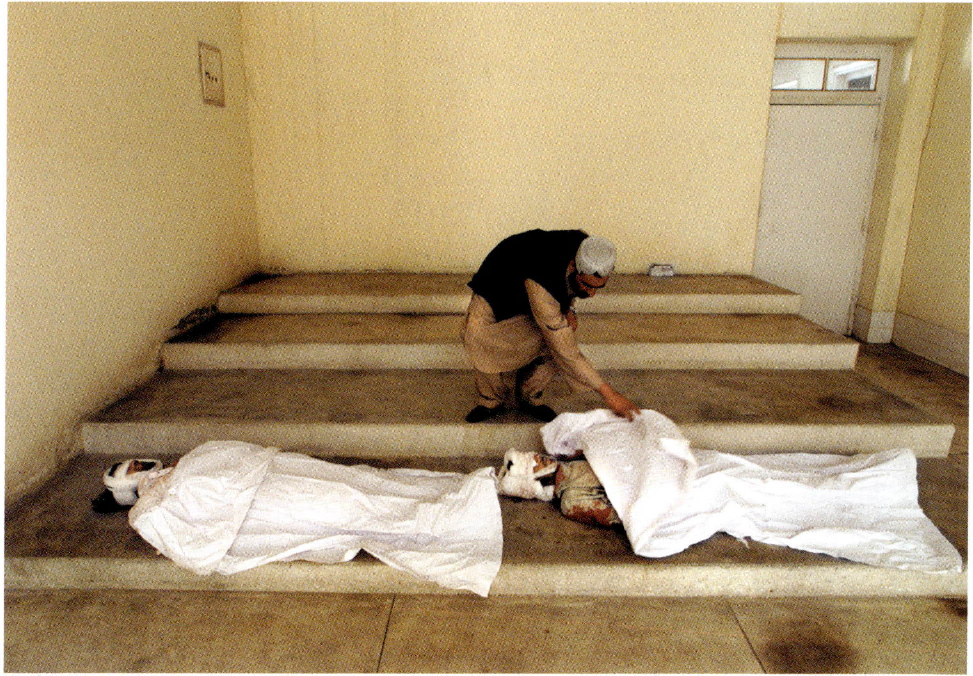

Two bodies.

After that, we went and made the foolish mistake of trying to go back to the town where they had been shot. The smart thing we did was tell the other journalists where we were going, even though it meant giving up our story—our "exclusive."

When the police met up with us, they were extremely angry with us for discovering what they had done. They tried to beat the crap out of us and at one point leveled AK-47s at our heads. In the midst of the chaos, we began to run.

Luckily, it was then that the other photographers—our friends—showed up and started to take pictures of the situation, which diffused it. Had those journalists not showed up, we could have easily been shot and buried with no one ever finding us. We would have simply disappeared without a trace.

SHOWING THE OTHER SIDE

The reality of war is that it's not always back-to-back fighting. It's not nonstop confrontation. It includes a tremendous amount of calm, peace, and apparent normalcy, followed by intense chaos, and horror.

Even in the middle of war, men still have to get their hair cut and beards trimmed. This image tells the story of how life goes on in wartime.

It can be very weird when you know that while people are dying and big missions are being planned, life must go on. Here is a simple scene of the exterior of a barbershop. It speaks of the culture and the peacefulness of the people that are necessary to counterbalance the chaotic elements of war, such as the crazy guys burning effigies in the street.

Men getting haircuts in Pakistan.

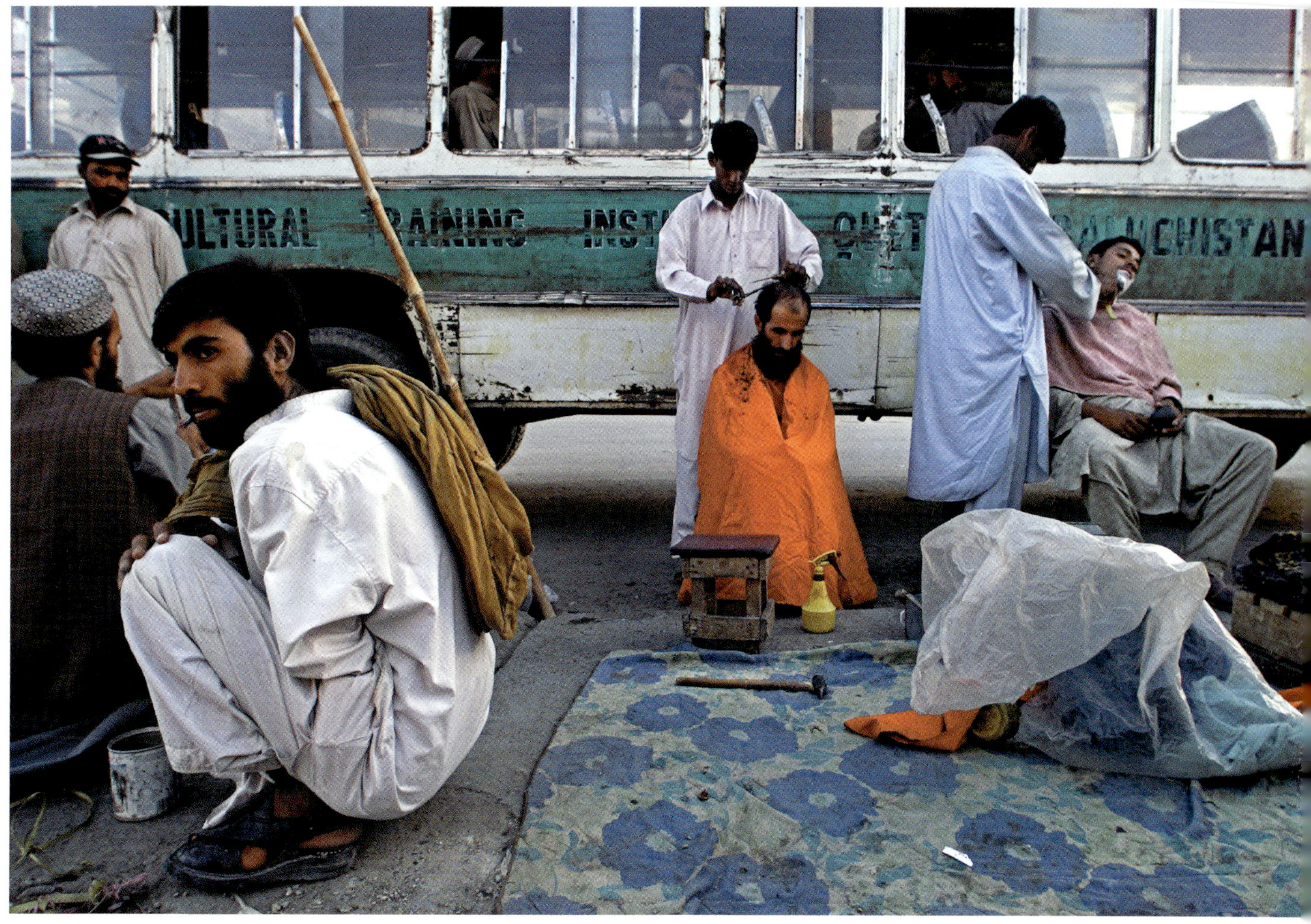

Aerial photograph of the devastation caused by the high winds and heavy flooding in the greater New Orleans area following Hurricane Katrina.

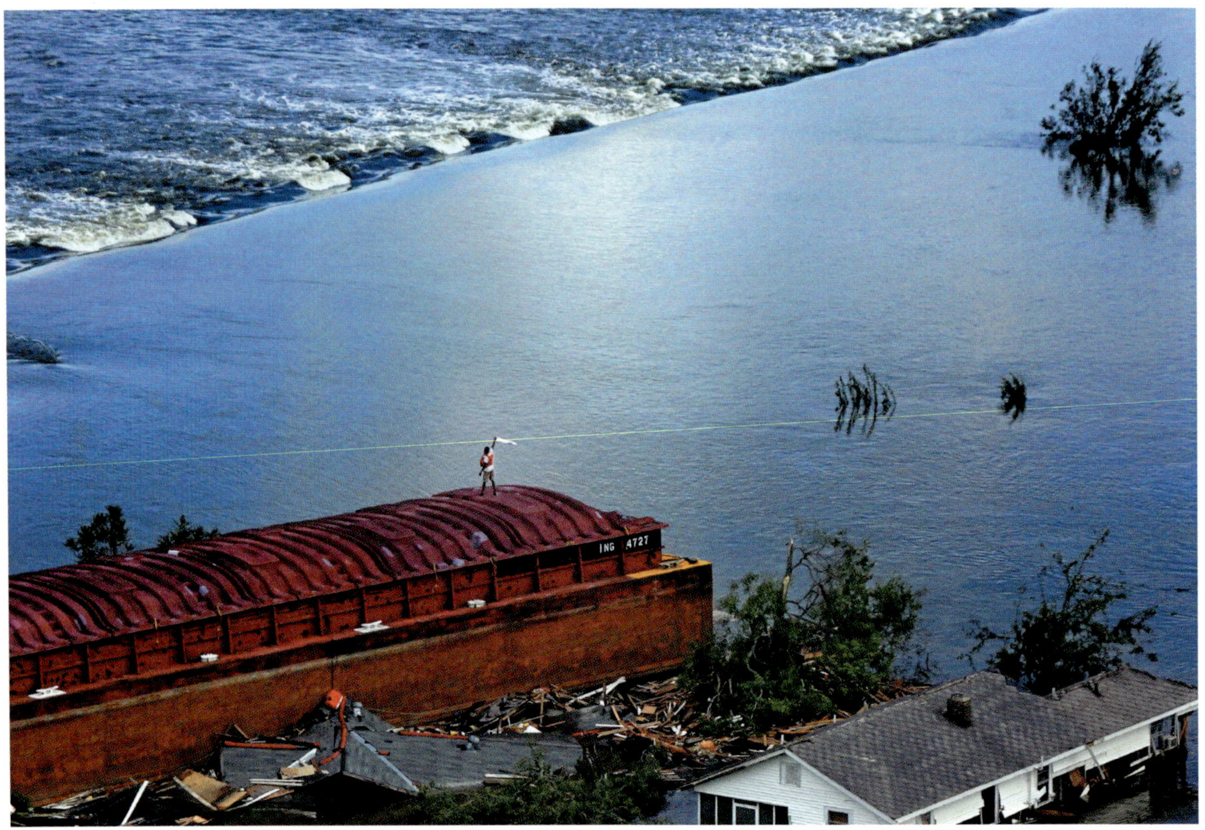

ISO 800 f/6.3 1/2000 200m

DANGERS AT HOME

Similarly, the setting of Hurricane Katrina back at home was absolutely as dangerous as a war zone. A primary reason for this was the complacency of journalists, and that there was absolutely no support for us.

I initially took on a different role in Katrina. Because I was one of the first people to arrive there, I became a kind of a logistics person, to a certain degree. And sometimes logistics involved very simple thinking.

When my friend and seasoned war photographer Tyler Hicks informed me that he was coming down to photograph in New Orleans, I asked him an important question: "Does your satellite phone work?"

"No," he said. "I'll fix it when I get there."

"What do you mean 'I'll fix it when I get in there'? Who are you going call and how?"

There were no working phones. There was no cell service, and if your satellite phone didn't work, you'd be stuck in the water.

It was the little logistical things like those that could kill you. And in New Orleans after Katrina had hit, the only working phones were actually the old phone booths, and you couldn't call collect.

I made sure reporters and photographers had a few rolls of quarters, a ton of water, extra fuel, medical supplies, and, of course, food and clothing. To charge everything from their cameras and computers, they used the power from a car battery.

I also made sure everyone had a paper map so they could get around, because most of the streets were under water, and GPS units had become useless.

A lot of the journalists had been working in Iraq and Pakistan and received marching orders to come back to Katrina, but if they didn't prepare, they were not only putting their own lives at risk but also they were going to be a burden to rescuers.

The infrastructure that we normally would have depended on had been literally washed away. So we had to figure out the logistics from scratch, and they were pretty massive in terms of documenting the impact of Hurricane Katrina.

GETTING ACCESS

After a few days of driving back and forth between New Orleans—or what was left of it—and Baton Rouge, we realized that having a helicopter would give me the advantage of showing a bit more of the scale of what was going on.

But what would have been easy to acquire in New York City was a difficult if not impossible thing to get during the aftermath of Katrina.

We had to make over 100 phone calls over two days to get a helicopter, because all of them were being used by rescue teams and the oil rig companies. Luckily, I was able to connect with two gentlemen from Kentucky who had come down to help rescue people. They were able to fly me around for a week. We've become very good friends.

They flew down from Louisville, Kentucky, just to help. It was a very small Robinson R44 helicopter, but it gave me the opportunity to reveal the scale of the submerged city and water damage from the air, a completely different perspective than what could be captured on the ground. It also gave me access to locations that were impossible to reach by boat or by car, or by any means of transportation other than a helicopter.

It allowed me to capture heart-breaking images including one of a woman being raised in a basket into a rescue helicopter. It's a pretty powerful image to me in that it reflects a sense of the scale of the disaster.

I've always thought about how it must have felt for that woman to be hoisted up in a basket in her T-shirt and jeans, leaving everything she owned and knew beneath her.

Our helicopter provided us the perfect view from which to witness the scale of the devastation. I remember turning to one of the men in our helicopter, whose face had turned as white as a sheet. We were all left speechless.

Helicopter rescue following Hurricane Katrina.

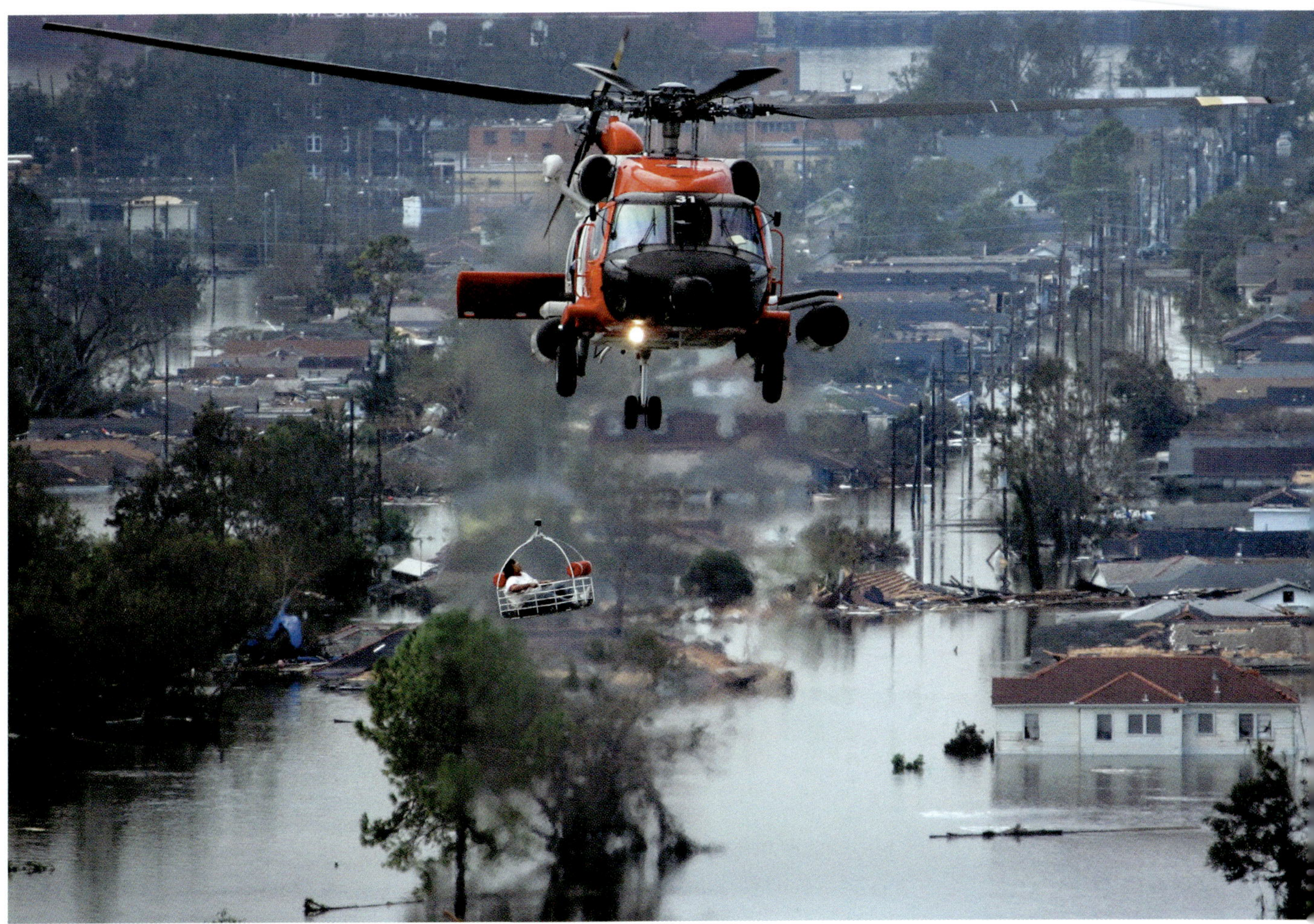

ISO 800 f/6.3 1/2000 300mm

New Orleans. One year later.

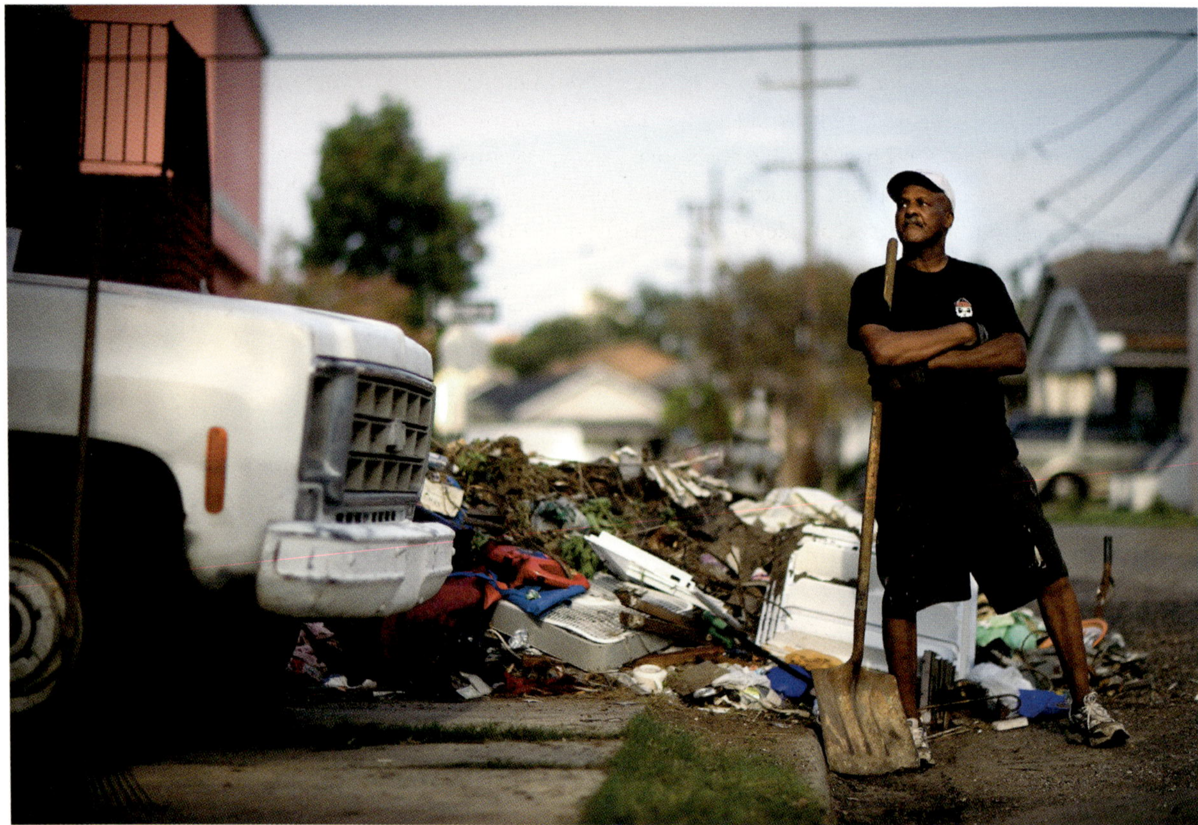

ISO 100 f/1.2 1/8000 85mm

PUTTING A FACE ON TRAGEDY

This is a photograph of a man who had stuck through the entire hurricane at a neighbor's house to watch it for them, and who a year later was still digging and cleaning out his own home and that of his neighbors.

He was one of the guiding lights for the community of New Orleans. He demonstrated the resilience of its people, as well as how much they love their fellow residents and their culture—their music, food, and heritage. It's absolutely insane that this man was still cleaning out his own home one year after the hurricane hit. You know, of course, he'd been helping other people out, but it gives you an idea of how massively destructive this thing was.

As a photographer, sometimes you have to document the devastation with an aerial image. But the risk is that when someone sees the immensity of such devastation, it can be too easy for them to just remove themselves and say, "This is too much." Everything is gone. Everything is destroyed.

The reality is that these were people's homes, their dreams, their lives, and that there were people like this man who were coming back and wanting to rebuild.

You absolutely need to put a face on tragedies, and on the story of that struggle and that kind of perseverance.

It's not just about making factual images. It's about documenting who, to me, are the real heroes—people who don't just give up and move away. It's much easier to leave your home if you have the means and go live somewhere else, or build a new one. It takes a lot more courage to try to dig out and rebuild a community that's been wiped off the map either by war or natural disaster. I admire those people so much.

It's moments like these that can easily and quickly lead to frustration and nervousness and fear. When you swell up with so much emotion, those very feelings will lead you to make a lot of bad photographs.

It's always important for me to remember that I'm not just making photographs for myself, to satisfy the desire of my own ego, but to be there to help tell someone else's story. It can be a big event like Katrina or Pakistan, but it could also be the everyday life of normal people. Those photos of the commonplace are important too, because they document our lives as we are today, in a very real manner. That's the beauty of photography: over time, those images can and do become incredibly valuable.

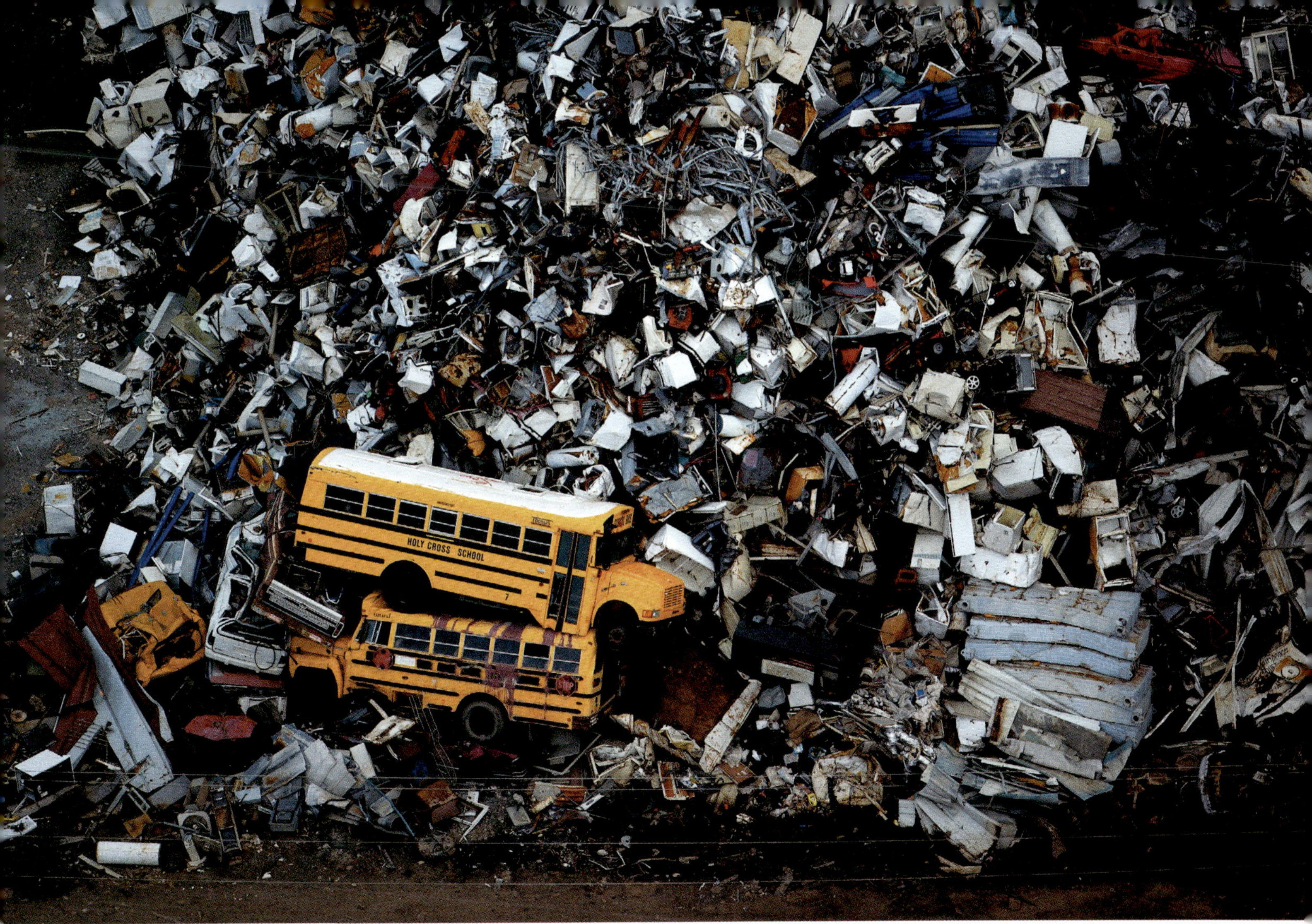

Aerial view of the cleanup of flattened vehicles, buses, and refrigerators in a dump adjacent to the Lower 9th Ward.

ISO 500 f/4 1/1250 500mm

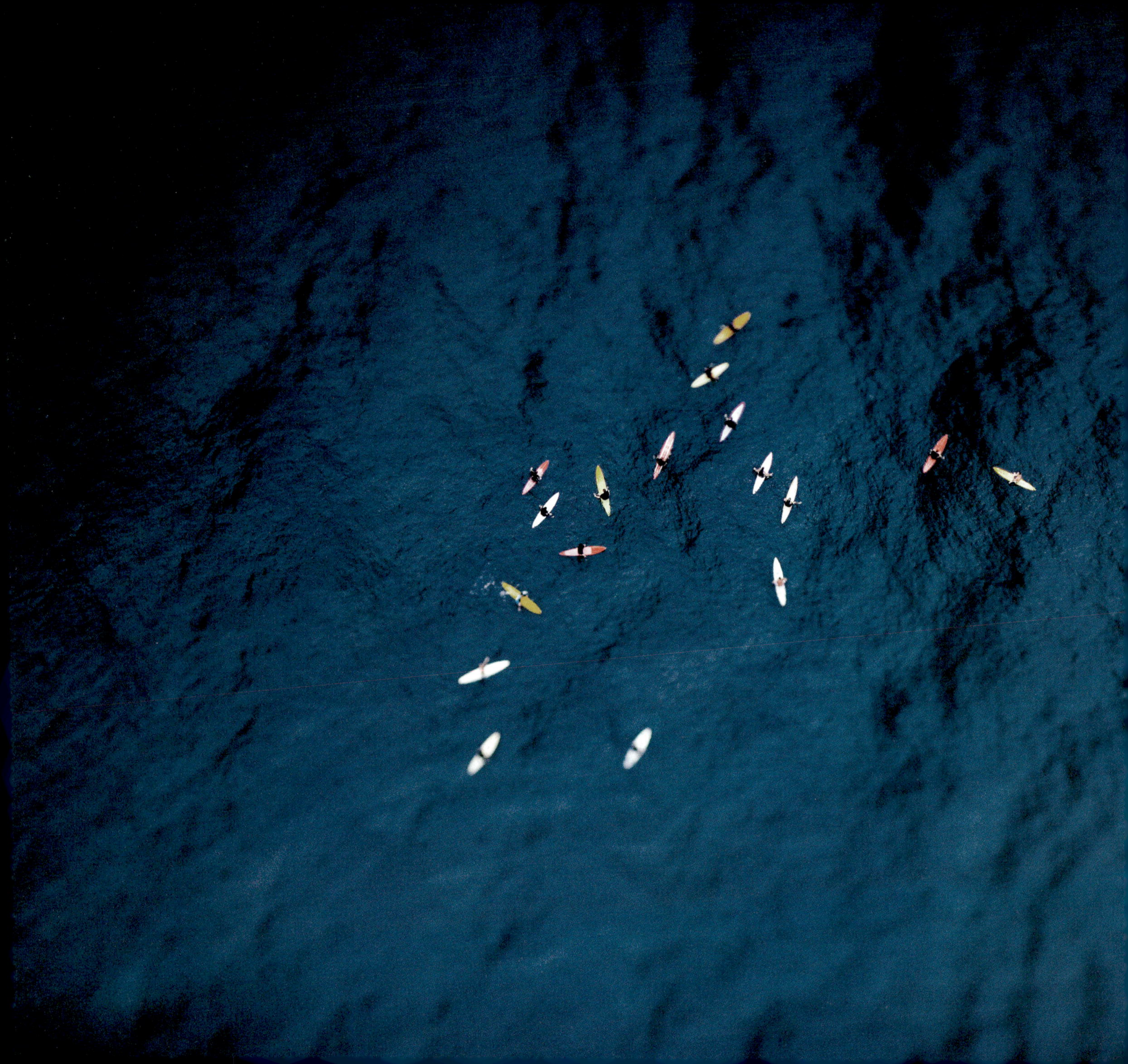

CHAPTER 6

KISS (KEEP IT SIMPLE, STUPID)

The photograph on the following page of a fencer winning the Olympic gold is one of the images that came as a result of everything I'd learned and practiced up to that moment. It is those lessons, both good and bad, that allow me to make bets and take a calculated risk.

I was photographing the Olympic women's gymnastics semifinals in Beijing in 1998, while one building away, the men's fencing finals were occurring. At a certain point, I knew I needed images from both events.

◀ Surfers wait for waves during the 2006 Rip Curl Pipeline Masters competition at the Banzai Pipeline on Oahu, Hawaii.

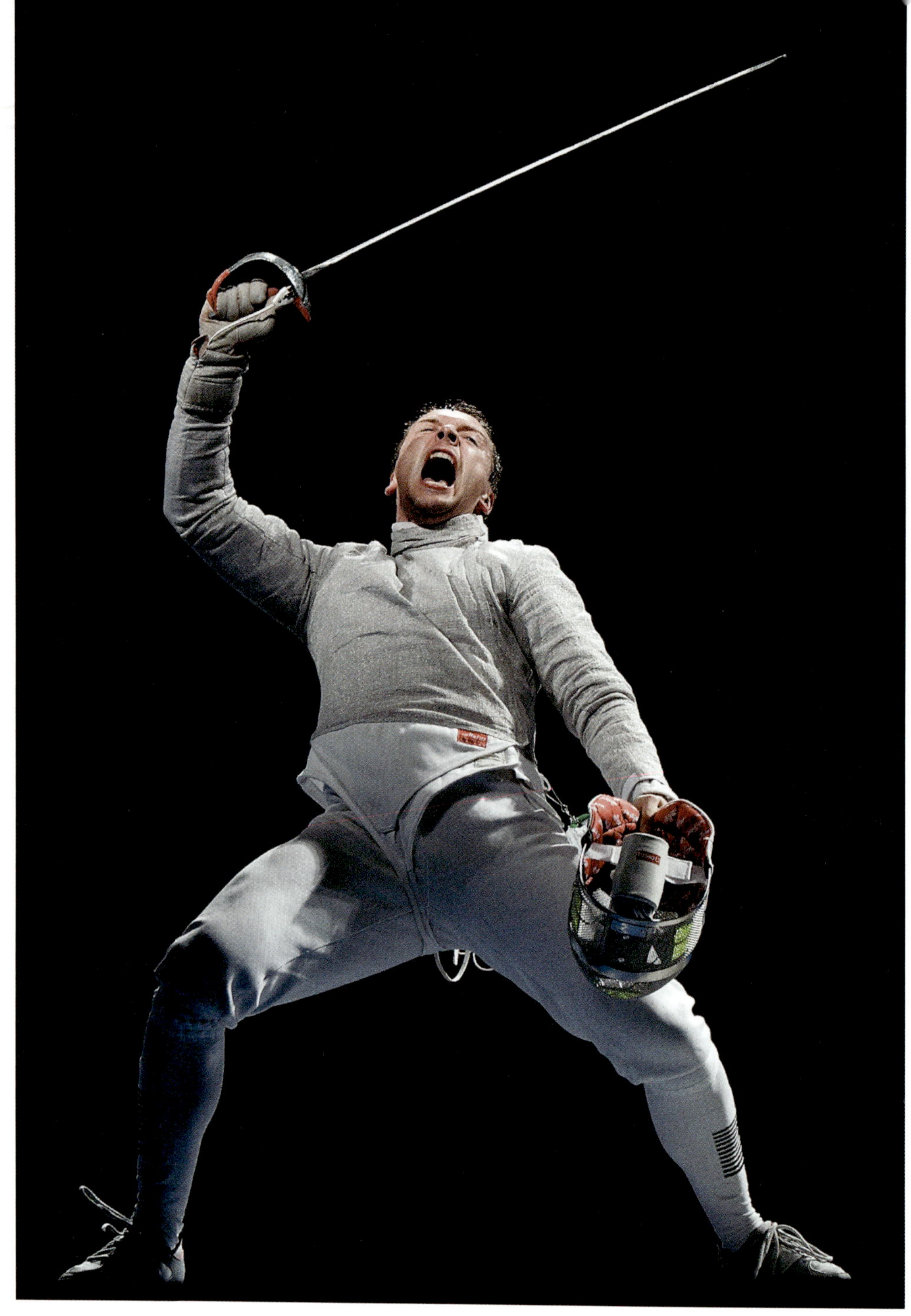

Julien Pillet reacts to winning the gold medal in the Men's Team Sabre final in the 2008 Summer Olympic Games.

ISO 1250 f/2.8 1/1000 200mm

I started with gymnastics because the preliminaries for fencing were irrelevant. However, photographers had been waiting at the fencing venue for five, six, or seven hours to secure their seat, to ensure that they would get the gold medal shot. And while they would shoot many images while they were waiting, it was obviously the gold medal moment that was the most important.

Since it was the semifinals for gymnastics and there would be no gold medals that day, I shot for about two hours, and I then took a risk and left early.

The other photographers were wondering where I was going.

"Don't worry about it," I said, and began to make my way through three security checkpoints just to reach the building across the street.

When I finally got up to the fencing venue, the fencers were in the middle of a match. I looked over to the fencing coach, who happened to be French, and I asked him in French, "What's happening?"

"It's the gold medal match," he said.

"Who's winning?"

"We are," he said. "Match point."

I literally showed up at the last fencing point—the match point, during a break in the action when people were allowed to get up and move. I still had my rolling bag in my left hand, and I had my camera in my right. I got down on one knee, raised my camera with a 70–200mm lens to my eye, focused, and got this picture. Could you ask for better?

All the photographers looked back at me with sheer disgust that I had shown up at the perfect angle, at the perfect time, and nailed the image while they had been waiting there for hours.

When you do the Olympics, you realize that even though an event lasts five hours, the really important things happen at the end. You definitely can't plan on showing up 30 seconds before the final and always expect to get the shot. But the important lesson was that by knowing my equipment and being prepared, I was able to get the shot when it mattered most.

STARTING SIMPLY

The best gift I received from my dad was one camera and one lens. He gave me a Nikon F3 with a 50mm lens and what was called a brick of Kodak Tri-X, which consisted of 20 rolls of film. That was the only lens I had, and when you only have one lens, you learn how to use it inside and out. You learn where it's weak and where it can be really strong.

At 15 years old, I didn't have the extra cash to spend on the luxury of photography. My mother was divorced, and my father was living in France and not making a boatload of money. So I went to shoot Bar Mitzvahs and weddings with the hope of making a few hundred bucks to buy the next lens. It took me a year or two to have a collection of lenses.

With each lens purchase, I would have the time to work exclusively with that lens for months. When I got the 24mm lens, I learned its sweet spot; and I learned that if I moved too far, it wasn't an effective lens choice, and if I was too close, the images suffered from too much distortion.

I began to learn that each lens, each choice of equipment, had to be rooted in what I was trying to achieve with the camera. Otherwise, I would be bringing everything and the kitchen sink with no guarantee that I would get the shot.

As much as I evangelize gear for the companies with whom I work, it's important to remember that gear alone never makes the picture. Gear that doesn't work or that you don't know well stands in your way of getting the photograph.

Sometimes you definitely need a specific piece of gear, because it's the only piece of gear that will allow you to make that picture, but people think that that's true a bit too often. The reality is that you can make a great photograph with virtually any lens or camera there is, but only if you know what you are doing.

Really, it's only their knowledge and experience with those lenses that will make the difference between getting the shot and not getting it.

New Orleans: one year after Hurricane Katrina (2006).

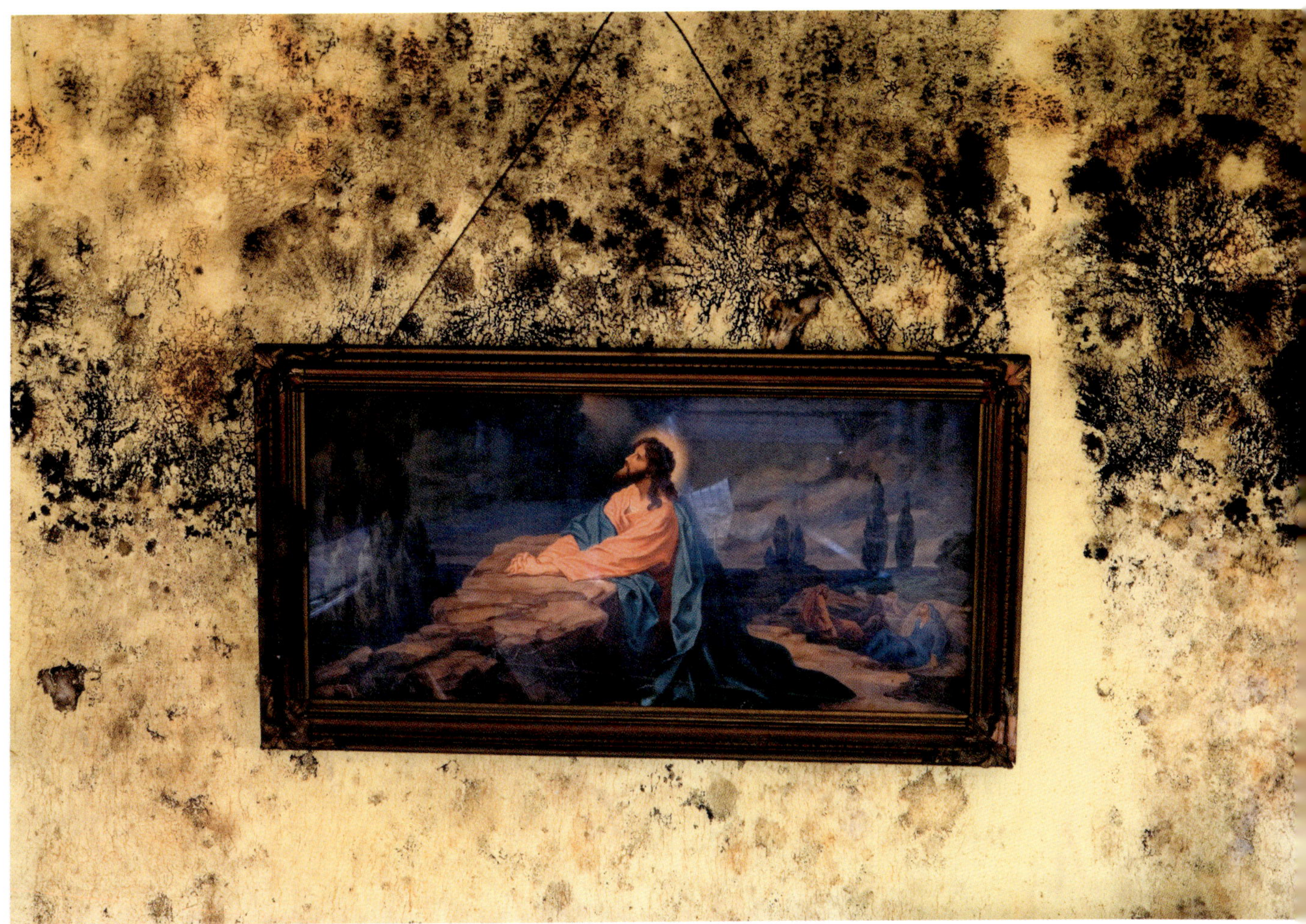

ISO 100 f/22 20.0s 57mm

Thousands of Afghans fled to Pakistan fearing for their lives, either from Taliban reprisals or bombs falling from above (September 9, 2001).

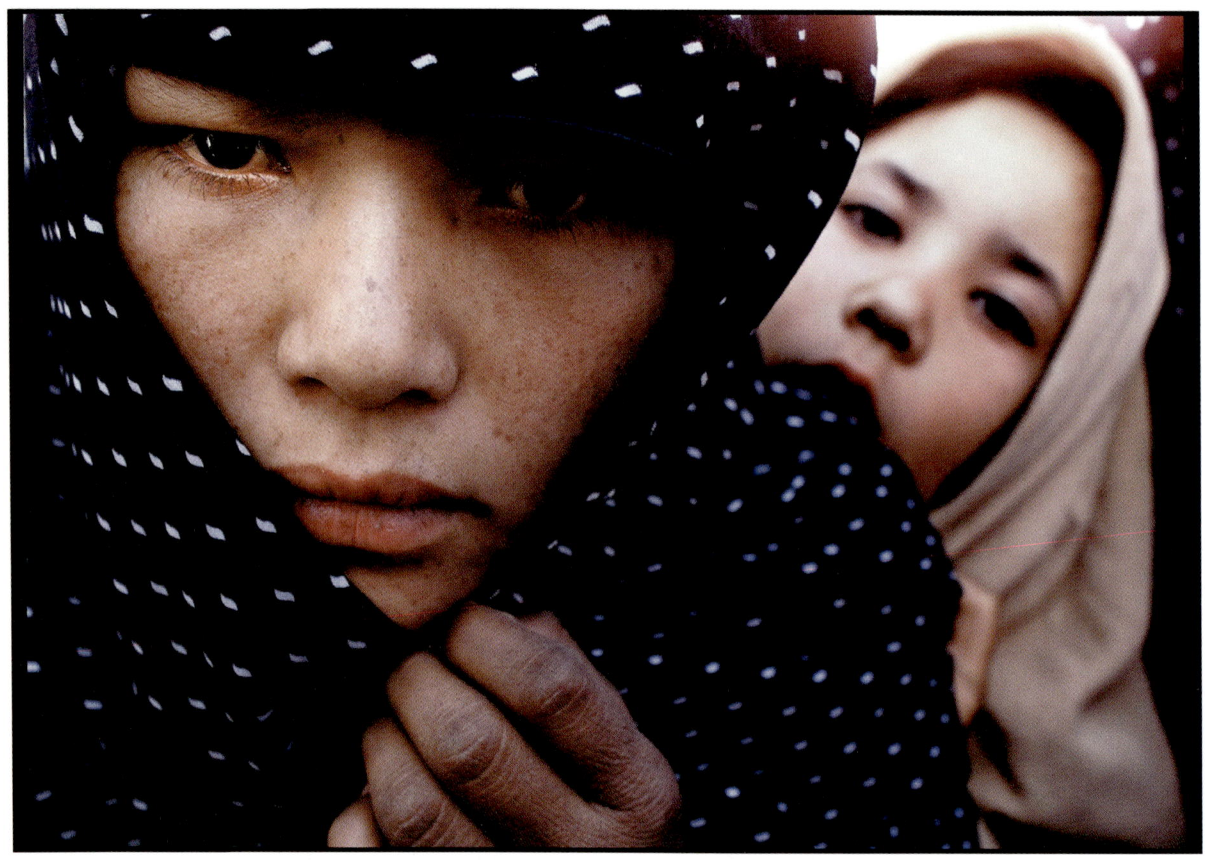

I moved in close with a 24mm lens and chose to fill the frame to eliminate all the potential distractions.

WHEN THE SITUATION DICTATES THE CHOICE

I was in a Pakistan refugee camp not long after 9/11, photographing under horrific noon light with an early-generation digital camera that did not capture Raw files. Many potential subjects were suffering from "chipmunk lighting," which is what I call it when you have horrible shadows under people's brow, nose, and chin. So the light was terrible and the camera had some challenging limitations.

Because of the high-noon light, my choices were either to shoot in open shade or to expose the shot to the sky and create a silhouette. I chose the former because this was going to be a very straightforward photograph. This is a mother who has left Afghanistan because she feared getting bombed by American B-52s. The Taliban shot her husband in the head in front of her and her daughter as they crossed the border.

She was talking to a reporter about her fear and showing him her passport, while I framed her and waited for her to take a pause. I then shot this frame.

The choice of the best lens for this situation was a simple one. We were in a very confined space. There were other reporters and TV crews around us. So I moved in close with a 24mm lens and chose to fill the frame to eliminate all of the potential distractions. Instead, the viewer focuses on the woman's eyes and those of her daughter looking over her shoulder.

DON'T BE OVERWHELMED BY GEAR

Master photographers like Henri Cartier-Bresson and David Alan Harvey walked around with a Leica and a 35mm lens, and maybe a second body with a longer or wider lens. That's it. And that's because they knew their style. They knew what they were looking for. They saw shots every second that could be shot with a 400mm f/2.8, but that's not what they were going for. They've made a conscious decision to let those shots go because of the style that they were pursuing.

Just because you can afford to buy a lens or have it available in your bag, it doesn't mean you should use it or even carry it around. When you take too much gear or, more important, when you overthink things, you can become your own worst enemy.

Sometimes the very best thing to do is just to bring one camera and one lens. It is then that you are completely free to move around, blend in, and not be distracted by having to put this big camera bag down every time you're ready to make a picture.

The philosophy I try to live by is KISS (Keep It Simple, Stupid), because while I'm busy thinking about the gear, the moment has come and gone.

And although missing a shot can be disappointing, it's always important to remember that this isn't rocket science. If you miss a photograph, no one dies on the operating table. No, one falls from the sky because you designed a rocket poorly. This is photography and it should be fun; at it's best, it's liberating.

SIMPLE IMAGE, SIMPLE CHOICE

The photograph on the facing page is from a series on how man interacts with nature, and I think this image is one of those beautiful, quiet moments. I was at the beach with my family. One of the most important rules of photography is always to have a camera with you. The photographer Chase Jarvis said, "The best camera is the one that you have with you." I think that's a great quote, and it's very true. In this case, it's a very simple image.

I was walking with a Leica M8 and a 35mm lens. I saw this man wearing a white hat and a white T-shirt walk into this body of water, and it became a very graphic moment. There's a lot of negative space with that one spot of light.

It's one of the few times I shot in aperture priority mode. In this case I turned the EV (exposure composition) down one-third to get a nice, rich negative (although in this case, I was shooting digital), and from there it was just point and shoot to capture the moment. There's no need to overcomplicate things. Sometimes the simple approach wins out, and I think this was one of those times.

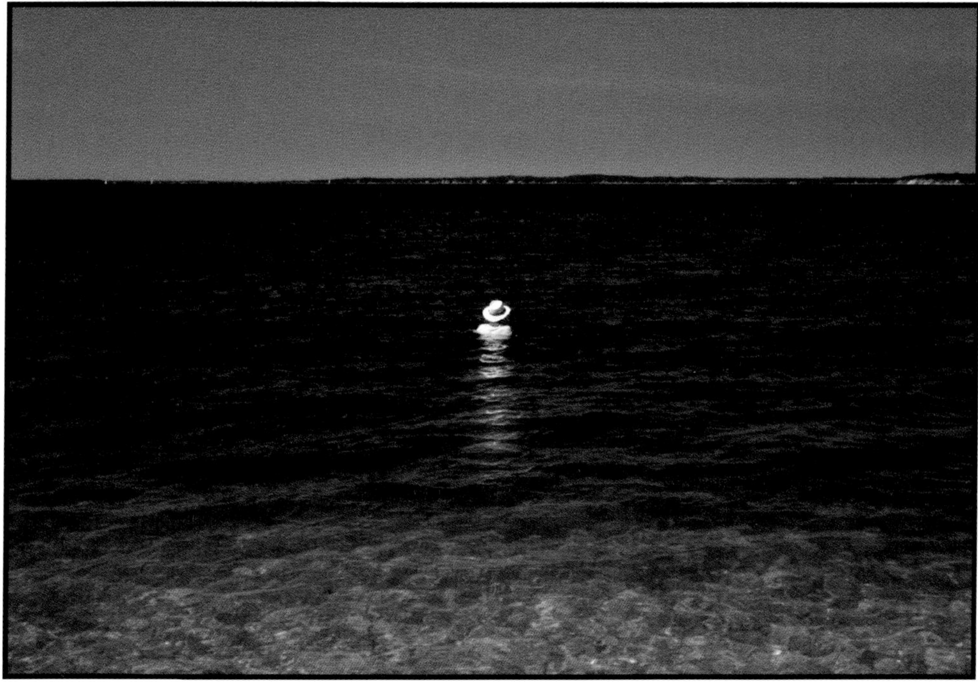

Lens: "Little Black Box," Sag Harbor, New York, 2007.

ISO 320 1/500 26mm

CORE EQUIPMENT

My core equipment would be one or two bodies that have full-frame sensors. If I had just two lenses to go to heaven with, they would likely be prime lenses. They would be a fixed 35mm and a 135mm. And if I could manage it, I would also include a 500mm f/4, because I really love super telephotos, which is what I use to take a lot of my aerial and sports images.

But for the average person I would recommend a 24–70mm f/2.8, because it covers a wide spectrum of focal length. And the second lens would be the 70–200mm f/2.8. Between those two lenses, you have enough range to cover practically anything in the world, be it fashion, nature, sports, or photojournalism. Those are the two mainstay lenses.

After starting with two bodies, each with one of those lenses, I would probably go to 16–35mm f/2.8 for a wider focal-length range and more dynamic imagery.

Weight and size are a huge factor, so the Canon 5D MK II series is probably my favorite body ever. It's the perfect size. It's close to weightless, rugged enough, and its battery lasts quite a long time.

The Canon 1D series bodies are the ones you take to the big assignments like the Olympics, a war, or any extreme shooting situation where you know that a quick trip to the repair shop is not going to be an option. The Canon bodies give you reliable performance that's insured by weather sealing and resistance to extreme heat or cold. They are the Rolls Royces of camera bodies but I think most people don't need them.

If I had just two lenses to go to heaven with, they would likely be prime lenses. They would be a fixed 35mm and a 135mm.

Bonneville salt flats in Bonneville, Utah (2005).

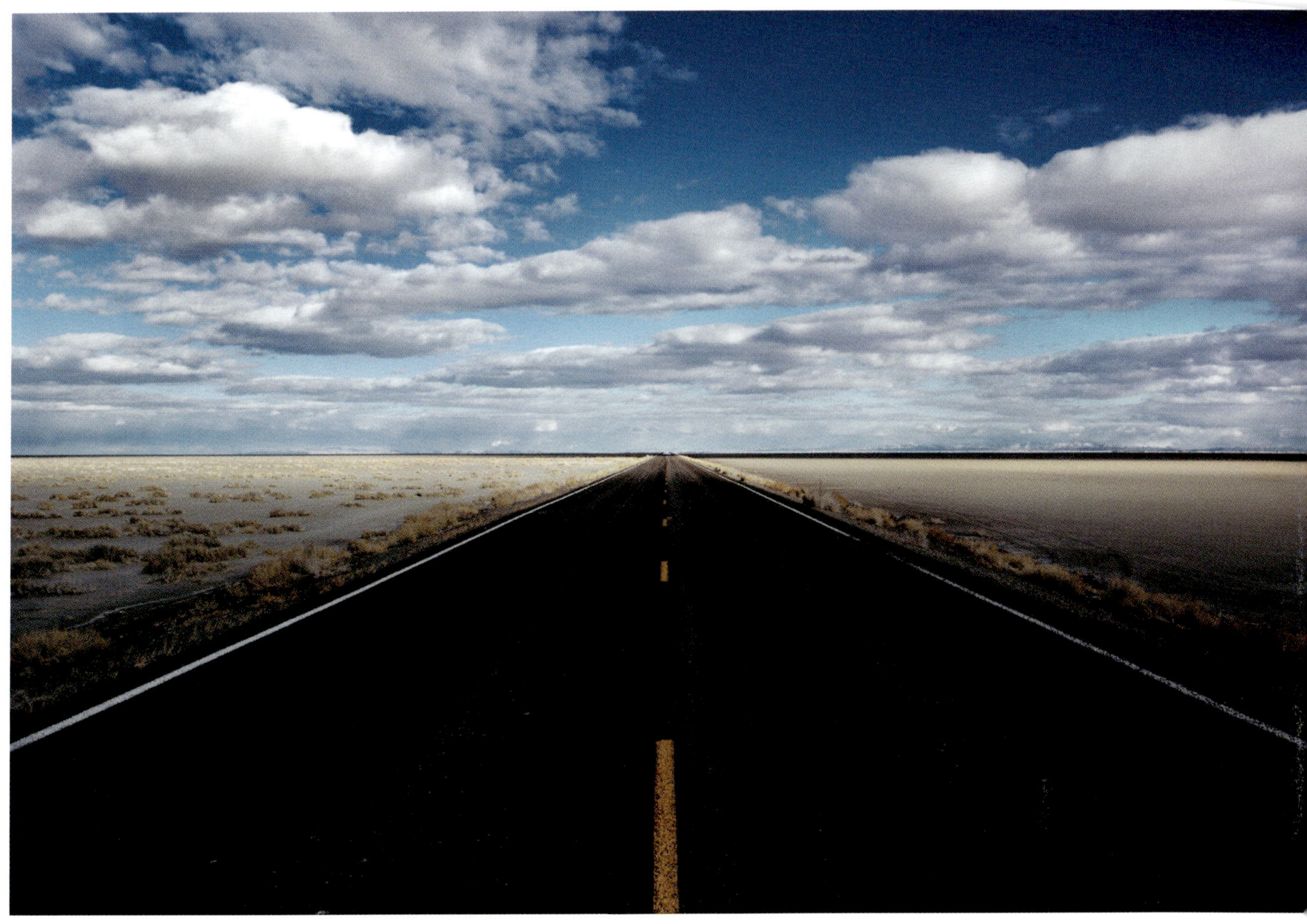

ISO 100 f/8 1/500 35mm

Hundreds spending their lunch hour in Bryant Park in April 2002, one of the first times New Yorkers had ventured out en masse to enjoy the sunny weather since 9/11.

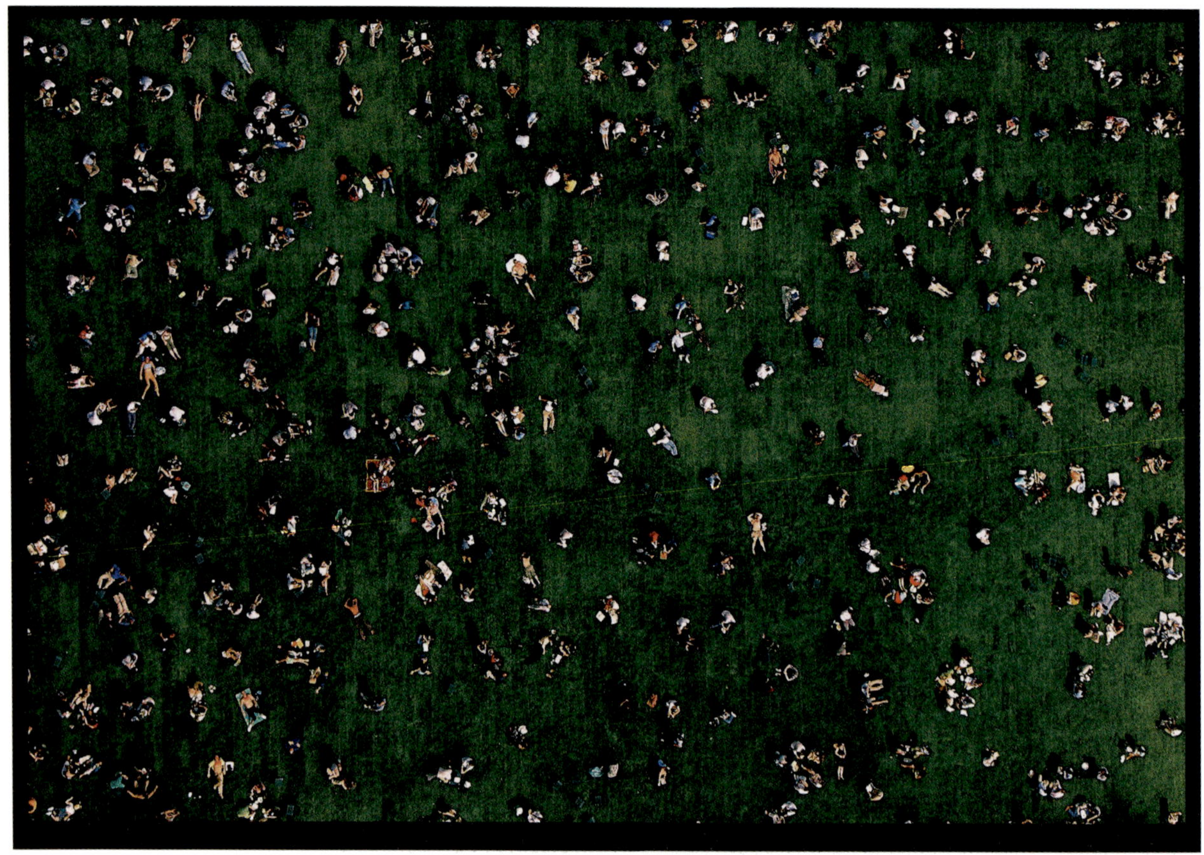

THE RIGHT LENS FOR THE JOB

This image of Bryant Park is actually not an aerial shot taken from a helicopter. When you don't have a helicopter in the budget, try to find a tall building.

This particular day was not a big news day and the newspaper didn't have a big news photo, so they had to find something to put on the front page. The deadline for the front page was 4 p.m., and I was rushing out of the office with only two hours to find an image for the paper.

I drove away from the office to Bryant Park, where I saw this mass of people out in the field. From ground level, a wide-angle lens would have made it very hard to show the number of people there. So I called the building manager I knew for the Verizon building and asked if I could go up and gain access to one of the office windows on the 50th floor.

I got up there and made a series of images with a 28–300mm zoom lens. The lens offers a pretty incredible range, and it's a very useful lens for news because you can shoot pretty much anything. When you're running around for breaking news, you don't have time to sort through three, four, or five cameras and ten lenses. You've got to move really, really fast.

I tend not to use that lens as much anymore because it's a bit slower with regard to f-stop, and while the optical quality is quite good, it's not as good as the 24–70mm or the 70–200mm. While I took this shot with a 28–300mm zoom lens, I had to make sure I had a fast enough shutter speed to freeze any sort of vibration, in this case 1/500th of a second or higher.

This was a really cool moment: It was the first spring after 9/11, and I think the photograph—which showed up three or four columns wide on the front page of the *New York Times*—really struck an emotional chord with New Yorkers because it was the first time they saw people going back to normal life.

I saw this photo cut out and hung in people's cubicles four years later just because I think it struck that chord that a newspaper photo can sometimes do. It has always meant a lot to me for that reason.

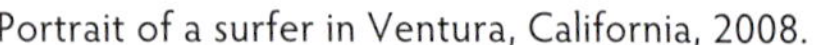
Portrait of a surfer in Ventura, California, 2008.

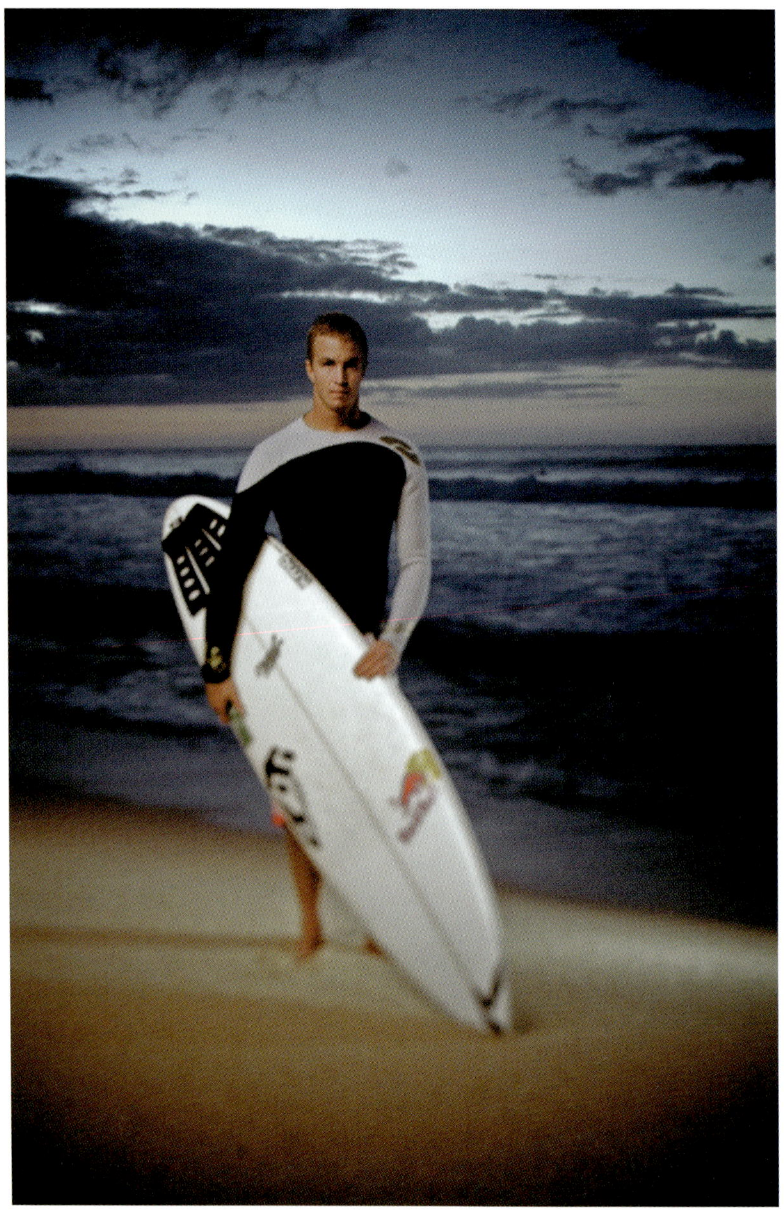

ISO 100 f/6.3 1/15 45mm

ACCESSORIES AND WORKFLOW

I always have extra batteries, and I always make sure to charge them before I go to sleep. No exceptions. Ever. No matter how tired I am, no matter what the excuse is, I never go to bed without making sure my batteries are charging.

I tend to have a dozen memory cards with me. I always keep the cards on me, usually in a fanny pack, in my pocket, or clipped to my belt. You never want your memory card or batteries more than a hand's reach away from you.

I also separate my memory cards into two wallets. I never have all my memory cards in one wallet. So, God forbid I should lose one pack, I have another set at the ready.

I place empty formatted cards face-up in my Think Tank Pixel Pocket Rocket card wallets. After I've used them, I flip them over so I see their backside. That way I never have to wonder whether a card has data on it or not. Once I've copied the files over, I put them face-up, but inserted vertically, so that in case the hard drive to which I've copied the files fails, I know I still have the files on the card.

Unless I'm doing time-lapse photography, I don't use the biggest cards available. I don't want to put too many eggs in one basket—you never want to fill your card fully; you always want to leave a little space, because that's where you have the potential to run into problems with data corruption.

You don't need many accessories beyond lenses, charged batteries, and memory cards. However, I recommend that everyone not walk around with their lens cap on their lens and instead keep them stored in your camera bag. The only time I ever use lens caps is when I'm protecting lenses from damage during shipping.

And without exception, the first thing, you should buy with every lens is a quality haze or UV filter such as a Schneider B+W or Tiffen. The purpose of such a filter has nothing to do with the haze or the UV; its purpose is to physically protect the lens. It's a barrier that protects the front element should you drop it.

I find it ironic that people would buy and attach the cheapest filter to a $2,000 lens, or that they would spend $5,000 on a camera body and then buy the cheapest CompactFlash (CF) card. When you think about it, it doesn't make much sense, considering the investment you've made and how much you are going to use that card or lens. If you are going to invest that much money on your camera or lens, don't compromise on the cards or filters you use with them.

Last, I always have a chamois cloth, because it can provide a little added layer of protection when I wrap my camera in it. I can also use it to wipe away any dirt or gunk that gets on the lens or camera body.

REMEMBER TO DIVERSIFY

One very important thing to keep in mind when you're doing a series of photographs is to diversify not only the lenses you use but also the type of photographs you take. This is an example of a macro shot—a detail shot of a spur inside a ranch for a commercial assignment on the paniolo in Hawaii. It was lit with two off-camera strobes and a macro lens. A macro shot gives the user kind of a break from the wide vistas or the super-long telephoto lens shots, and it's a really important element to any series.

This image was made with the 24–70mm f/4.5 lens; one of the lesser-known features about this lens is that it's an incredible macro lens. Not only is it a fantastic general-purpose lens with which you can shoot pretty much 90 percent of the stuff you'll ever want to shoot, but also it shoots in macro, and that's quite important.

One very important thing to keep in mind when you're doing a series of photographs is to diversify not only the lenses you use but also the type of photographs you take.

A detail shot of one of the spurs in the paniolo stables in Waimea on the Big Island of Hawaii for an essay on the Hawaiian cowboy, or paniolo, in January, 2006.

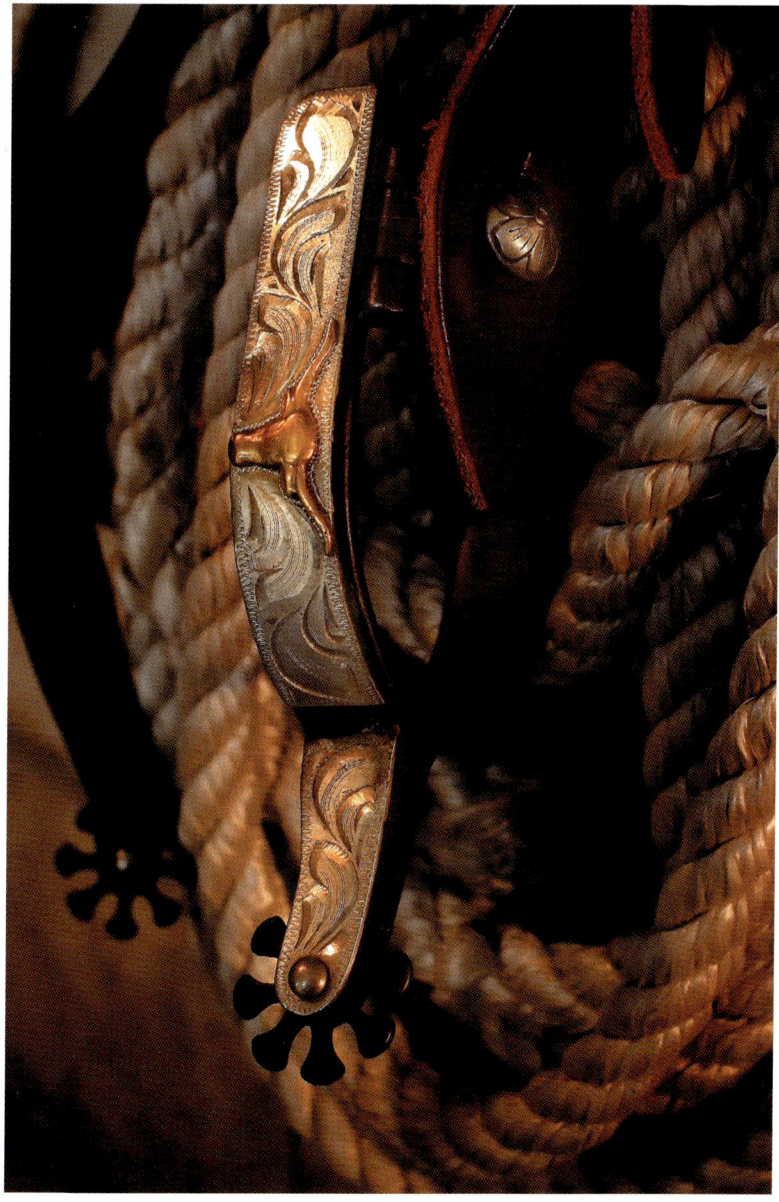

ISO 100 f/4.5 1/3 24-70mm

BRINGING IT ALL TOGETHER

Pulling off this photograph of an engineer atop a gargoyle on the Chrysler Building took me seven months and 14 contractual rewrites with the Chrysler lawyers. And when it came down to actual shooting time, I had only one back-to-back sunset and sunrise in which to make the photograph happen. So, knowing my equipment was absolutely necessary. There were no second chances.

There were eight gargoyles to choose from, but this is the one I chose because it had the best point of view, where I could get both a sunrise and a sunset shot. I knew it was critical to get the camera lower, so I had to devise a way to see what the camera was seeing, because I couldn't put my eye to the camera's viewfinder.

The issue with this photograph is that when you stand on the 77th floor, level with the gargoyle, it intersects the city skyline, which is distracting. So I brought a Manfrotto Mega Boom, which provides up to a 10-foot extension arm with rotating pan-tilt head. I lowered it and controlled the camera using an Ethernet cable to my laptop computer. A wireless system wouldn't work because the Empire State Building's radio antenna was emitting more than 14 million watts of frequency, which created too much interference.

I was forced to compose by making small adjustments, frame by frame, as I viewed images on the screen of my laptop. There was no LiveView back then.

I chose to shoot this with my 24mm tilt-shift lens, but not for any reason other than it's a very sharp lens.

As well as shooting at the right time of day, I realized that even though the silver on the gargoyle would pick some of the color of the sky, the engineer would have been rendered close to black. To solve this, I put two Profoto 7bs battery-operated strobes about ten stories down, pointing up with CTO orange gel to light the bottom of the gargoyle. I put one 7b behind him with the grid, also the CTO, to rim-light his back and arm that you can see.

Then, because I didn't want to go out there, I had him put on two Canon Speedlights with orange gels set off by remote wireless triggers to provide illumination for his face.

So, there's a lot of technical stuff going on in what is ostensibly a simple image.

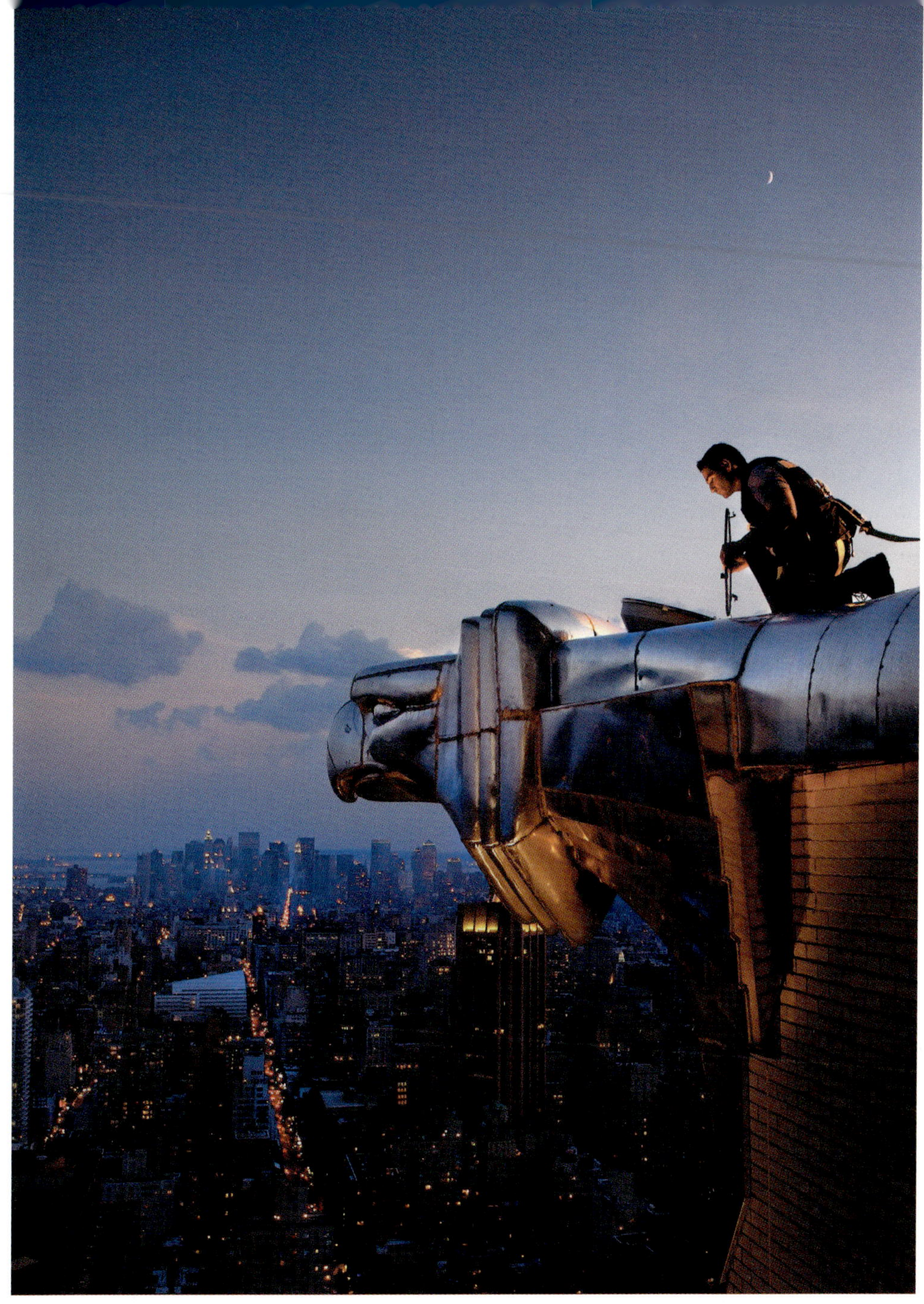

An engineer kneels on a gargoyle on the Chrysler Building in New York City (2006).

ISO 160 f/5.6 1/250 24mm

IT'S THE SMALL THINGS

A shot such as the one of the Chrysler Building could have been ruined by virtually anything that went wrong, but the reality is it's the small things that almost always get you.

If you study 95 percent of the failures to see what happened, you'll quickly find the rules to live by. You missed a photograph because the card wasn't properly formatted, so consequently you make a rule always to format your cards before beginning a shoot. The one time your camera runs out of battery power, you make it a rule that you never go to bed without putting your battery on a charger.

The choice to take care of those little things is not just an option, it's imperative, because proper preparation prevents poor performance. It comes down to discipline. There's a lot of discipline in photography, from knowing your gear to using it all consistently, but it's all there to serve a singular pursuit: to get the photograph.

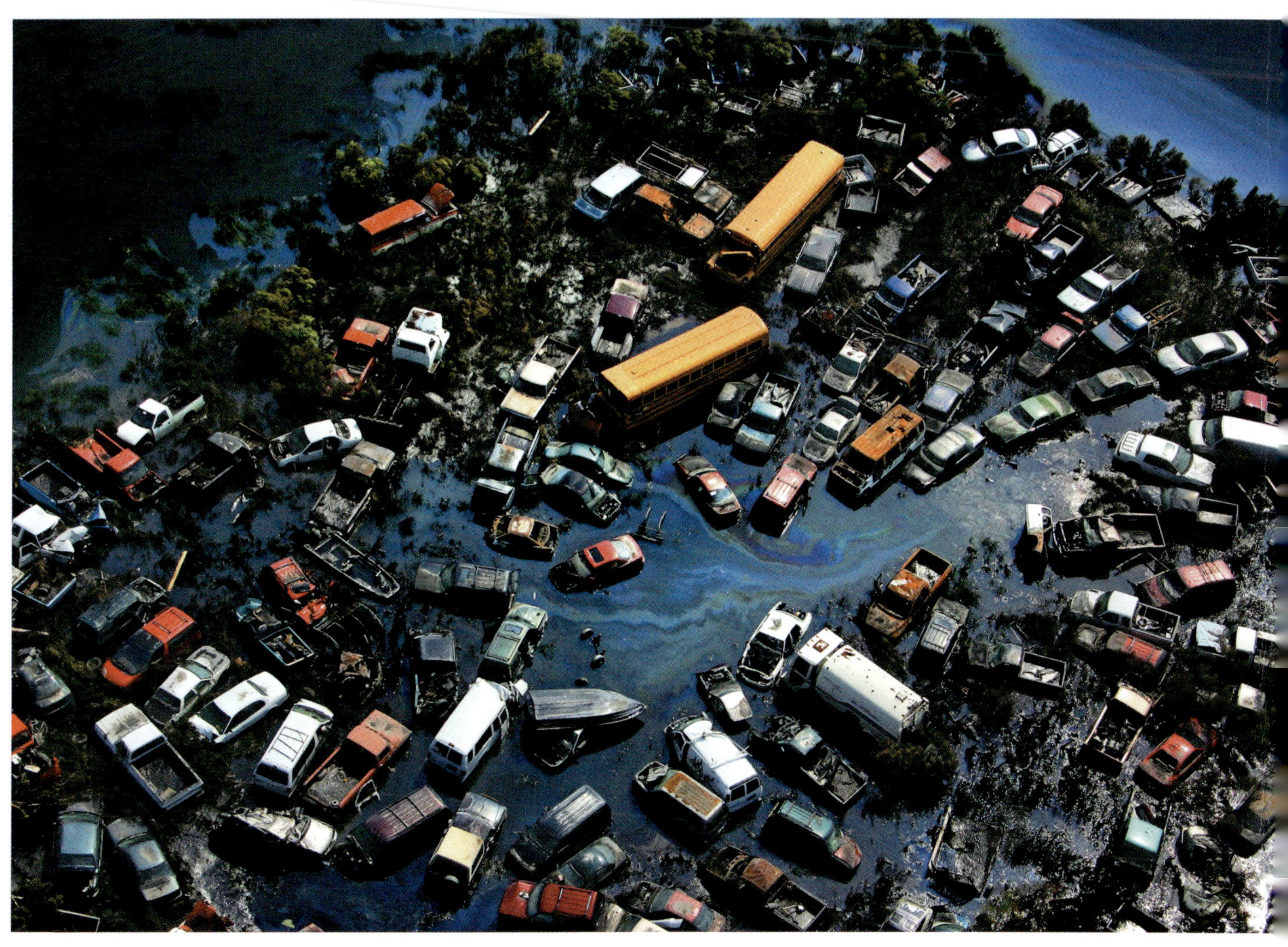

Aerial photograph of the devastation caused by Hurricane Katrina in 2005.

ISO 250 f/9 1/1600 60mm

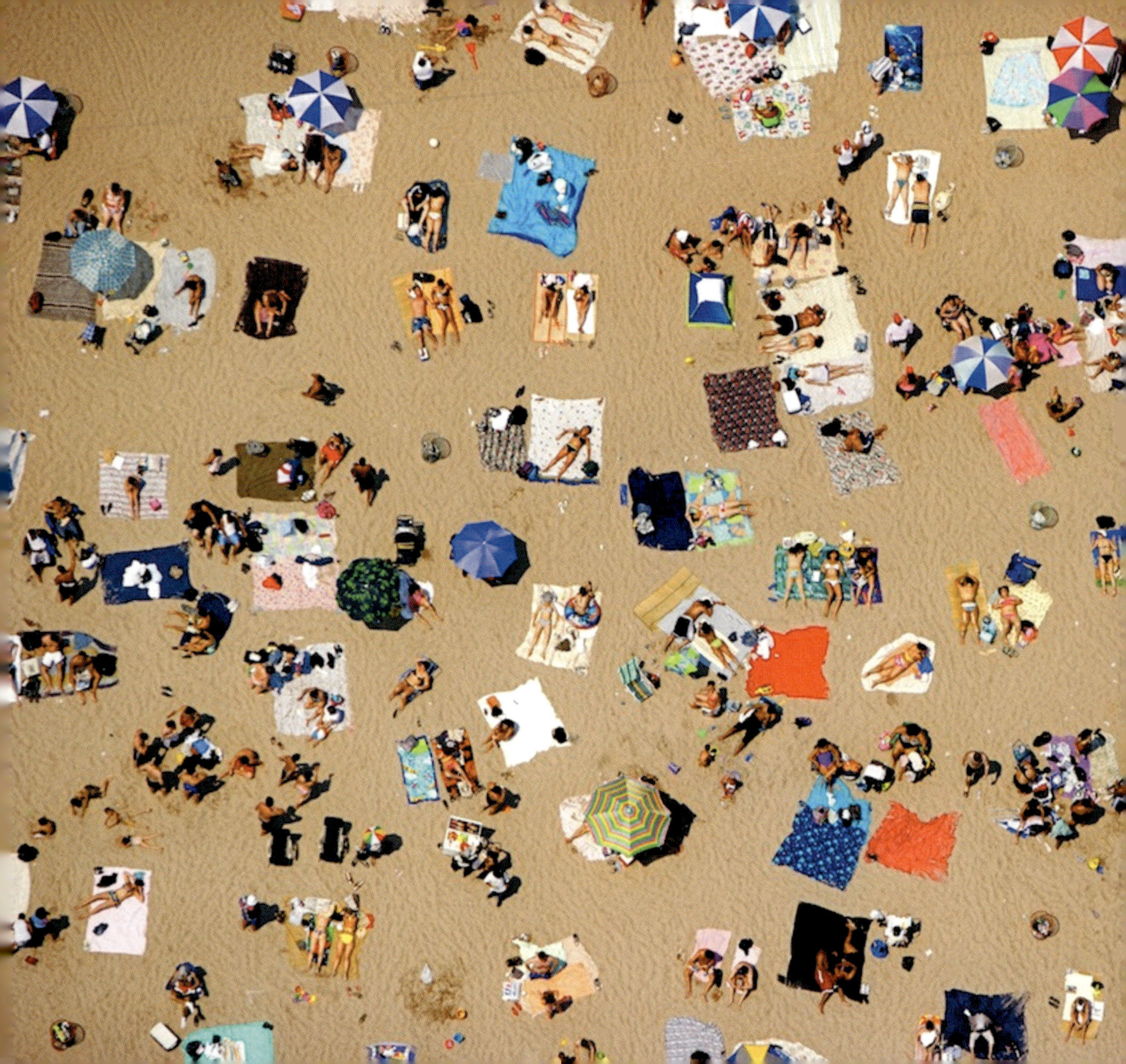

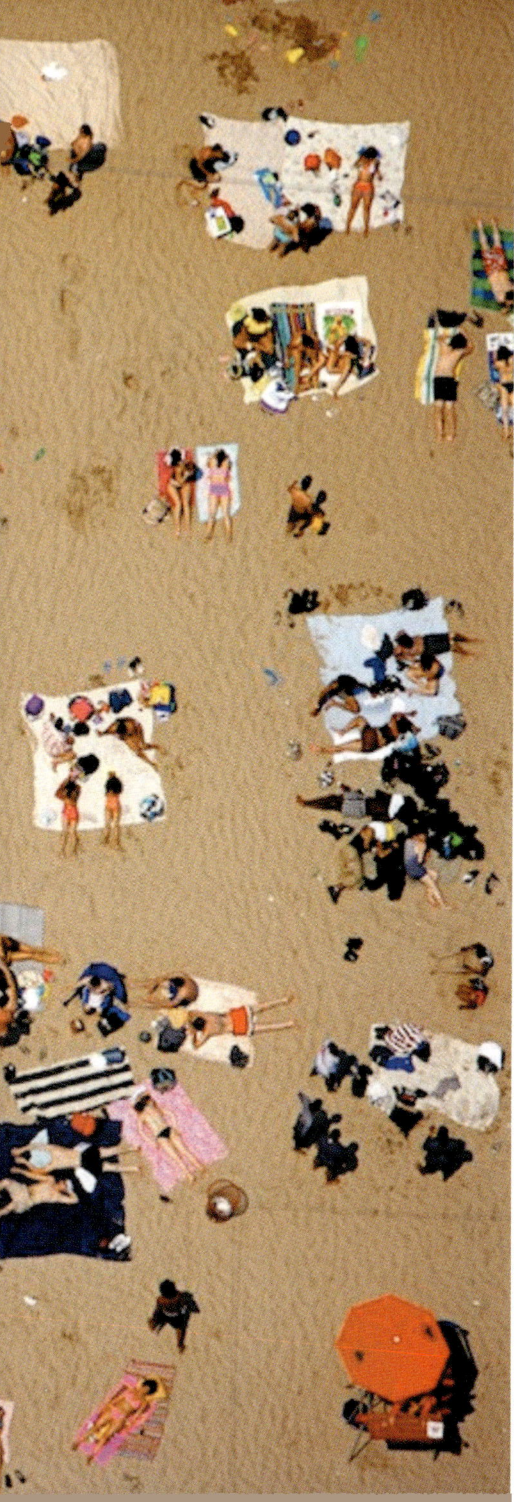

CHAPTER 7

IN THE AIR

Aerial photography has to be one of my favorite things to do as a photographer. I definitely fell into it—I never knew I was going to become an aerial specialist.

I had a background in sports photography, which involved using long lenses and capturing the moment. With sports, there's only one chance to capture that key play; you don't have any second chances. So when I was put up in a helicopter for the first time, I was already conditioned to capture that moment the first time.

◀ Coney Island in 2006.

ISO 160 f/5 1/2500 200mm

Helicopters or planes tend to loop around subject matter, and if you see something happening, you've got to nail it on the first try. The wonderful thing about being up in the air is that you have a totally new three-dimensional appreciation of the world, as you see environments that we all see every day on the ground, from a new perspective. I love going up there and finding different geometrical elements—lines, curves, and shapes made by man or by nature.

I find it funny that if you take a picture of a scene from 5 feet away, people will look at it and quickly move on. But if you take a picture of that same scene from 2,500 feet away, people are somehow more likely to stare for a long time and study it. The "Where's Waldo?" element might be part of the reason, but somehow I think that fascination speaks more to how human beings relate to their environment and how the environment affects them. New York is a good example of that.

THE CHALLENGE IN THE AIR

This image speaks a lot to who I am as a photographer. It's made with a 7.5mm fisheye lens, a highly unusual lens. The camera was actually at the end of a monopod beneath the skids, and if you look carefully on the bottom left, you'll see a bit of the skid in the frame, given the incredible field of view I had to work with.

You can't shoot this photograph from the door. I had to place the camera beneath the skids at the end of a monopod. The camera was connected via FireWire to a laptop in my helicopter so I could see what I was shooting, because for security reasons the helicopter couldn't hover above the Empire State Building.

It was an incredibly physical act and a huge coordination effort between the pilot and me. I was feeling a lot of Gs just grasping the monopod. I had to be precise. A quarter-inch rotation of the monopod clockwise or counterclockwise, frontward or backward—or to any direction—completely messed up the geometry of the frame. And not only did I have to fight the wind, but also I had to perfectly compose the top of the Empire State Building in the center of the frame.

I shot at a time of day that made it tough. There was little light in the city, so I had to nail the exposure to get this to work. I think it's the perfect marriage of high tech, knowledge of exposure, geometry, and aesthetics.

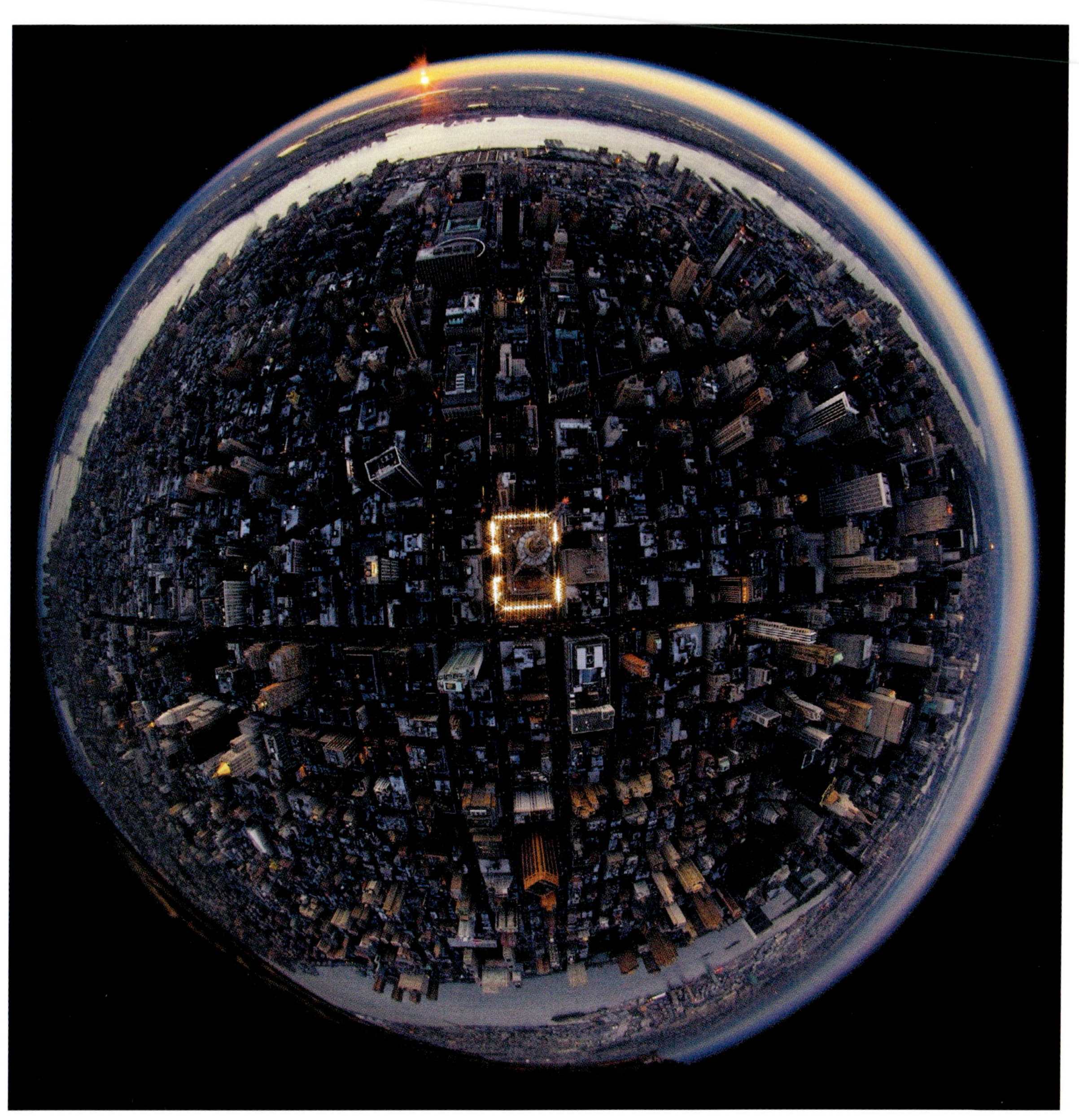

Aerial photograph of Ground Zero at sunset almost five years after the 9/11/01 terrorist attacks.

ISO 800 f/5.6 1/320 7.5mm

AN INTIMATE PERSPECTIVE

The first few times you're in the air, you want to shoot wide panoramic images. What I did is the exact opposite. I took my sports background and shot as tight as I could, because I didn't see many photographs taken from the air with a 500mm lens.

I don't just shoot landscapes from the air; I also photograph human beings and their environments—specifically, urban environments. Street-level photography is fantastic and has its place in the photography realm, but aerial photography of people, especially in a city like New York, is special in that it gives you a unique perspective on human beings and their relationship to their environment.

When you think about New York, you see and imagine it from how it looks on the ground, with the tall buildings towering over you. But from the air, you see human beings differently, with a sense of scale relative to the city from above. It helps you to appreciate the three-dimensionality of the city.

What's absolutely fascinating for me is that there are many times when you're 2,500 feet above someone, but there is zero potential for interaction because they can't see you. They can hear the helicopter, but there's no way to make eye contact. There's no way for them to feel comfortable or uncomfortable. Yet somehow that removal from them allows you to have a unique interaction, because you can see them and their relationship to the world in a way they could never imagine.

You can get lost in that world. When I look at photographs of people taken from the street level, I don't find myself studying their clothes or body language as much as when I look down from the air. I study what people are wearing, what they're reading, what they're doing, how they lay their body on the ground. It says a lot about them. It says a lot about their class, about how tensed or relaxed they are as human beings. I see how they interact with others, if they keep their distance or cuddle up with other people. I find it to be a very fascinating sociological study of human beings.

SHOOTING TIGHT

Due to my sports photography background, I tend to shoot very, very tight from the air. Most of the time I'm shooting with a 200mm, 300mm, 400mm, or 500mm lens, and these allow me to isolate little parts of the geometry as I compose, to get very rectangular images, and to look for those special images, the golden nuggets. When you're up in the air you see everything, and the challenge is to pick that one little section that just sings.

This image over Coney Island captured just the right ratio of the number of people in one frame relative to the beach and the size of the frame. It was a challenge because I was doing this while we were flying at well over 70 miles an hour.

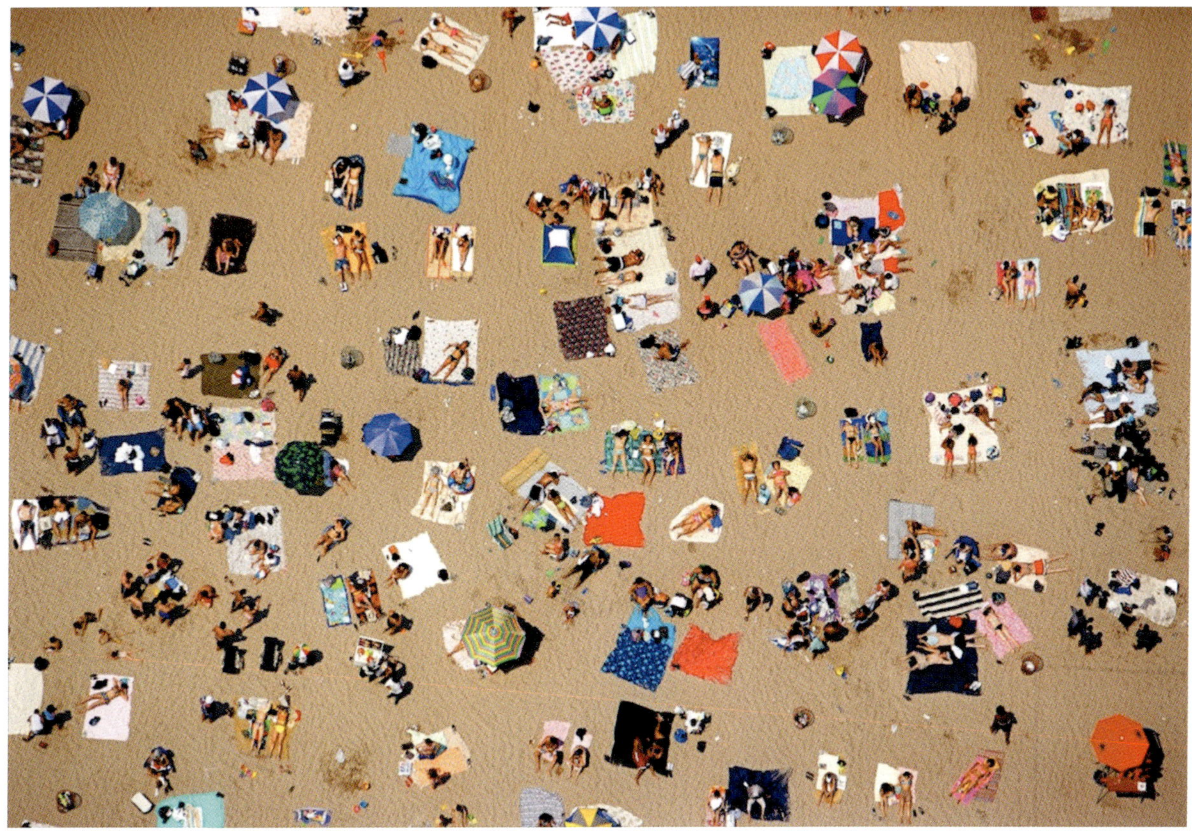

Coney Island in 2006. ISO 160 f/5 1/2500 200mm

Sometimes I ask the helicopter pilot to hover, but in this case I didn't want to create too much noise. And with so many people below us, safety was just as important a consideration. If you want to remain safe, you want to keep moving.

So I was flying with my head sticking out of the helicopter, trying to frame this as quickly as possible using a Canon EOS-1Ds Mark III with a 70–200mm lens. This is the perfect lens for this type of photography: sometimes you want to go loose and sometimes you want to go tight, and when you're flying faster than 70 miles per hour, it's tough to debate it and make a decision on the fly.

What I often do is zoom in and out repeatedly until I find that perfect moment. That's why I find that the 70–200mm is my go-to lens for a good 50 percent of the images that I shoot.

I believe this is an image that you really want to study. It's one that you could print large on your wall so you could step back and scrutinize every single person—the people walking off the beach, the people in their tents, the people lying on their towels, the kids playing. That's one of the wonders of still photography, as opposed to video: you can stop and just stare at something and really study it.

WEATHER AND PREPARATION

Generally I feel comfortable shooting just about any aerial photograph, but there's one thing that always makes me nervous, and it's the one thing I have no control over: the weather. This plays an incredibly important part in any aerial photograph.

If it rains, usually you just can't fly. It's not safe, and sometimes you can't see anything. When it's overcast, it's 50-50—sometimes it leads to a nice result, sometimes not. Patchy clouds can be great if the subject you want to shoot is in the light.

The one thing that is horrible for flying is a hazy sky. Most of the time if you know it's going to be hazy, you don't bother taking off. In this case we had to, and as I often say, "Try to make the best of any situation; try to take a negative and turn it into a positive." You can see how the haze in this image created a very dreamy quality. This is how I put into practice my approach to do the best I can with what I have at all times.

A strong haze overtakes lower Manhattan as the Empire State Building peeks out slightly in the distance (2006).

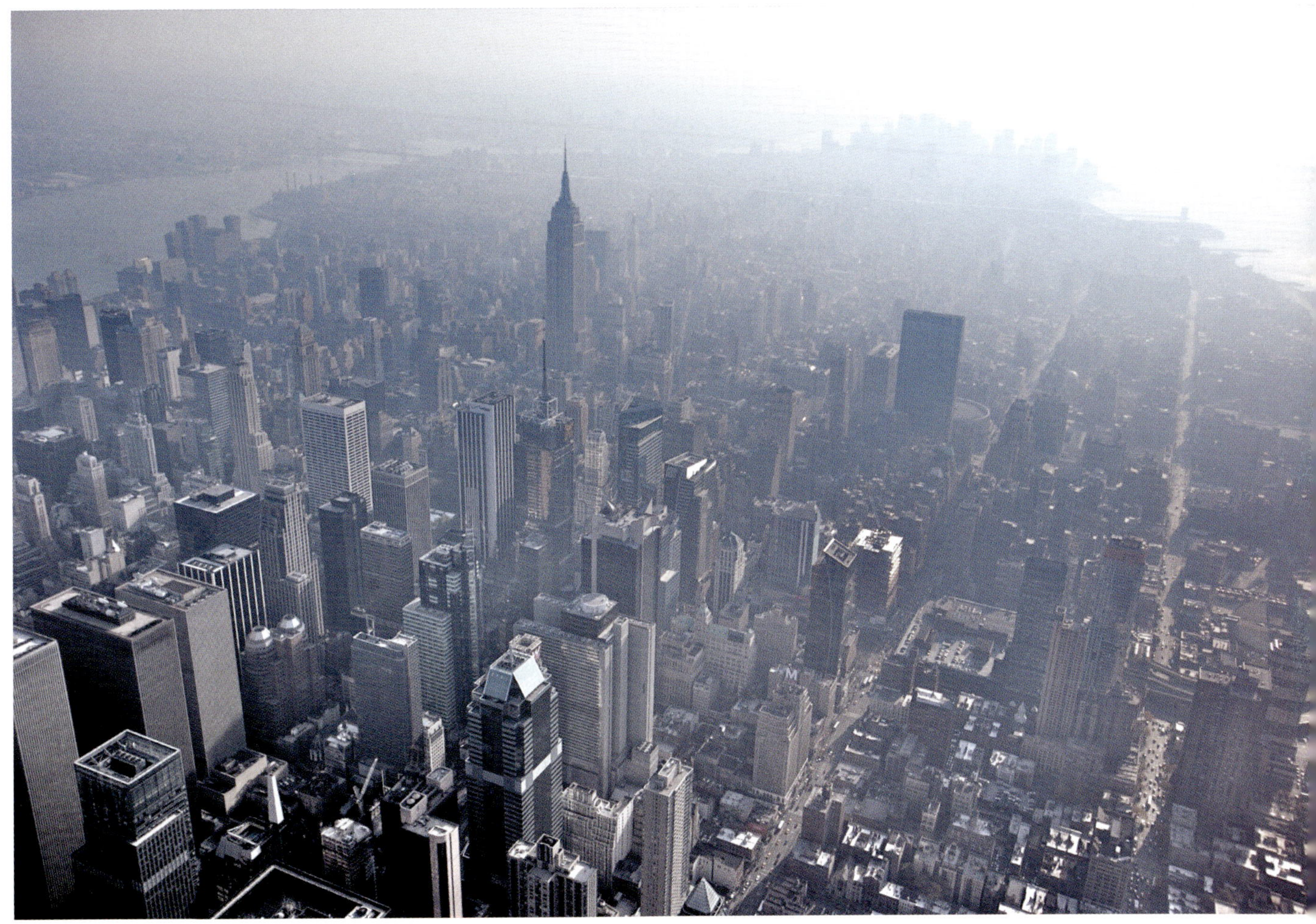

ISO 100 f/4 1/600 30mm

But awareness of weather is just one of the important things you have to do to prepare for an aerial shoot. This kind of photography requires a lot of time and money, and you have to do a lot of research to make that kind of investment pay off.

When I photographed aerials in New York, I researched what was going on in the city at that time of year. For example, what time does Rikers Island let out its prisoners for their daily stroll? Are there some fairs going on? Is there going to be an event at Coney Island this weekend?

If it's an outdoor event, what's the temperature going to be? If it's cold or raining, no one's going to show up. If it's 85 degrees and sunny, they are going to get slammed. Research is a must.

Coordinating the pilot was also highly intense because every move had to be recorded for the local airports—LaGuardia, JFK, or Newark. You can't just say, "Stop right here." You can say, "I would like to stop a mile ahead, and I'd like to hover a few hundred feet," and the pilot had to clear such requests with the airport. That's the ultimate in terms of preparing a few steps ahead.

You also have to be aware of the helicopter's movement, the wind movement, and how you can be positioned relative to the wind. If you have your back to the wind, not only is it dangerous, but also the heat waves fly toward your camera and create blurry images.

Safety is another crucial consideration. When I go up in the air, I usually have a door either off of the helicopter or slid back, and I'm wearing a harness, so I'm strapped into the helicopter. All of the cameras are harnessed to me. So if we hit a bump and I have to let go of the camera to grab onto the helicopter frame for balance, the camera's not going to go anywhere.

If you're flying over a very heavily populated area, you want to take every possible precaution to ensure that nothing ever falls out of the helicopter. Nothing should ever be loose in your pockets, and you should never stick your head out with eyeglasses on.

We take safety very seriously. So while it's easy enough to get into a helicopter, if you're going do it as a professional photographer, make sure you know what you're doing and ask other photographers who have done it before.

After all is said and done, it goes back to having one shot at everything, for the most part. To make it work, you learn to think about what the pilot needs to do, what he can and cannot do, what's safe, and what you need to make your photograph. It's a high-level dance happening thousands of feet above the ground.

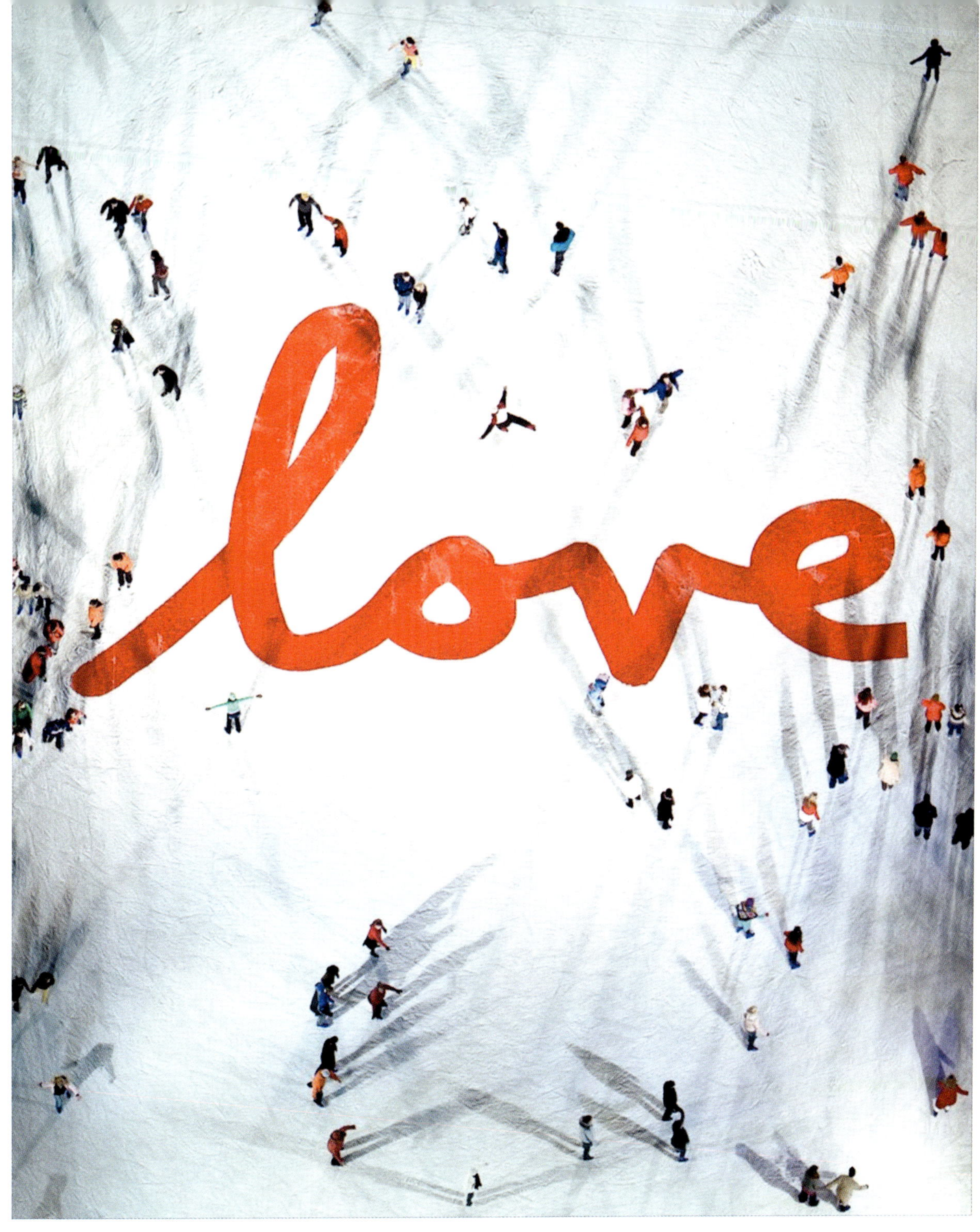

Aerial of the ice skating rink in Bryant Park, 2006. ISO 800 f/2 1/160 135mm

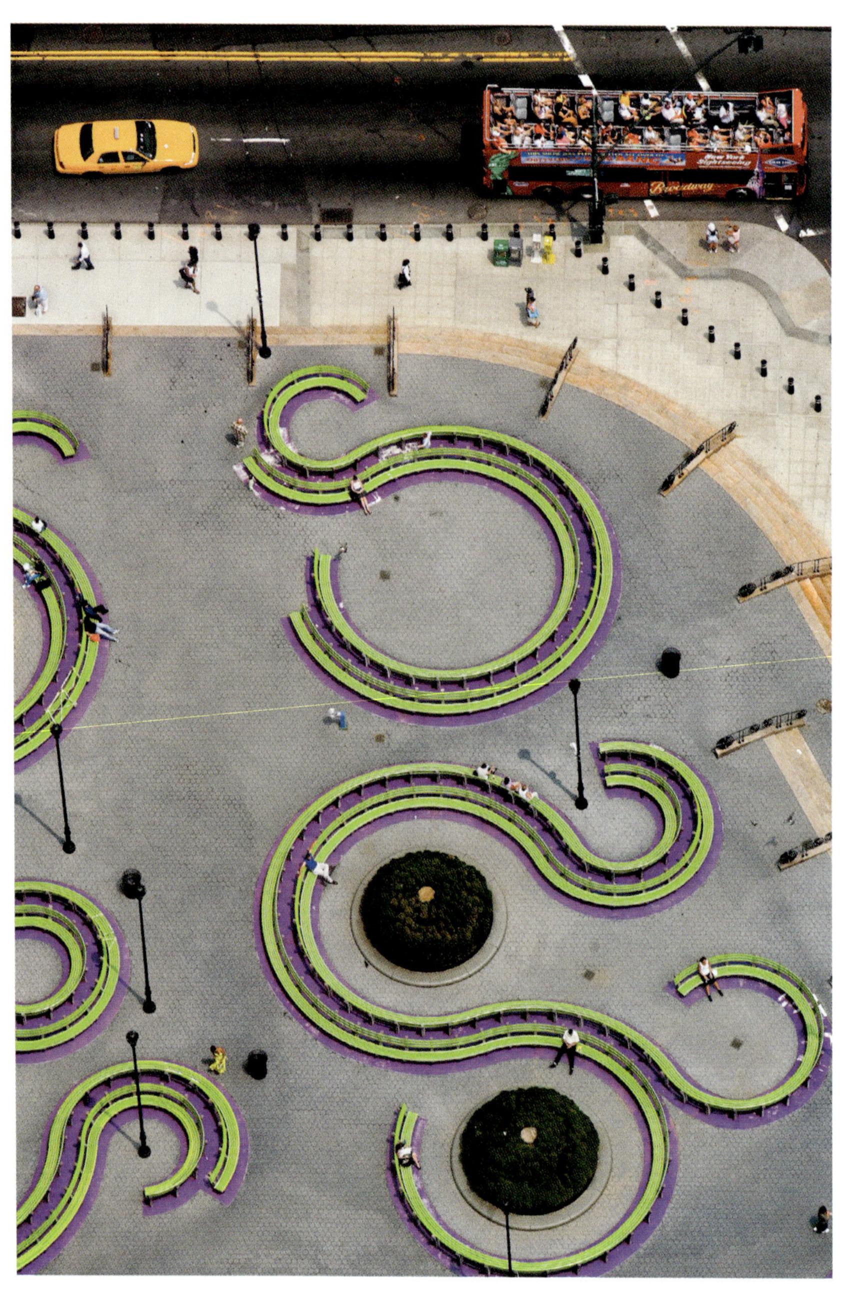

Benches in downtown Manhattan, 2006. ISO 200 f/5.6 1/2000 300mm

ASKING FOR ADVICE

Another piece of advice I have is if you go up in a helicopter, always ask the pilot to let you know if she sees anything special. More often than not, the pilot has flown over that area more than you have, and provides another pair of eyes up in the sky.

For this photo, Rich Carozza, the pilot, saw this image and said, "Hey, Vince, do you see that? Is that interesting?" And I said, "Yeah, absolutely."

These are benches in downtown Manhattan at the Jacob Javits Convention Center Plaza, arranged in beautiful geometrical curves. They're painted lime green and have a bit of a purple around them.

I shot a little bit looser to include (at the top) the cab and tour bus, which lent a bit of a sense of place. You know you're not in just any park; you're probably in New York City. And if you look very closely at the bottom left of the image, you'll see a woman in a yellow dress. I wanted that little extra touch.

This photo was shot in less than perfect conditions, which can be the case for New York City in July, with its often-murky skies—but I didn't give up. You can generally pump the contrast up a bit in postproduction and get rid of some of that haze or take a bit of the blue out, and that's what we did.

I shot a little bit looser to include the cab and tour bus, which lend a bit of a sense of place. You know you're not in just any park; you're probably in New York City.

Guests enjoying the relative calm of the roof deck at the Soho House Hotel in the Meatpacking district of New York City (2006).

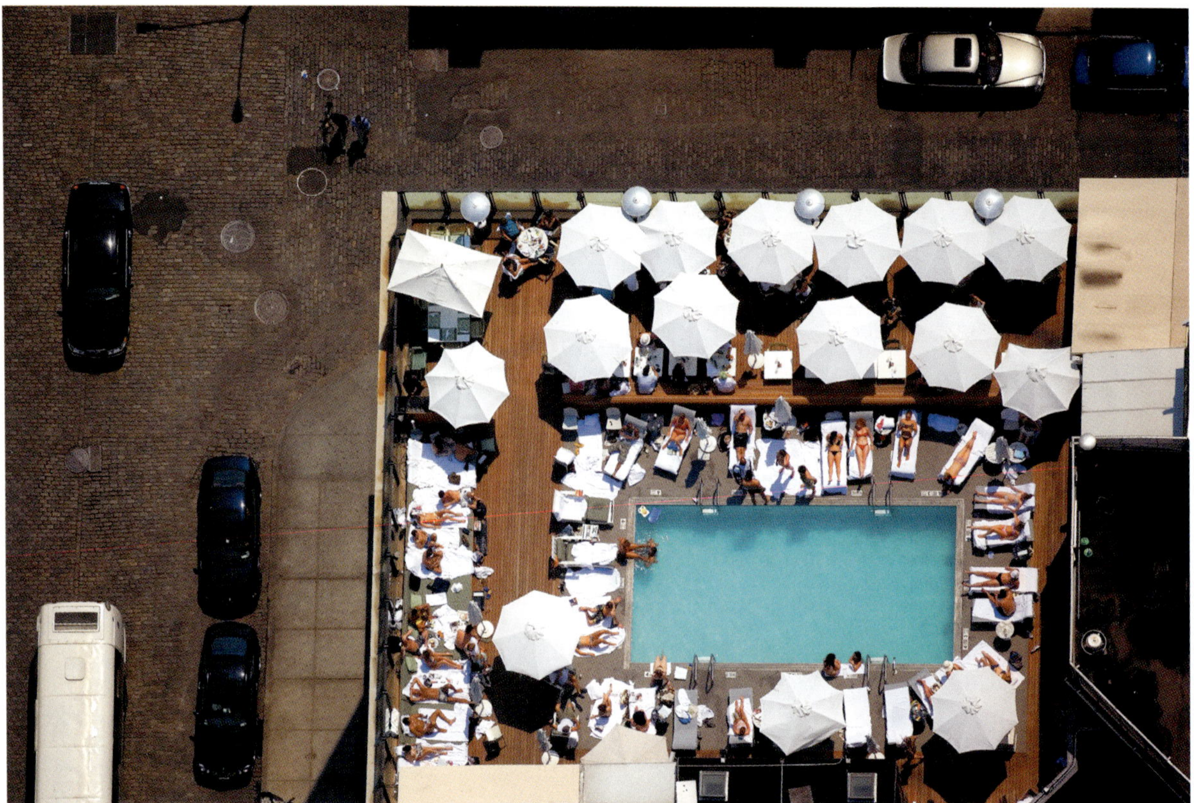

ISO 100 f/4.5 1/2500 500mm

What you're trying to do as a photographer from the air is to isolate that geometry in a way that looks beautiful in that two-by-three format.

USING THE GRAPHIC EYE

The photograph of the Soho House in the Meatpacking district of Manhattan is a great example of what I'm often trying to do as an aerial photographer. Imagine looking at Manhattan on Google Maps. You'll see the seemingly endless number of buildings and realize the majority of them are set up in a grid. What you're trying to do as a photographer from the air is to isolate that geometry in a way that looks beautiful in that two-by-three format.

For this shot, I had this cobblestone street making an L at the top and left side of the image, and then I had this very clean, modern-looking rooftop of a hotel. I think it's a good study in finding that right balance of elements and paying close attention to the geometry.

Keep in mind that if the helicopter were a few hundred feet off, the geometry would have completely fallen off in the wrong direction. The lines of the top edge of the hotel would not have lain parallel to the top edge of the frame. I had to be perfectly positioned, and that's what made this very challenging.

Once you've framed your image, you can get lost in the details and see the various cars on the streets, and the contrast between the cobblestone street and the clean rooftop. If you look carefully, you'll see there's a couple romancing one another at the edge of the pool. For me, those details are what make an image from the air.

Even though you're 1,500 feet or more above ground and have no direct connection with what's happening below, you're somehow able to capture those subtle little moments.

GETTING LUCKY

Every once in while you get really lucky, and this is one such image.

This is a series of private jets stacked together at Teterboro Airport. I've come to call this image "Rush Hour for Billionaires." It depicts a traffic jam at a small airport, where all these jets were getting ready to leave for a weekend in the Hamptons.

When I saw the jets, I knew I had to find a way to make a unique image. I shot super tight, eliminating the bottom and top parts of the scene. I just had to make sure not to clip the airplanes' wings. If I had shot this a little wider, the image wouldn't feel so compact; you would see more of the empty runway or more of the empty airport. It was slammed with planes trying to take every quarter-inch that was left on that tarmac.

That's the story I was trying to tell with the image, and the long lens compressed everything to make the planes look even more tightly packed together than they were.

If I had shot this a little wider, the image wouldn't feel so compact; you would see more of the empty runway or more of the empty airport. It was slammed with planes trying to take every quarter-inch that was left on that tarmac.

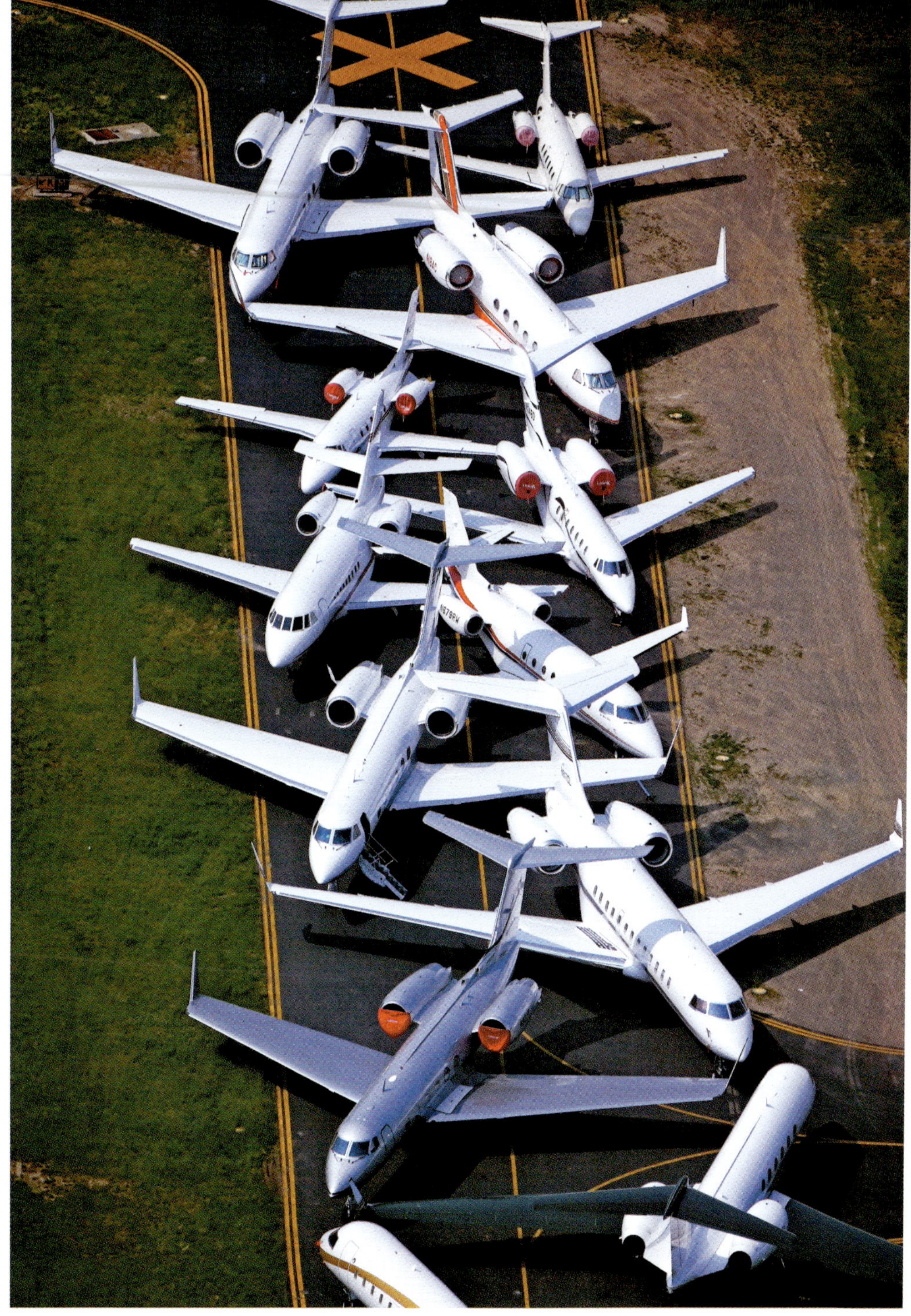

Private jets embroiled in conjestion at a taxiway at Teterboro Airport in New Jersey (2006).

ISO 100 f/5.6 1/5000 500mm

You've got to kind of pick your moments. There's another shot of a similar scene that I made with a tilt-shift lens at Teterboro Airport. That lens choice resulted in an entirely different feel. Which lens to use is one of the most important decisions you can make when you're up in the air; other crucial decisions are how tight or how wide to go, and what you want to include or exclude from the frame.

One of the biggest questions I ask myself when composing the photograph is: "What is it that I want inside that frame?" In other words, I need to decide what will add to or detract from the picture. It's an important rule that I tend to live by.

With a great aerial shot, you want to lure the viewer to take in the details, but creating a sense of place is just as important. I think aerials do that, and that's why I find them so fascinating.

A tilt-shift lens used to capture the conjested planes at Teterboro Airport (2006).

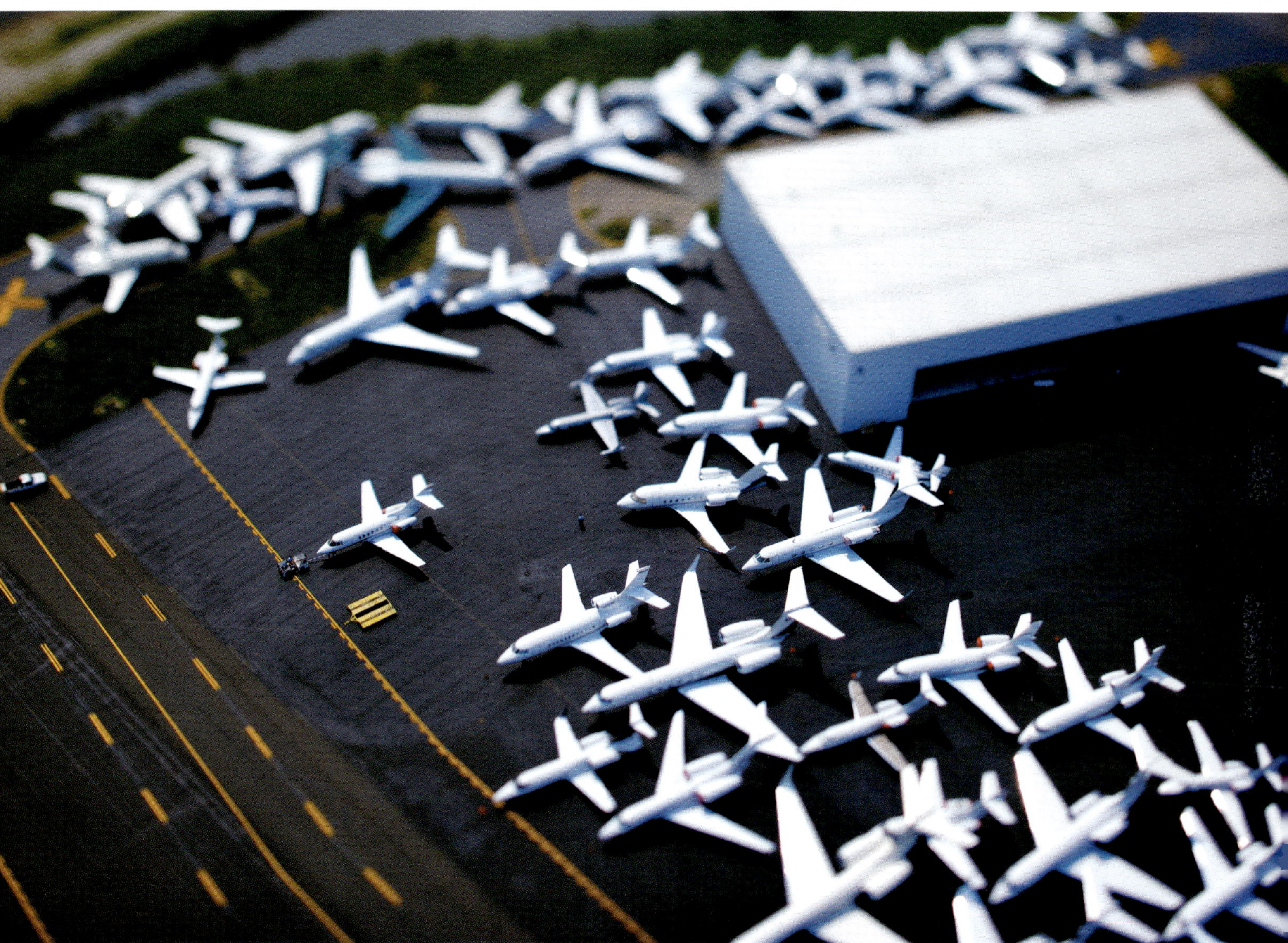

ISO 50 f/4 1/6000 45mm

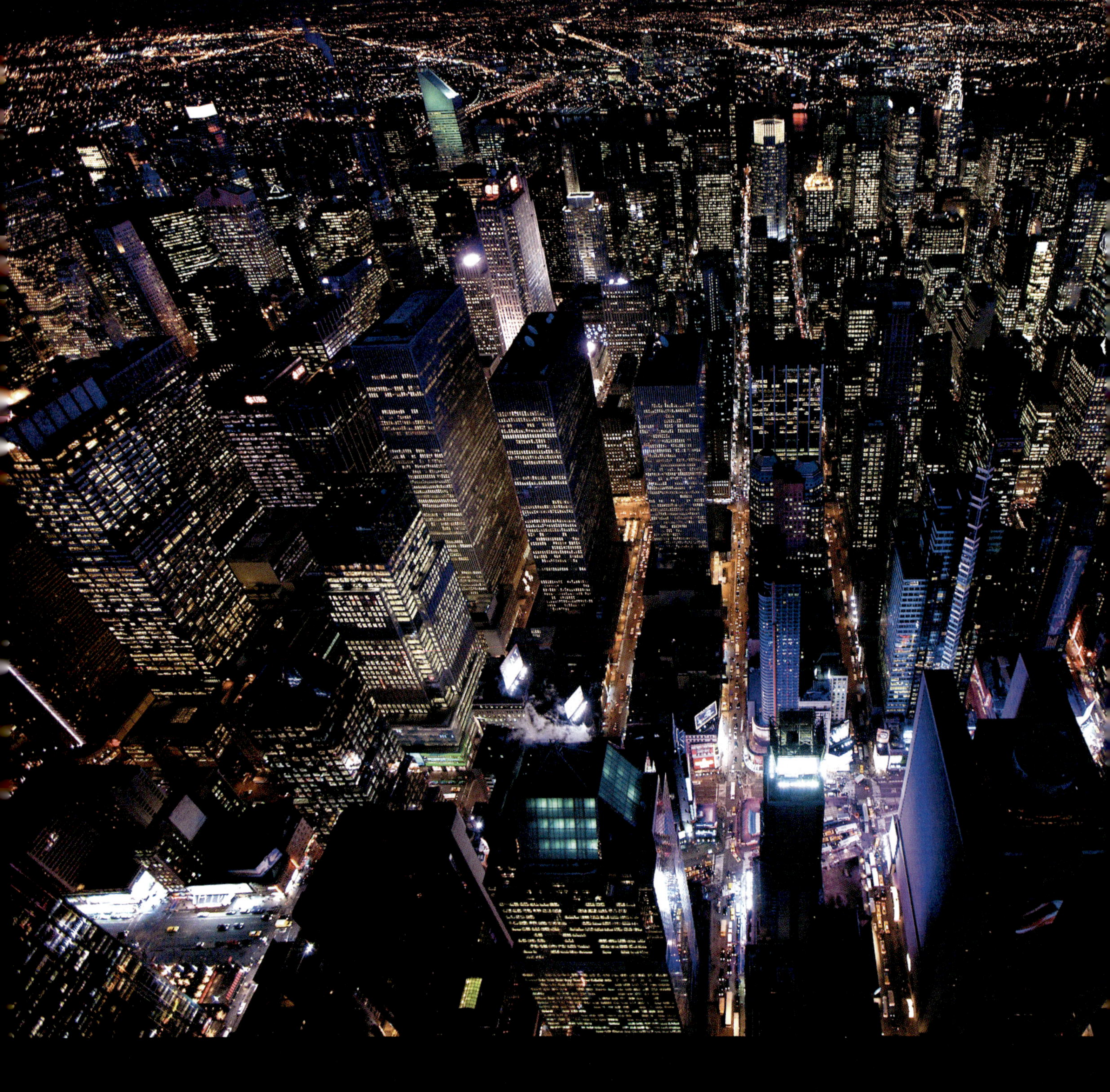

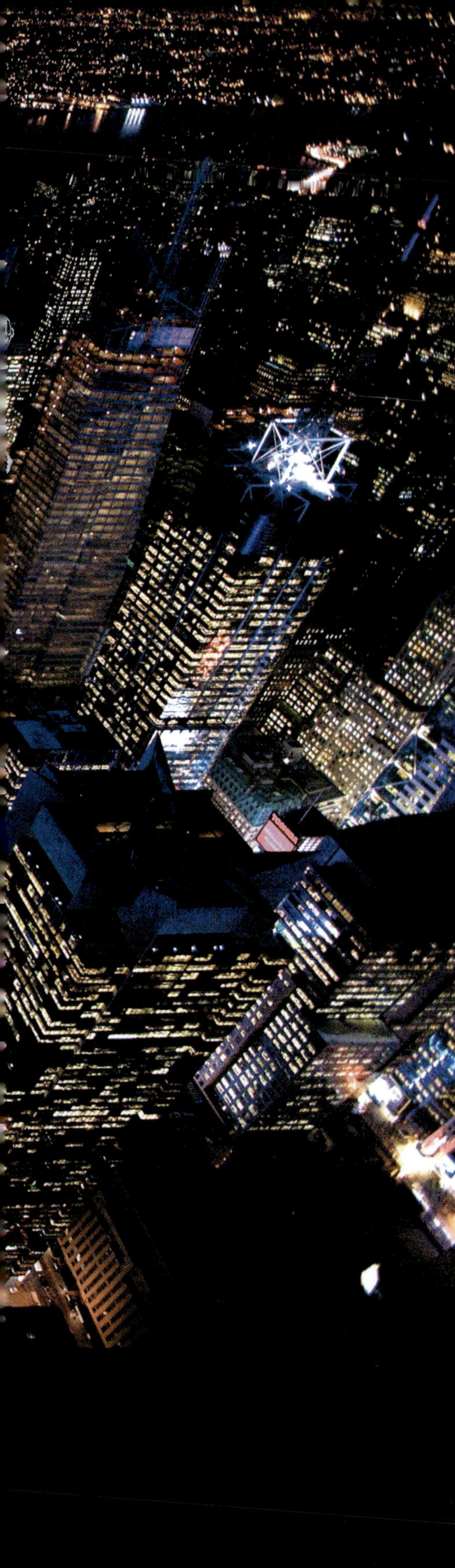

CHAPTER 8

A LOVE AFFAIR WITH NEW YORK

New York is my only true home in this world. From a young age, I've always been a traveler. I lived in Switzerland and Paris, but I have always considered New York to be my city.

I grew up there from the age of 5 until I was 18, returning as a young adult for seven years during my stint at the *New York Times.* So I've spent over 20 years—more than half of my life—in New York City. It was the only anchor I ever had in terms of a home and a family.

◀ Times Square and Midtown Manhattan after dusk (2007).

ISO 1600 f/2.8 1/40 16mm

To me, New York is the center of the earth. It's a city that seems to be a magnet for some of the most talented people in the world. I'm not sure you can say that about any other city. Paris is a romantic city. Rome is a historical city. I think Shanghai and Beijing will be bigger, but in my opinion, New York is the epicenter of the world in terms of creative talent.

And there I was in my 20s working for *the* paper of record in the world—the paper of the city, the *New York Times.* There was no shortage of challenges while working there, but I was very comfortable with what I did and what I shot, mostly because of the feedback that I got from the people who read the paper. My years at the *New York Times* were some of the best years of my career because I felt like I was documenting a town, a city. And I got feedback from readers on a regular basis that allowed me to appreciate that how I was seeing the city was resonating with my fellow New Yorkers and people all over the world..

WOMAN IN STRIPES

In 2007 I was walking the streets the same way I did when I was 15 years old, with only one lens and one camera. For seven weeks I went out with a Leica with a single lens.

I was just looking for New York moments and walking near the corner of Fifth Avenue and Central Park South when I saw this woman in stripes pushing a stroller. I noticed the pattern of the crosswalk that lay in the direction she was heading, and I ran at full speed after her, being careful not to run into her or scare her. I was only able to capture three frames.

I saw her and anticipated the moment, but I only had seconds to react and make the photograph. Thankfully, I captured one frame with her legs outstretched, emphasizing the stripes of her dress. It's a messy image. It's not perfect, but it works.

Once you see something like that, you can't hesitate or decide not to make a photograph. As long as you're not bothering the person you're trying to photograph, you keep a healthy distance, and you don't scare or startle her, you can fall into the vibe and make the photograph. She was never aware that I was there.

This is all about framing it, shooting it, and getting it. You can't think it over too much. It's not going to happen ever again, and it never did. Asking her to turn around and do it again was not going to be an option.

Exploring patterns of New York City's street life in a 12-week column for the *New York Times*

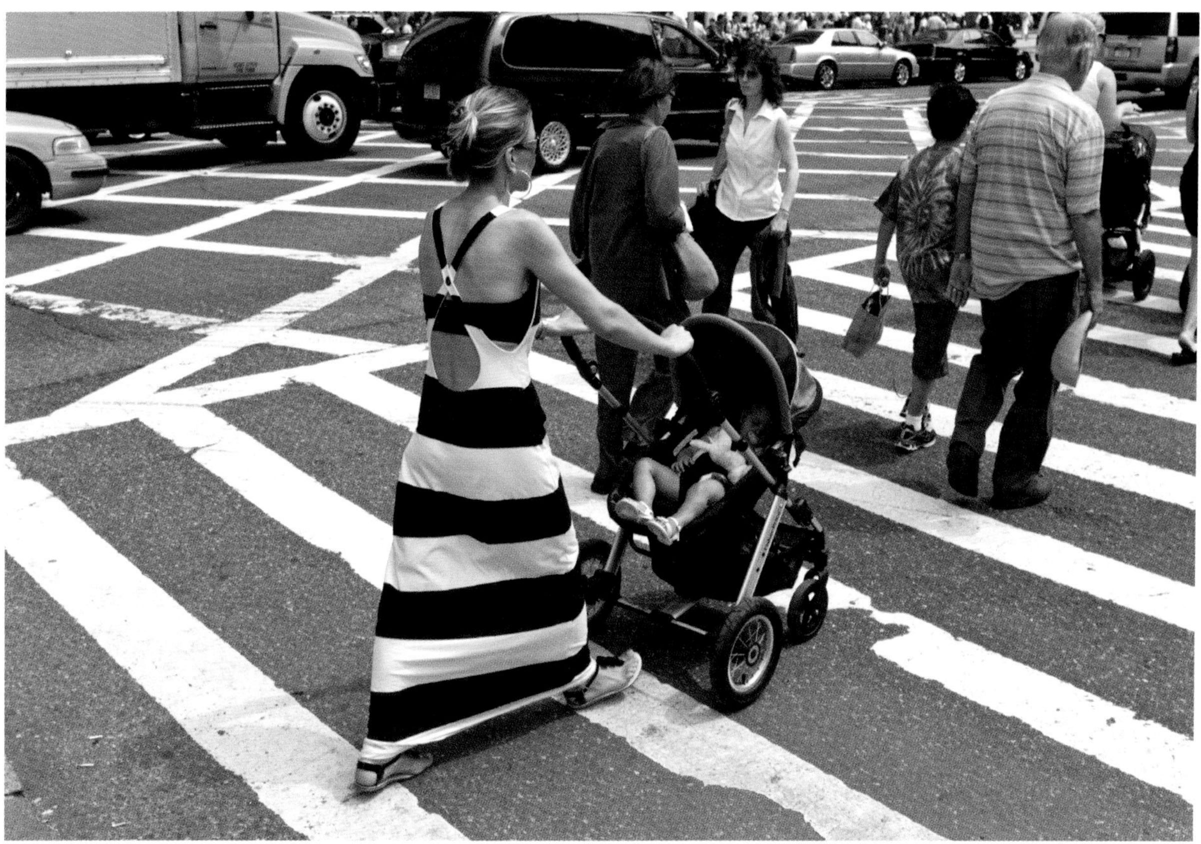

ISO 320 1/750 28mm

FRONT PAGE BEAT

Despite my visually graphic tendencies, I landed the front-page beat for the *New York Times,* which was often reserved for hard news events rather than visually pleasing images. So if there was no big story that day, or no great pictures to illustrate a story, it would go to an image of New York City. And between my aerial photographs and street photography, it became my beat for a full two years of my six years at the paper.

I had to find an image that spoke to the news of the day. If it centered on the weather or the season, the image had to illustrate that it was hot or cold, or muggy, or reflected the turn of a season. It couldn't just be a pretty image. It had to be an image that either spoke to the climactic change, the time of the year, or the events of the season—whether it was a holiday or spring.

So I had to become very attuned to the city and what happened in it. And what ended up happening was, because of my graphic eye and the images I made, I discovered that I had a style.

The best letters from readers were rarely about my best photographs—I kind of knew which ones were good, and my colleagues would often tell me as well. The best letters were in response to photographs that I thought were terrible, or lacking. I realized that as a photographer, the true of magic of photography is that every photograph, every piece of art, means something different to someone else, and everyone connects to it differently. And I found that utterly fascinating.

AVOIDING CLICHÉ

The challenge I faced doing this beat for the *Times* was to photograph something that was recognizable enough that readers knew it was New York City. But it had to be photographed in a way that was aesthetically different enough to make it a unique image, not a cliché.

This is an image of a young boy playing in the water jets in front of the planetarium at the American Museum of Natural History. It's a simple image, but I've always loved it because geometrically speaking, it's a plethora of shapes and contradictions.

You've got this great structure with the planetarium and its perfect spheres of the planets. With this shot, you've got a very rigid, geometric world in the back contrasted by the very fluid body motion of the child.

To me it just feels very free, like what it feels like to be a child or a young man. Here he is playing with a jet of water, which was my favorite thing as a kid. And then you've got light and dark—the brightly lit spheres and shapes and building, and he's in perfect silhouette. It's a wonderful play on geometry, of light and dark, lines and shapes, gesture and movement.

The American Museum of Natural History (2007).

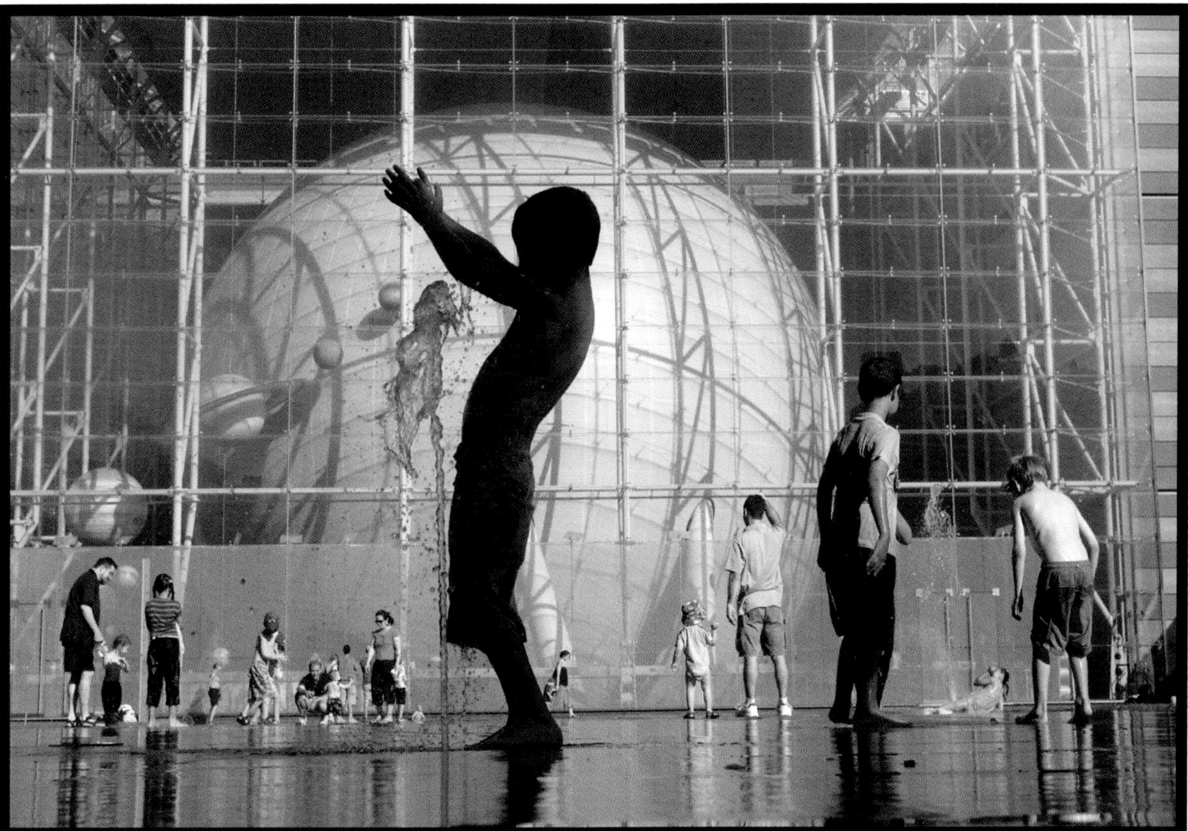

ISO 320 1/750 35mm

Financial district in New York City on July 30th, 2007.

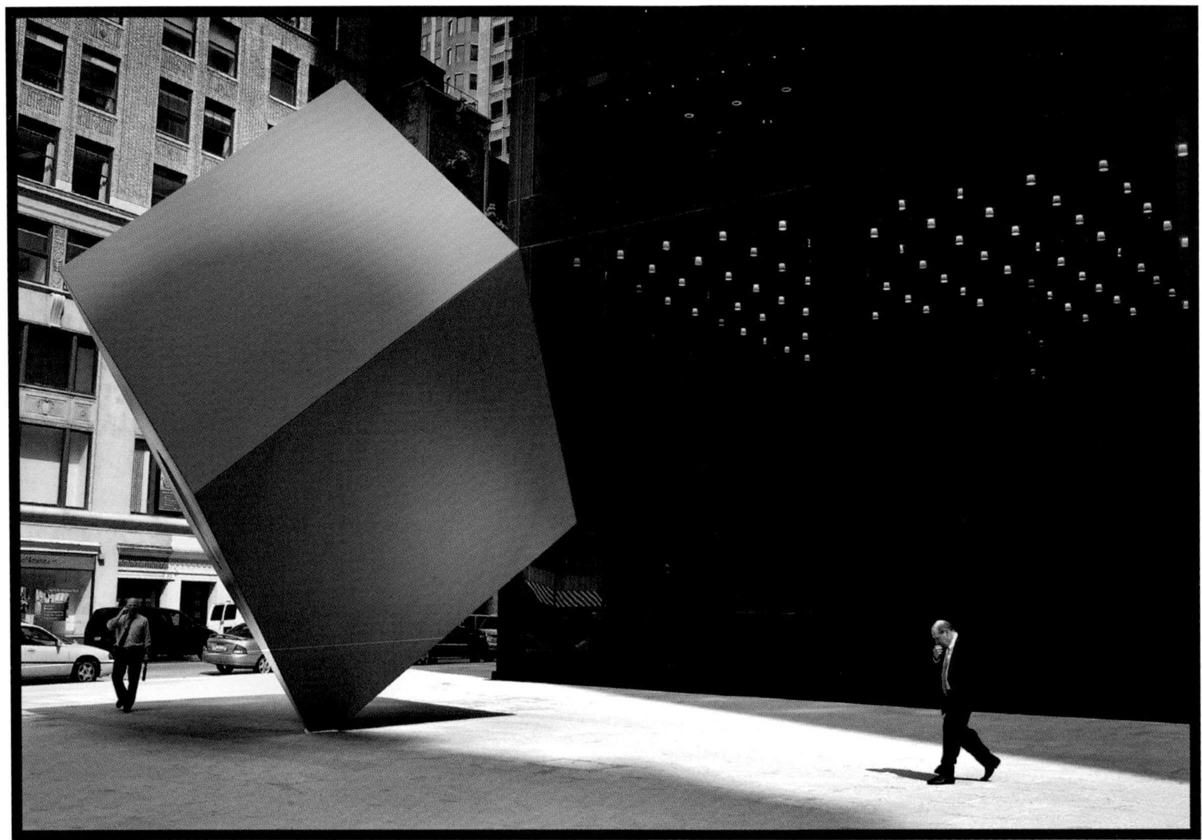

ISO 320 1/90 28mm

SEEING POTENTIAL

I love this image. It was made on Wall Street during the financial crisis that began in the summer of 2007, and to me the cube seemed ready to squash the older man who'd probably had a very bad day, because everyone on Wall Street was experiencing bad days that week.

Then there is also the quality of the light and the graphic elements in the frame. There's a shaft of light and the play between light and dark. There's the beautiful pattern of the building's interior lights. The building across the street has small squares in the windows, which visually repeat the shape of the cube. And then you have the guy on the other side of the cube, which helps balance the entire composition.

It's very clean. It's very simple. It's all about geometry. It's all about motion. Obviously, he's not in a great mood. Looks a bit downtrodden. And thank God there wasn't a hotdog stand in the middle of that frame.

The point with an image like this is that you see the potential for something and you just wait. That's a lesson I learned from studying the work of Henri Cartier-Bresson. There's a famous image he captured of a descending staircase with a bike passing by in Hyères, France. I saw his original contact sheets. He shot 36 frames of the exact same composition, and only one of them included the bicycle.

A lot of photography is about finding that environment and waiting. In some documentaries of Cartier-Bresson, you may see him jumping around like a bumblebee taking pictures from every angle, but that's what he wanted you to see. The reality is that he waited, and waited, and waited.

You find the right set of circumstances with the right light and geometry, and you sit, pray, and try to blend in. It's like a hunt.

JUST MAKE THE SHOT

This photograph was taken the same day as the previous image. They were made within an hour of each other, and again it was across the street from Wall Street.

This image is all about layers. The focus of the image was not primarily the kid looking up at the sky and the geometry of the shadow; the key thing that made this image work is the reflection of the stairs inside the man's sunglasses. The repeating lines are everywhere, and the human beings appeared chaotic and dynamic within a very linear world.

When you're in New York it's such a chaotic environment. The only anchors in New York are those buildings. So when I'm doing street photography, I'm paying attention to the shape and lines created by those buildings and the way they cut off or reflect light. Those buildings served as my background but also informed my sense of geometry and composition.

Look at the geometry of the buildings in this photograph. Pretty much what I did as a photographer was compose my frames as cleanly as I could with those lines in mind. When the man with the sunglasses walked into the frame, it completed the scene and I made the photograph.

There's just the right amount of motion with the man entering the frame. That's why I think 1/125 second is the magic shutter speed when practicing street photography; it's just a quick grab—click. 1/250 second freezes too much, and 1/60 second is too slow.

With moments like this, you just react. I think at a certain point you feel it. You just have to let your gut and your heart say, "Make the shot." You can't overthink it, especially in moments like this. You can't plan these moments.

I was the happiest guy in the world photographing every day in New York, and people still talk to me and say things like, "The paper hasn't been the same since you left. I miss the aerials of New York. I miss your views of New York." And all I was doing was following a tradition of what photographers had done for decades.

It's just that these days it's less common to have kind of a love affair with the beauty of your everyday world. Granted, New York City is a mecca of sorts, but my goal as a photojournalist at the *Times* was just to see the inherent beauty in the everyday and to share that discovery with the world in a photograph.

Across the street from Wall Street, New York City, July 30th, 2007.

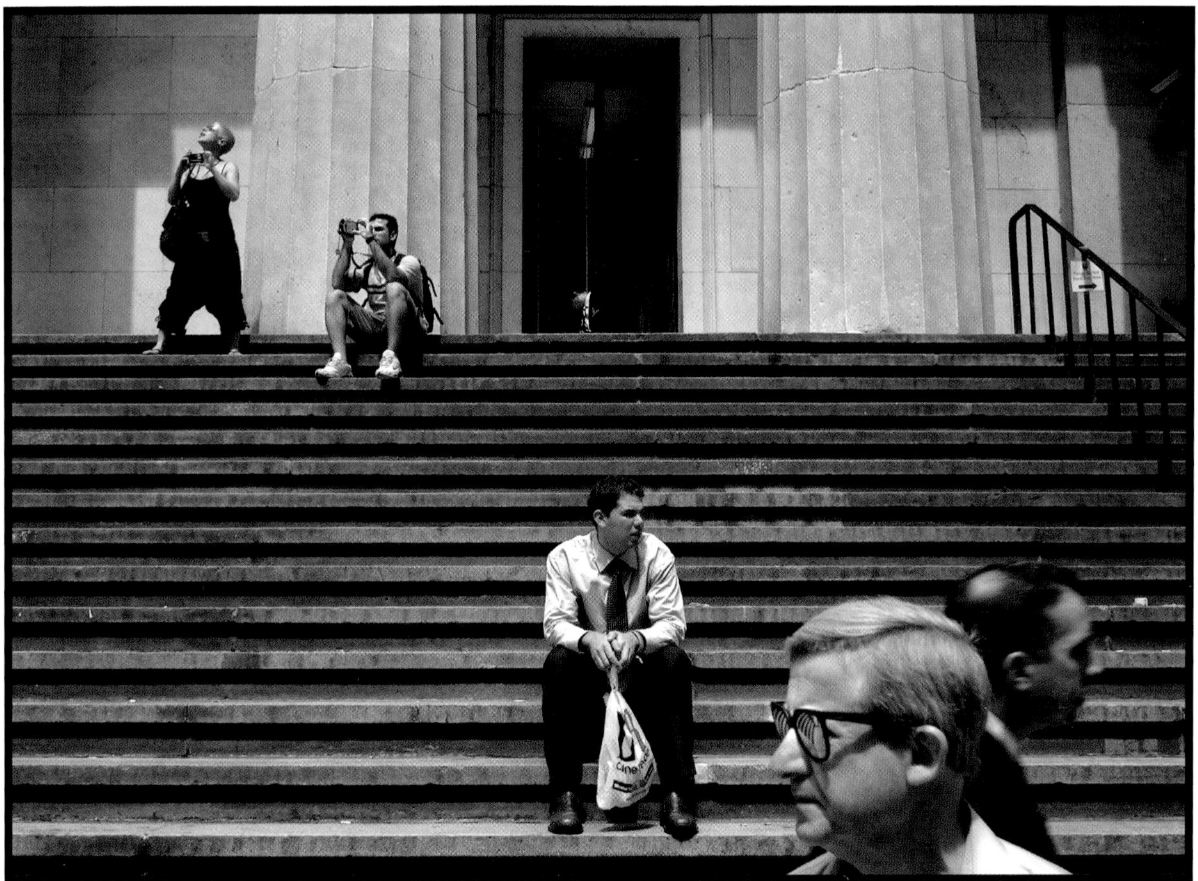

ISO 320 1/125 28mm

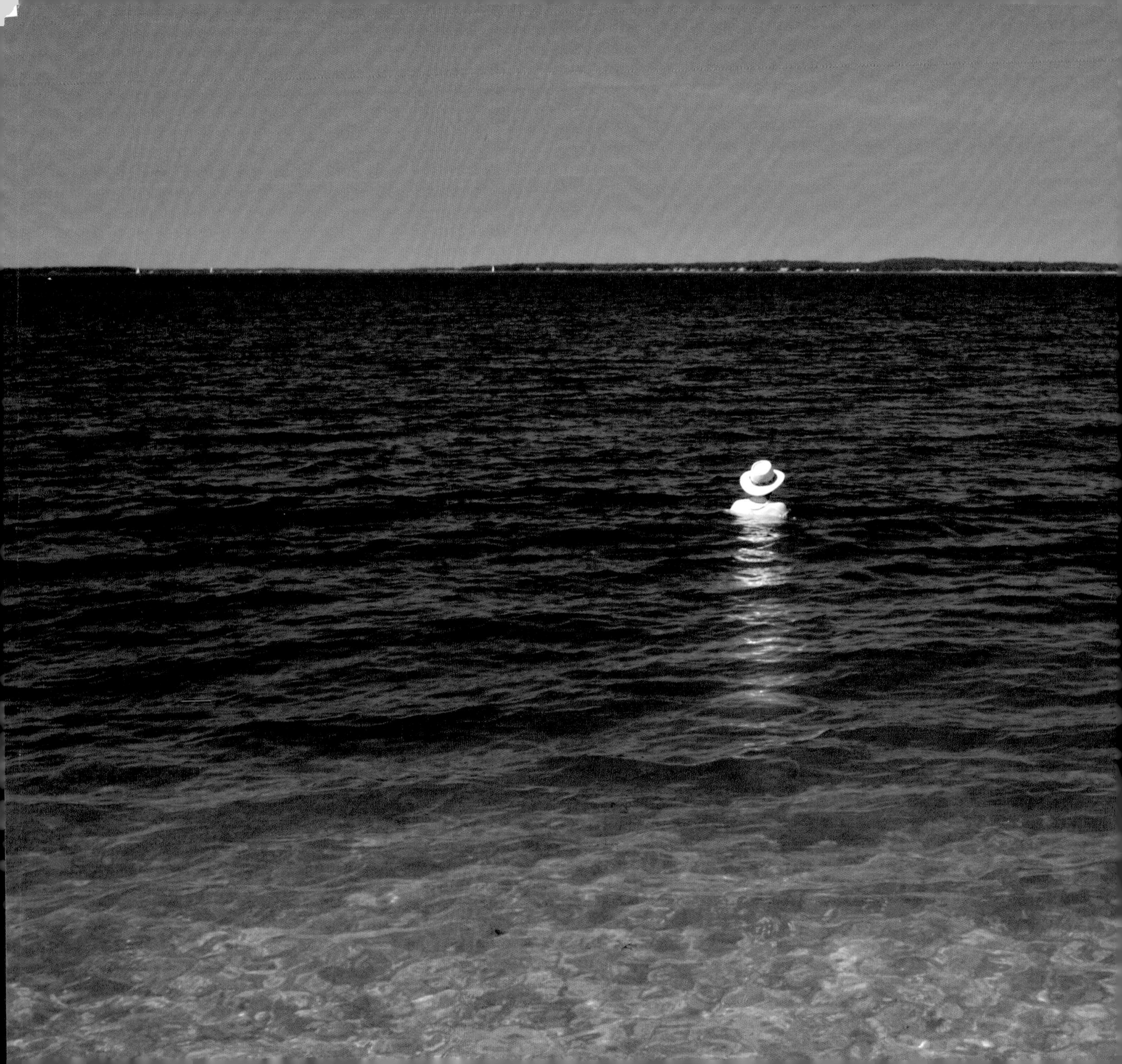

CHAPTER 9

THE ART OF LENS CHOICE

The reality of photography is that there are always infinite possibilities in front of you. And if you think you're probably missing a million photographs every time you take one, it is easy to feel overwhelmed. This makes lens choice even more of a consideration.

◀ Lens: "Little Black Box," Sag Harbor, New York (July 2007).

ISO 320 1/500 26mm

There will be times when you choose a wide-angle lens and then, for example, you see an image on top of a hill that would require a 600mm lens, possibly one of the best images you've ever seen, but you made a conscious decision not to bring that big lens because of its weight. You can't kill yourself over that choice, because the alternative is to become a walking equipment closet. With that much weight, you are immobilized. You get tired, and then you just get lazy. You just have to accept that you've missed that shot and that's OK.

Part of the discipline of photography is asking the question, "What do I really need?" To answer that question, often you first have to ask yourself, "What am I looking for? What is my vision for the photograph?"

LEARNING LENS DISCIPLINE

One of the best things that shaped my career was that I didn't have a lot of money when I started photography, and all I had was one camera with a 50mm lens. I didn't have access to the zoom lenses that I have now, so I was forced to learn how and when a single focal length would work and when it couldn't. It forced discipline.

I used a 50mm lens for this image of an opium smoker. It was for a photo essay on how drugs and the drug world financed the Taliban in Pakistan. You can't ask for more striking symbolism, a man smoking himself to death in front of a tombstone.

The choice to use the 50mm lens was based on my desire to get a sense of place. Had I shot this with a telephoto lens, I wouldn't have been able to see the moon or much of the cemetery. Everything in the background would have been blurred, and the overall composition would have been too tight. Had I shot with a wide-angle lens, the foreground and the setting would have dwarfed the background.

With a standard lens, the scene appears as it would to the human eye. You can see the mountain, the moon, and the graveyard. It gives the composition an important sense of balance.

When you make a conscious decision about a focal length, you are deciding what to include or exclude from the frame. You are composing an image with nothing extraneous in the frame that would distract your viewer from what you are trying to convey. At the same time, you don't want to make the image so tightly composed that it cuts out relevant information.

Opium smoker in Quetta, Pakistan, 2001.

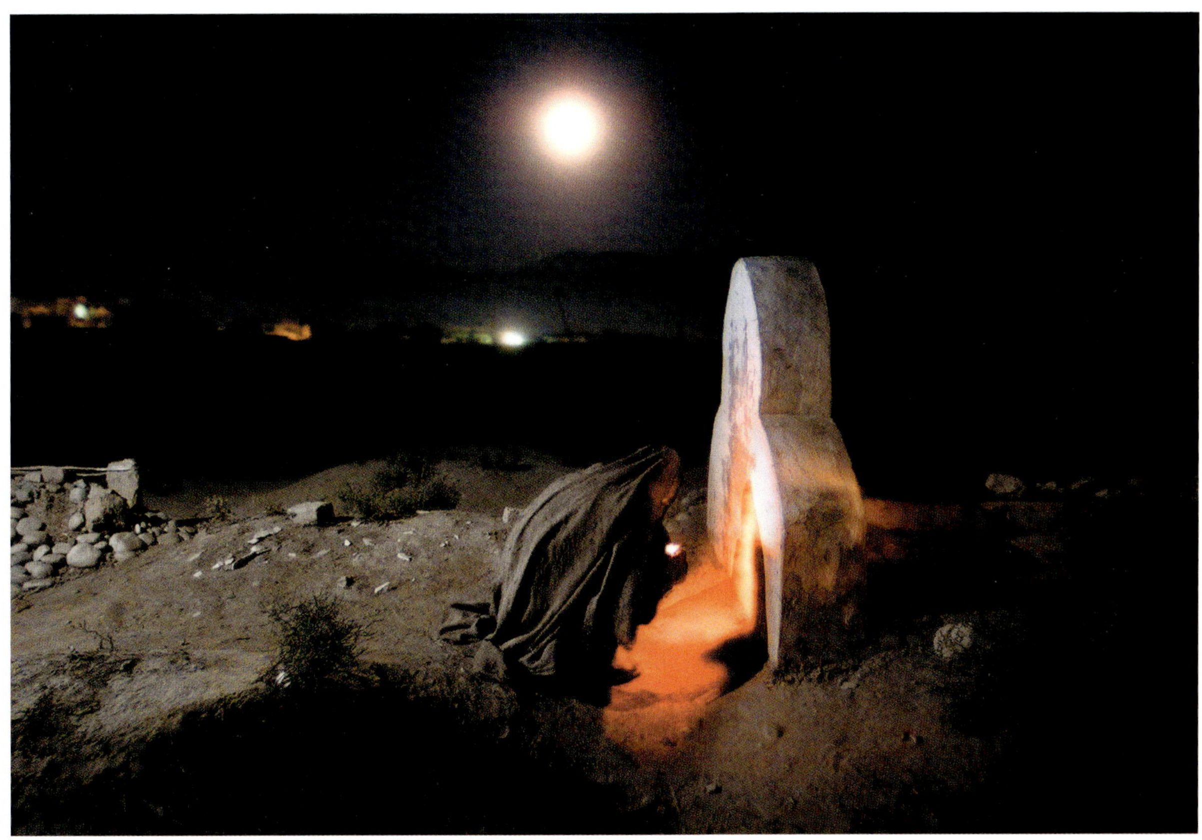

When you use a fixed focal length or even a zoom at a specific focal length for a period of time, you're forced to learn the sweet spot of every lens and where it fails. You discover when it's going to be too tight and when it's going to be too short. You quickly get a sense of what the focal length is going to give you even before you've raised it to your eye.

THE POWER OF PERCEPTION

Lens choice is really about depth perception. It's about understanding that a 14mm lens can make a small room appear gigantic, or that a 300mm lens can make two objects appear closer to each other than they actually are.

One of the principles that I haven't heard too often, but that informs much of what I do with my photography, is not to make a lens choice based on how far my subject is or how wide or tight I want to shoot. I choose a lens based on compression, how the lens impacts the relationship between the foreground and the background.

If I want to create the impression that the foreground and background are closer to each other than they may actually be, I choose a longer lens, to at least a 200mm.

For this image made aboard the *USS Abraham Lincoln,* I knew that the telephoto lens would make it easy to create a very clean, graphic image. By some slight adjustments to my camera position, I was able to isolate certain key elements, while blurring others out.

There's nothing to look at in this image except for the group of guys, the pilot, the setting sun, and the plane. There are just those four elements. There are no potential distractions at the edge of the frame. It's extremely clean and graphic.

However, it is the compression provided by the telephoto lens that makes this shot possible: those four elements appear to be closer to each other than they really were, thus creating a relationship in the viewer's mind.

It looks very much like a painting to me, because the composition is so clean and there are no distractions. It's what you could call a very *commercial* image, because there is just no messiness to be found in it.

The *USS Abraham Lincoln* at sunset (2003).

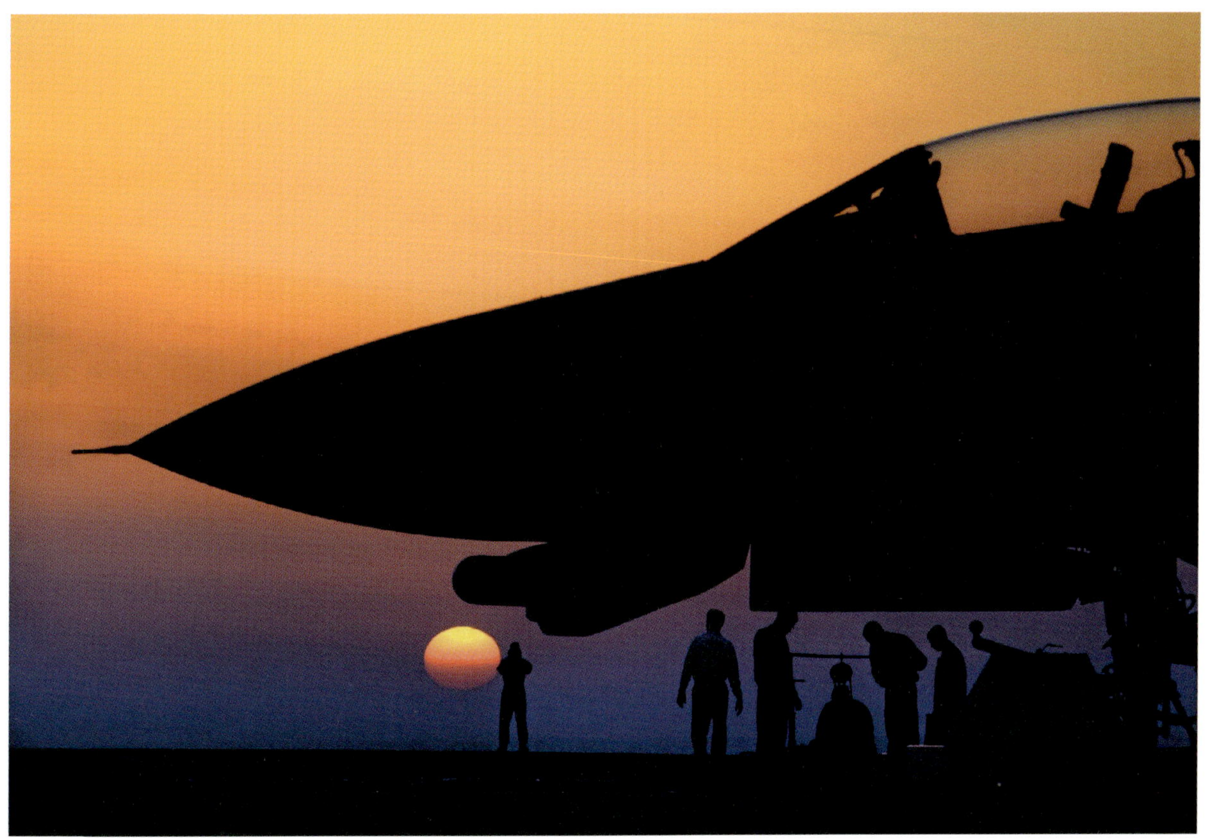

ISO 100 f/8 1/125 190mm

That's the real issue with the ultrawide-angle lens: distortion. It can be your friend or your enemy.

With a wide-angle lens, you would see everything, including all the mess that was on the ground. If I had made the image with a 24mm lens, this would have been a very different photo.

Where a telephoto lens creates compression, a wide-angle lens creates a different kind of distortion between the foreground and the background. In this image of two men working on the antenna atop the Empire State Building, I was shooting with a 14mm lens.

You can see the antenna expanding through the frame toward the top and bottom, and it's made to seem enormous when in reality it's only about as wide as two human arm spans. In the frame with a wide-angle lens, it looks humongous. The foreground is tremendously exaggerated.

Just below the crewmen is the 110th floor; the observation deck and the tourists there appear as nothing more than specks. Even the surrounding buildings around these men appear smaller. That's obviously not a realistic representation of scale.

And that's the real issue with the ultrawide-angle lens: distortion. It can be your friend or your enemy. If used incorrectly, it's incredibly unflattering. If used correctly, as in this case, it makes the image more dynamic. You can see how the buildings look as if they're out of a pop-up book. Obviously, the buildings on the edges of the frame don't actually lean over. They're not the Tower of Pisa.

The reason this image works and why others might not is that it has a visual anchor; in this case, the two engineers. An anchor has to be pretty close and become a substantial part of the frame in order to make itself relevant and to work.

The challenge here is that because you are so close to your subject, if the subject moves a half foot toward or away from the camera, it suddenly becomes too big or too small in the frame. As a result, you have to be very nimble with a wide-angle lens, because of its ability to focus the attention of the viewer on the subject or foreground element and to play with that sense of scale. You quickly start to understand why it's such an important creative decision.

Workers repair the antenna atop the Empire State Building in 2001.

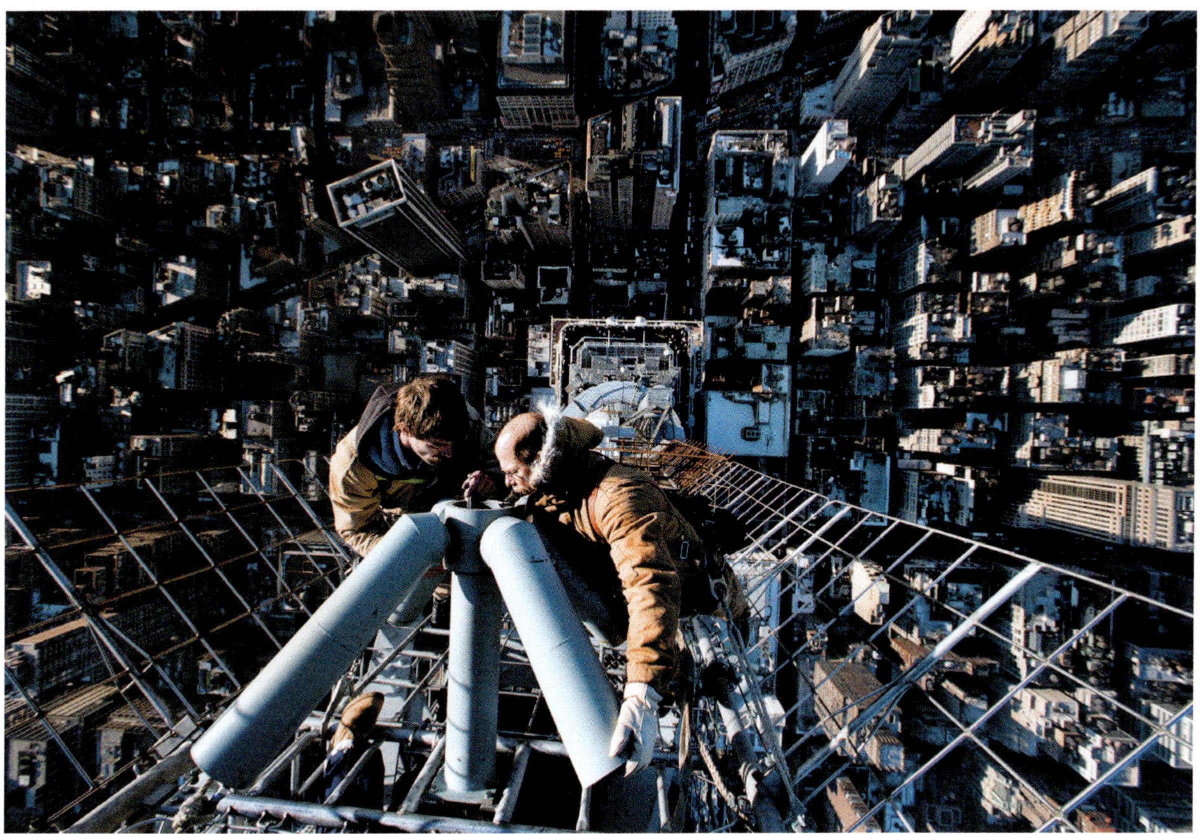

ISO 200 f/5.6 1/1000 14mm

Swimmers on the Santa Monica beaches at sunset.

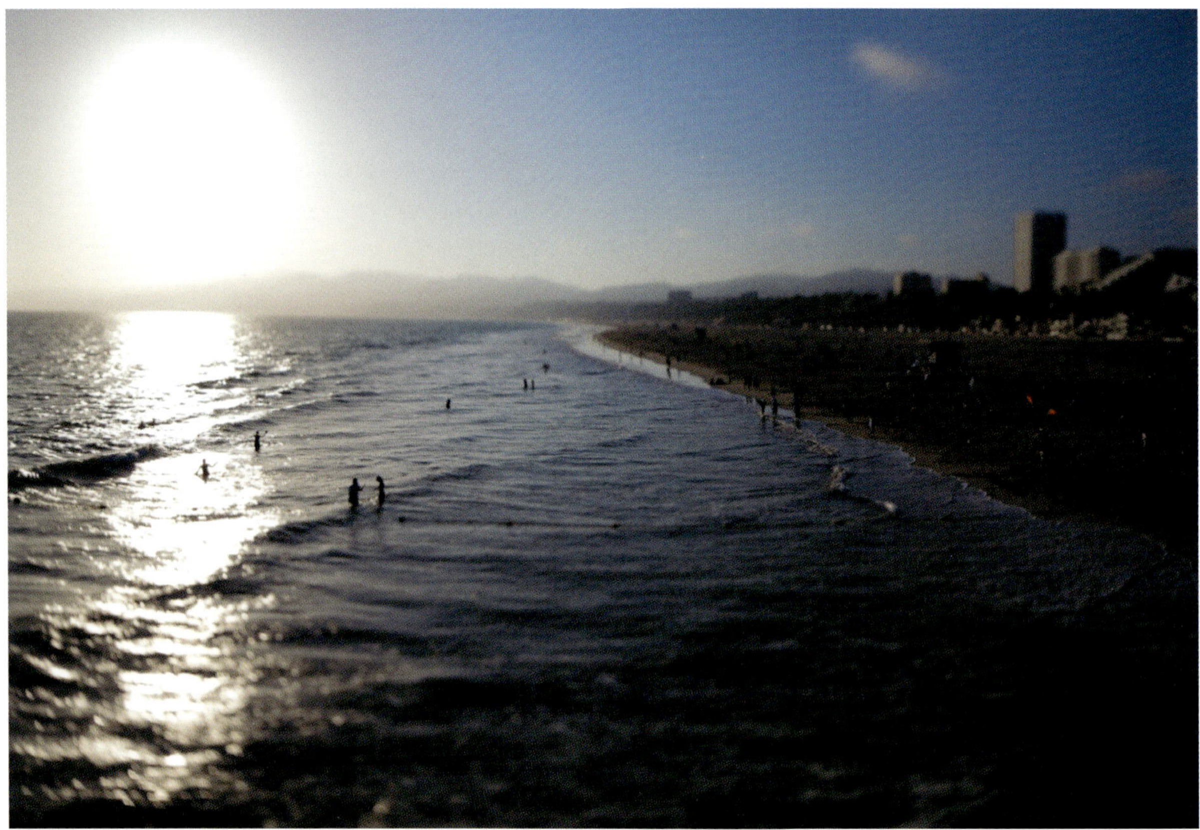

ISO 100 f/3.5 1/6400 24mm

BAG OF TRICKS

The reality of shooting photojournalistically is that a lot of the stuff that we shoot isn't always very graphically interesting. A lot of what we shoot is part of the everyday, and sometimes it's just not pretty, not very geometric, not that aesthetically pleasing. My solution for that is often found in my lenses, my little magic tricks.

These lenses allow me to create geometry out of the stuff doesn't naturally pop out at me.

When you see a painted wall with two red circles and a woman in a yellow dress walking by it, it doesn't take a genius to see the geometry in that. But when you are faced with an everyday street scene, there is rarely a lot of clean geometry. Instead it's often busy and chaotic.

Using a wide angle allows you to find the geometry, but it also lets you emphasize that element or subject in the foreground. In fact, you can even use that wide-angle lens to hide a distracting element in the background right behind the subject, if you are close enough to your subject. You can't do that with a telephoto lens, but by using a wide aperture and a limited depth of field, you can blow out the background.

One of the tricks that a photographer has to practice is simply moving around. Whether you are using a wide-angle or telephoto lens, you need to adjust your position constantly as you look through your viewfinder to discover and force that geometry into your images. You are constantly looking to emphasize and de-emphasize all these disparate elements within the frame.

So, if I am shooting with a 35mm lens and I take a half step to the right, the foreground elements remain relatively the same, but the background changes quite a bit. I find myself constantly dancing around and finessing things as a photographer, trying to make all these elements line up in some sort of geometric way that adds meaning.

It's something that I find much easier to do with a wide-angle lens, and when that doesn't work well, I will often revert to a telephoto lens.

ZOOMS VERSUS PRIMES

Zoom lenses for me are a convenience. It's nice to be able to walk out with two cameras and two lenses and know they will cover every single range. Having to change lenses, especially when you're in a new and fast-paced situation, can cause you to miss a lot. But when you're walking around with a 24–70mm and a 70–200mm, you can cover the world with just those two lenses.

With those two lenses and two cameras, you don't need the camera bag anymore. All you need are your memory cards and extra batteries, and you're good to go. With prime lenses, on the other hand, you have to carry as many as you need, and the idea for me is never to travel around with more than three or four lenses if possible. If I am walking around with too much equipment, it just gets too heavy and cumbersome.

That being said, some of my best work has been shot with prime lenses, because after having done this for more than 20 years, I am very familiar with how prime lenses perform and what they offer me. I know their sweet spots.

It's important to learn the sweet spot of your lens, particularly a zoom. What I often do with my students is have them put gaffer's tape on their zoom lenses and force them to shoot at a specific focal length for two weeks. They are not allowed to move it. They are forced to learn the sweet spot of that particular focal length on that lens, as well as discover when it fails.

LENSING AS A PRACTICAL CHOICE

I used an 18mm lens for this image of a homeowner returning for the first time to his home in the Lower 9th Ward in New Orleans. It was a full year after the storm had hit and the levees had fallen, and it was only now that he was able to return to salvage what he could, which was nothing.

I was very physically limited while making this shot. I could only go so far back, thus forced to use a wide-angle lens to capture the scene.

Louis Simmons came back to his home for the first time since his rescue three days after Hurricane Katrina struck (August 2006).

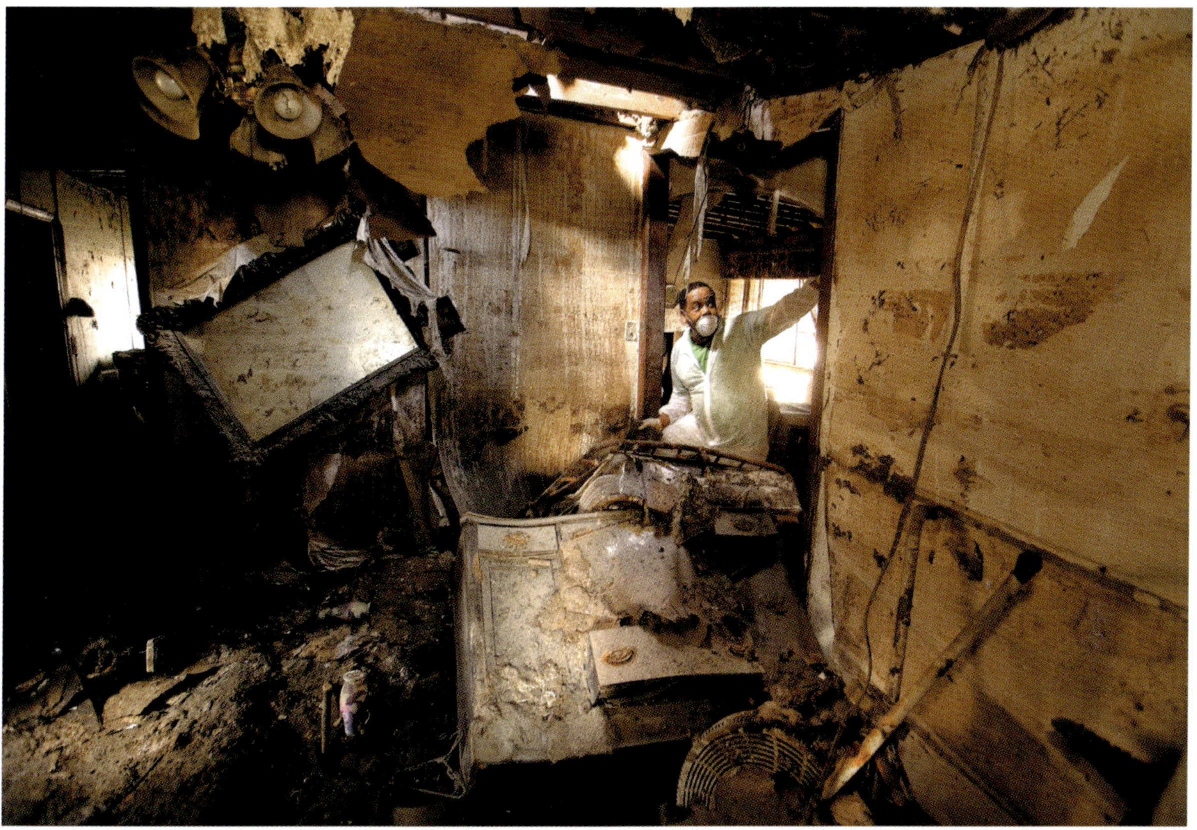

ISO 640 f/4 1/10 18mm

So I had to use a 16mm lens to capture this very small room. The same image with a 50mm lens would have resulted in a very different photograph. With a normal lens of that size, you could never get the sense of all the content in that small space. The 50mm would produce a very limited field of view, and you would just see the man. I would have probably lost the mirror and the fan on the floor. Most important, the photograph included the hole in the ceiling, which is the very opening out of which he had to climb in order to be rescued.

The wide-angle lens not only allowed me to include all that, but also helped me illustrate how dwarfed he was by the devastation around him.

OWNING YOUR FRAME

When it comes to choosing the lens and composition, I treat the frame as if I were painting. One of the first things I was taught when learning to draw was that you can't just put your pencil on a piece of paper and start drawing. It's what you want to do, but you shouldn't.

When I simply started drawing, I'd get some fantastic results as I begin, but when I'd reach the edge of the paper, I realize I didn't have the discipline to think about how the image would fit at the edge of the paper. When you reach the edge of the paper or the canvas, there's really nothing more that you can do.

I think composing a photograph should be treated in much the same way. Those four edges and corners are ridiculously important, and you see how they are transformed and impacted by your lens choice.

The goal is to find a way to accept the limitations of the equipment or the situation and to begin engaging in the act of art. Each of us has to aim for that space between the technical and the artistic, where discipline and knowledge mix with talent and luck.

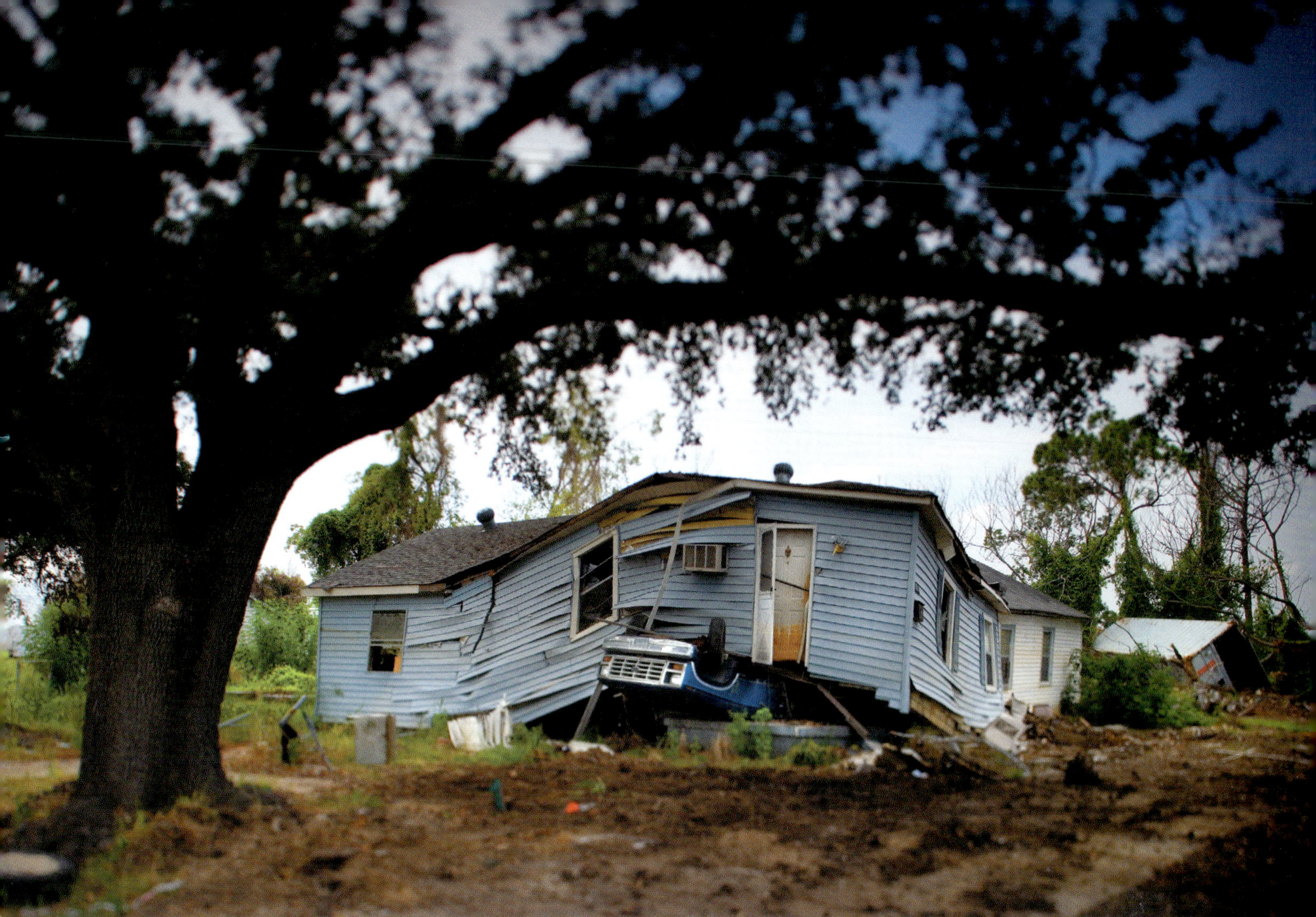

New Orleans: one year after Hurricane Katrina struck (2006).

ISO 200 f/5 1/320 24mm

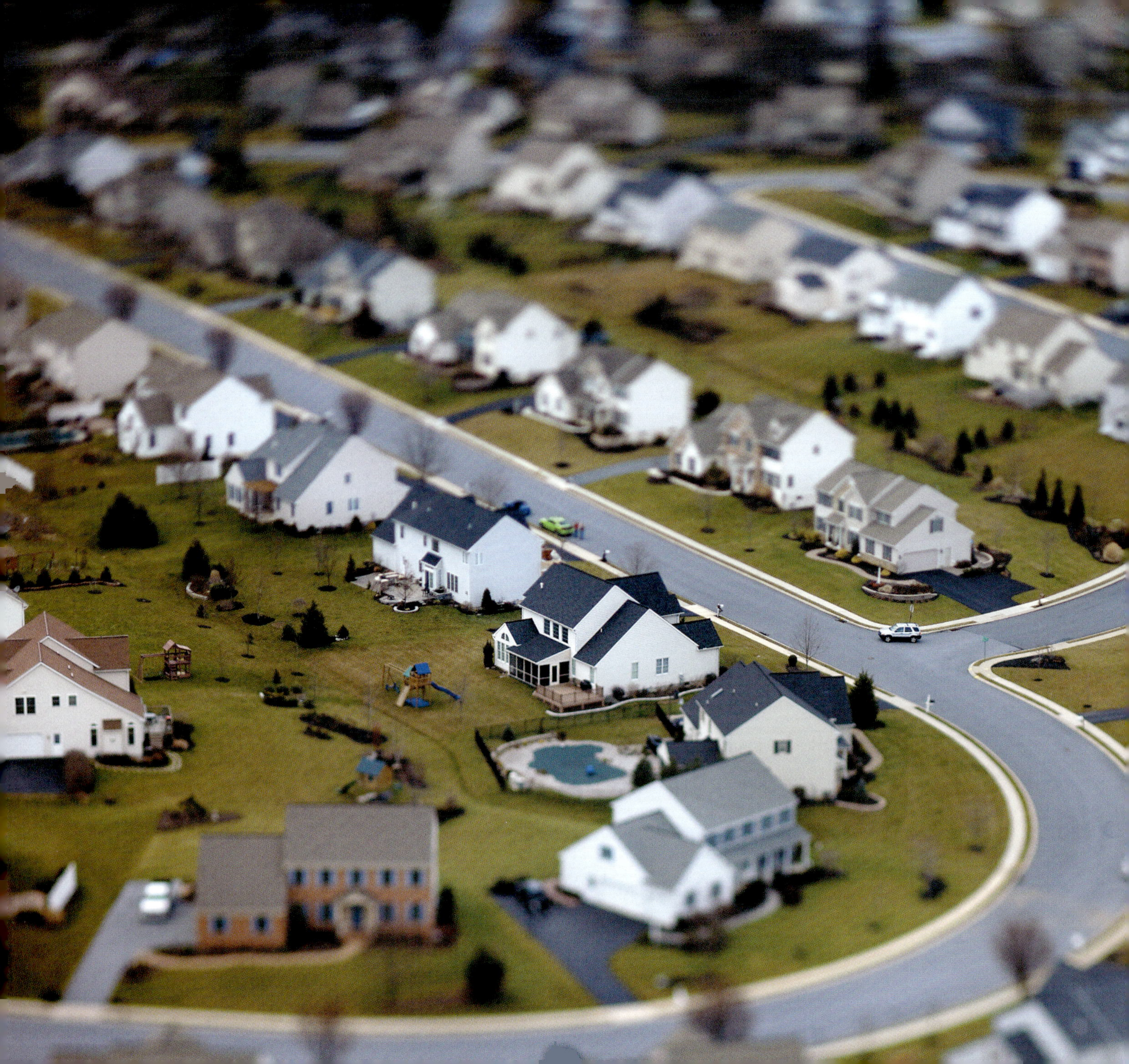

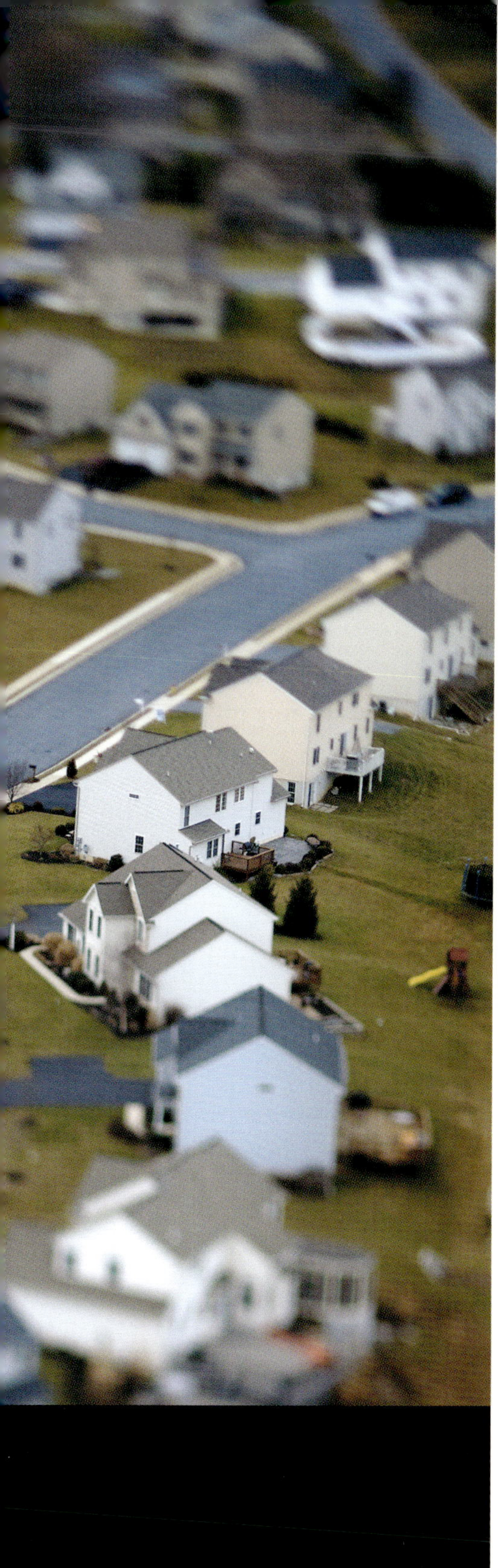

CHAPTER 10

THE WORLD THROUGH A TILT-SHIFT LENS

Every time I look at the image on the next page, I remember thinking at the time I wouldn't come back with a single image from the assignment.

This was Super Bowl XLI, the Chicago Bears versus the Indianapolis Colts, and the rain never let up during game time. It was a record-breaking game in terms of rainfall; the only time it finally stopped was during halftime, when the musician Prince performed.

◀ Southridge Farms, a suburb of Lancaster County, Pennsylvania.

ISO 400 f/2.8 1/1500 90mm

Super Bowl XLI.

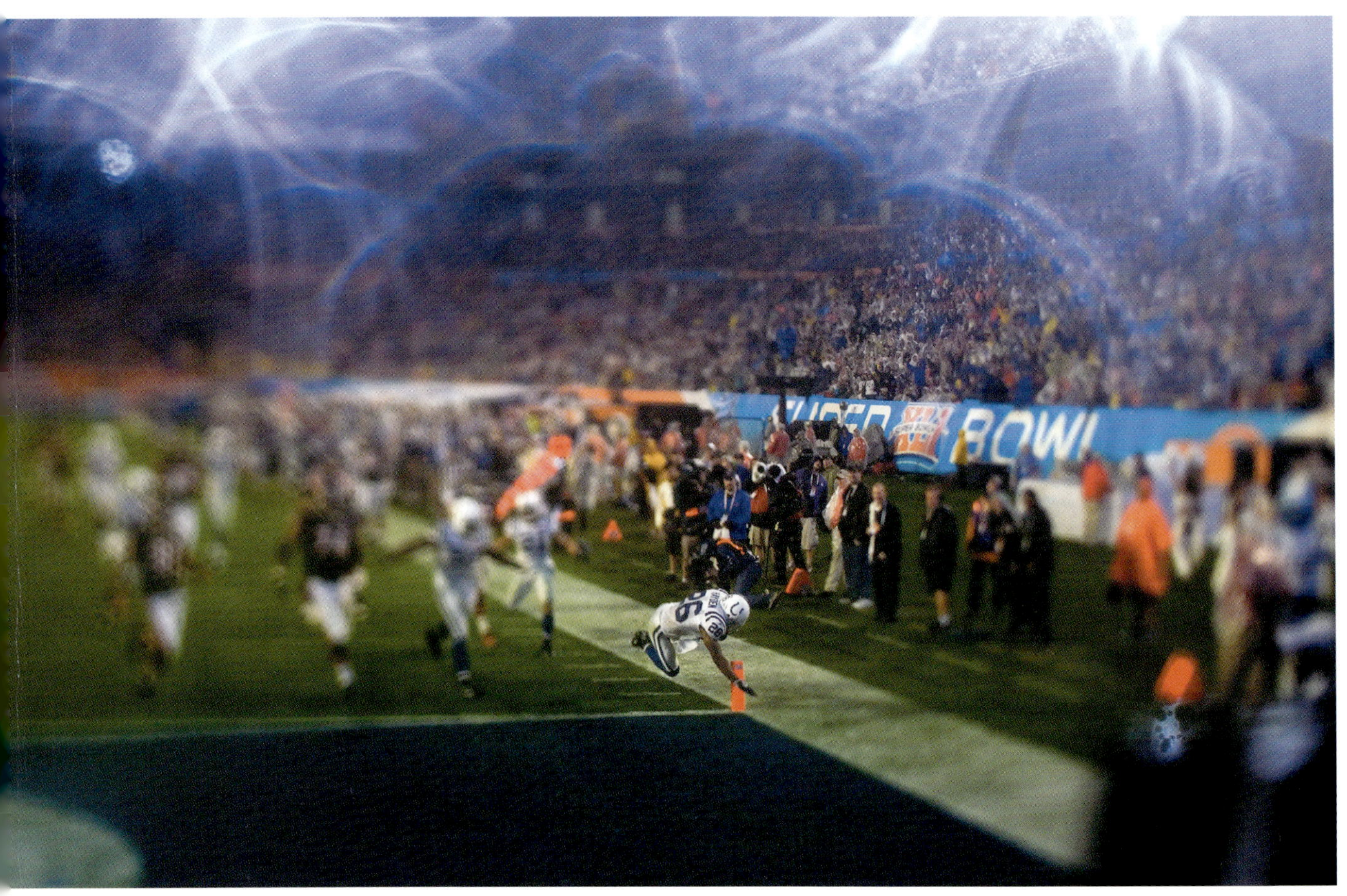

ISO 800 f/2.8 1/640 45mm

It was the worst time to be using a 45mm tilt-shift lens: a wide-angle lens that you purposely tilt up had no protection from the rain. I had a horrible time. My glasses were fogging up repeatedly, which also made using a manual focus tilt-shift lens a pretty hard thing to pull off.

I left that game thinking I had absolutely nothing, and I was distraught because I was drenched, and thought I had probably destroyed a few cameras (though they actually survived the dousing).

When I went through the photographs, I had only two usable images. One was of Peyton Manning winding up for a pass—nothing special. The second one, thank God, was that of the game-winning touchdown.

If it was at all possible to pick a lucky moment to be at the right place at the right time, this was definitely it.

THE SURREAL IN THE REAL

A tilt-shift lens allows you to rotate the front lens element either left or right, or up or down; and when the front lens element is no longer parallel to either the sensor or the film plane, the only area in focus is where the focal plane intersects with a sensor or the film plane. Everything else appears gradually out of focus.

A tilt-shift lens lets me create photographs that make people stop and examine the world more carefully, because the resulting image doesn't look real. It arrests you. It reminds me of how as a kid I would photograph my toy train station using a 50mm macro lens.

Images created with a tilt-shift lens force people to explore the photograph. They are looking at a real scene, but one that has a touch of the surreal in it. Many people can't tell what you've done, while others wonder whether you created the surreal effect with a computer. But in either case, they are completely drawn into the image.

Every lens you use distorts reality in a certain way, depending on its degree of compression and depth of field. A camera lens doesn't see the world the way your naked eye does, and tilt-shift lenses push that to the extreme. Using one is no different than using an old 8-by-10-inch–format camera, which has a bellows and a movable front and rear standard.

The Washington State Ferry makes its way toward Seattle. The ferry's capacity is equivalent to that of five Boeing 747 airplanes, about 2,500 people.

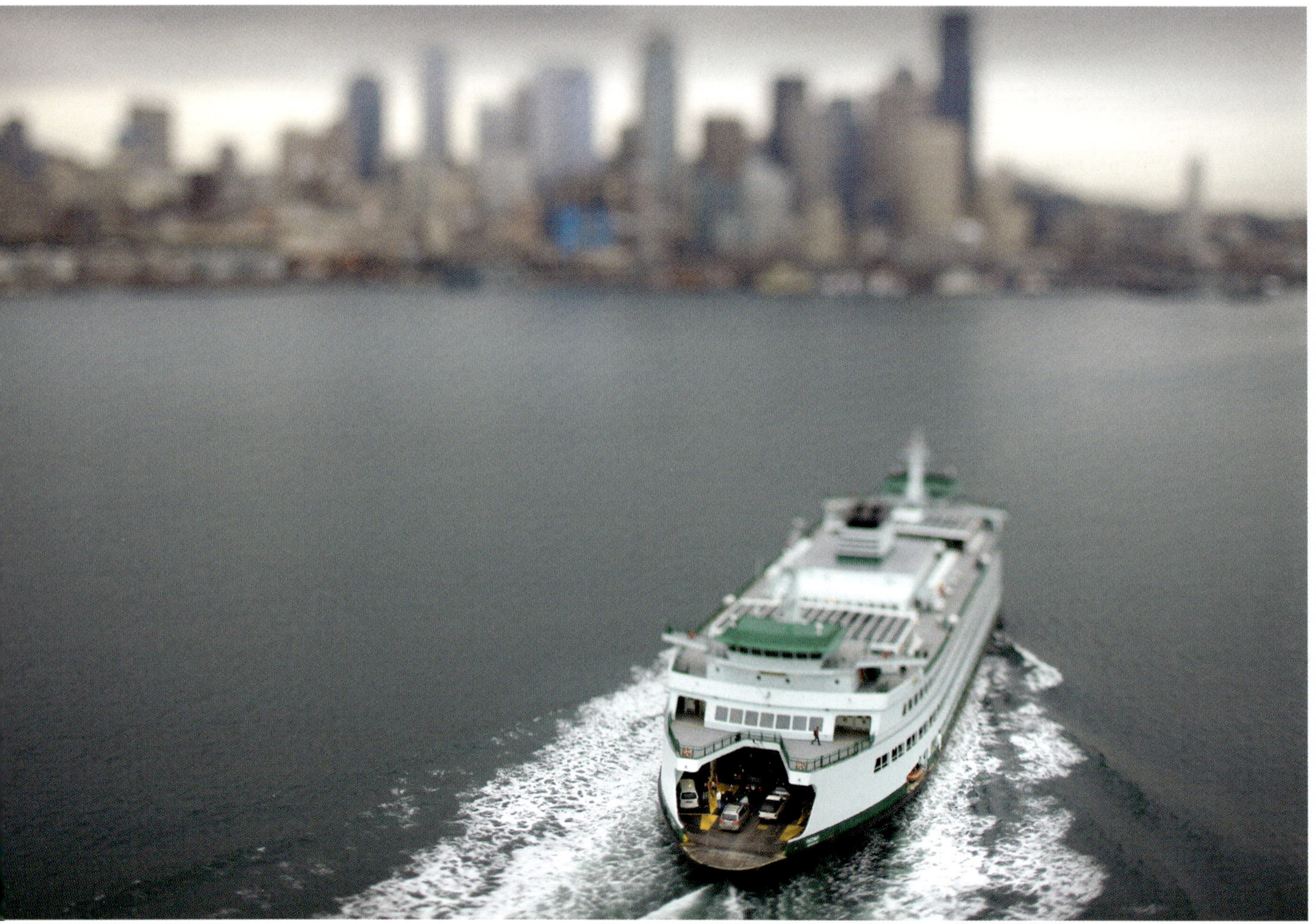

ISO 40 f/2.8 1/500 24mm

I appreciate the fact that the effect was done in-camera with optics, rather than with software. Beyond the look of the photograph, it allowed me to elevate what I was able to do with subjects that lacked inherent drama.

For example, in the commuter series that I did for a magazine assignment, I was faced with one of the most boring subjects you could imagine shooting: commuting. It's an everyday event that happens all around the country, a hundred thousand times a day, and the challenge was to capture it in a way that was unique.

That's why I chose the tilt-shift: it allowed me to create a very wide image of a scene, and still have a way to emphasize the people—the commuters. The wide-angle, tilt-shift lens provided me with a good sense of scale and perspective, yet I could sometimes narrow the focus down to that one individual who would otherwise get completely lost in the frame. That's what I loved about it.

It's important to point out that I don't think I could have shot this way for the *New York Times*. I think it's more acceptable for feature photography in magazines—photography that's meant to illustrate ideas and concepts.

I don't really see tilt-shift photography as being appropriate for hard news events. I wouldn't shoot with a tilt-shift lens in Pakistan. That being said, as my career matured and grew, I was naturally leaning toward taking more chances and pushing that envelope, stepping away from pure editorial photography. I found it was tremendously limiting to creativity not to be able to use different tools, and to light things in certain ways.

Images created with a tilt-shift lens force people to explore the photograph. They are looking at a real scene, but one that has a touch of the surreal in it.

SERVING THE STORY

With a tilt-shift lens, the focal point has to be perfectly placed. It's a much more fine-art approach, like that of using an 8-by-10 field camera. You continually refine the composition until you're blue in the face, and you have one frame to fire.

You can never trust your light meter when making a tilt-shift photograph, because of the way the path of the light changes as it travels through the lens. The light no longer passes through a straight path as it does with other lenses, so you can't trust the automatic-exposure controls of the camera or what you might see on the back of the LCD.

To ensure that I achieve focus accurately, I magnify the image on the back of the camera to double-check my focus, because it is extremely hard to see where I had focused with the tilt-shift lens by using just the optical viewfinder. And because I tend to shoot tilt-shift photos wide open, I have to make sure the focus is right.

This is another image from the tilt-shift series on commuting. I shot it in Amish country in Allentown, Pennsylvania, and I've always loved the small details in this image. If you look really closely between the two houses, you'll see an elderly Amish man with a white beard and straw hat, a touch that gives a beautiful sense of balance to the photograph. It's one of my favorite images.

When shooting from the air with a tilt-shift lens, you should first consider position and elevation relative to your subject. You have to realize that while you're waiting for a moment, you're trying to make the photograph live off the aesthetic.

Shooting from the air with a tilt-shift lens compounds the challenges, especially as you try to stay in focus. But it's also exciting: after more than 15 years of practicing photography, I could get to the point where everything was sharp because I knew how to use my camera system. Since the autofocus system isn't a viable option with a tilt-shift, I had to go back to focusing manually and trusting my skill and experience.

The Amish and Mennonite horse-drawn buggies share the road with modern vehicles near Lancaster, Pennsylvania.

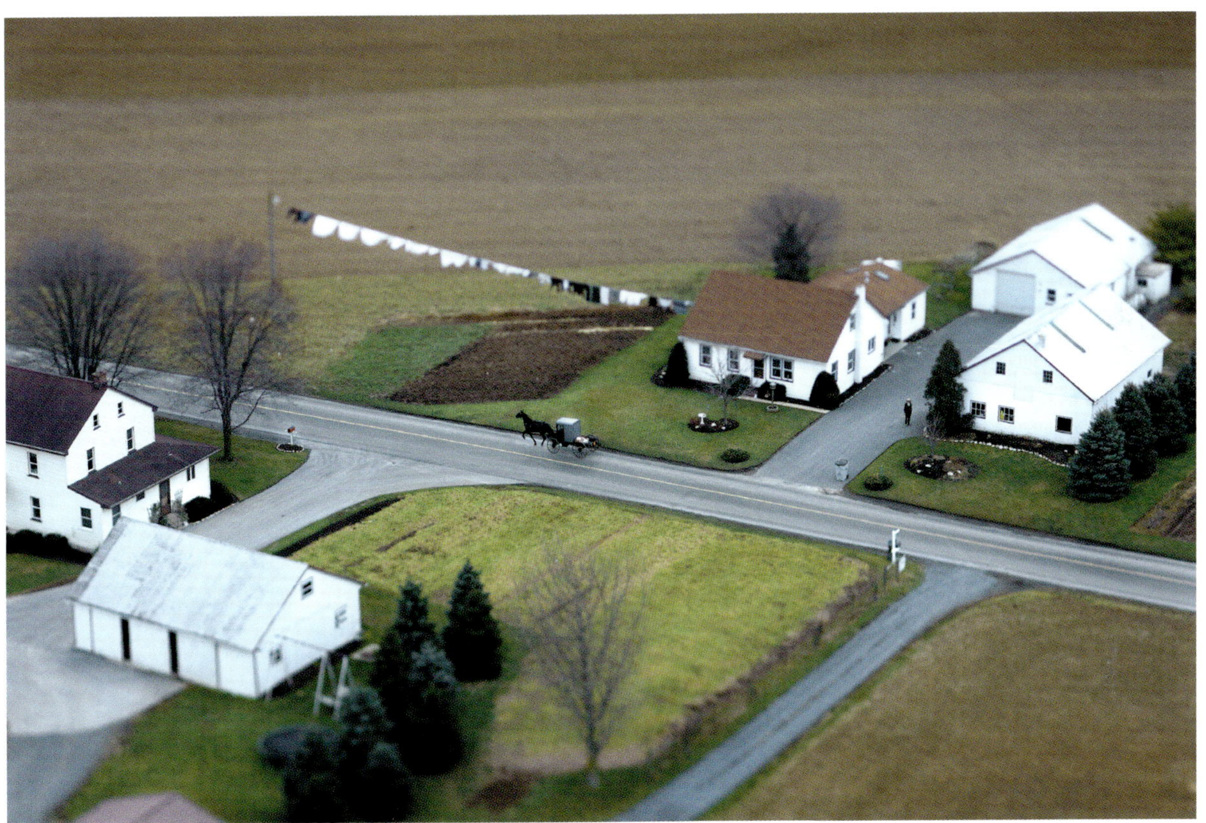

ISO 400 f/4 1/1000 90mm

TILT-SHIFT AS A GIMMICK

This distinctive look eventually led to a tilt-shift photography craze, including tilt-shift iPhone apps, which has resulted in a lot of images created using tilt-shift lenses for no apparent reason; they're just done in a gimmicky way. I think any technique should be used to help tell a story.

In my tilt-shift images, no matter what, there was always a very clear point where the focal plane crossed the sensor, so I was forcing the audience to look at something. It was never a random point picked without a subject. I was highlighting a subject, and purposely deemphasizing everything that extended away from it.

You should use a tilt-shift lens for a reason, and with a purpose—to augment or tell the story in a better way—and make sure you always choose a specific focal point to help accomplish that. If you just use it as a gimmick, then you're just destroying it for everybody. It's an utter waste of time, in my opinion. Most of the tilt-shift photography I find doesn't really express anything, except calling attention to the technique itself.

This first image shown here was made during the World Series when the Detroit Tigers were playing the St. Louis Cardinals. As always, I tried to tell a story with the tilt-shift technique. In this case, I tilted the lens and rotated it a little bit so that only the pitcher and the batter were in focus. In baseball I think there's a big duel between that duo, and that's what I was trying to portray.

The Detroit Tigers and St. Louis Cardinals compete during Game 1 of the 2006 World Series at Tiger Stadium in Detroit, Michigan.

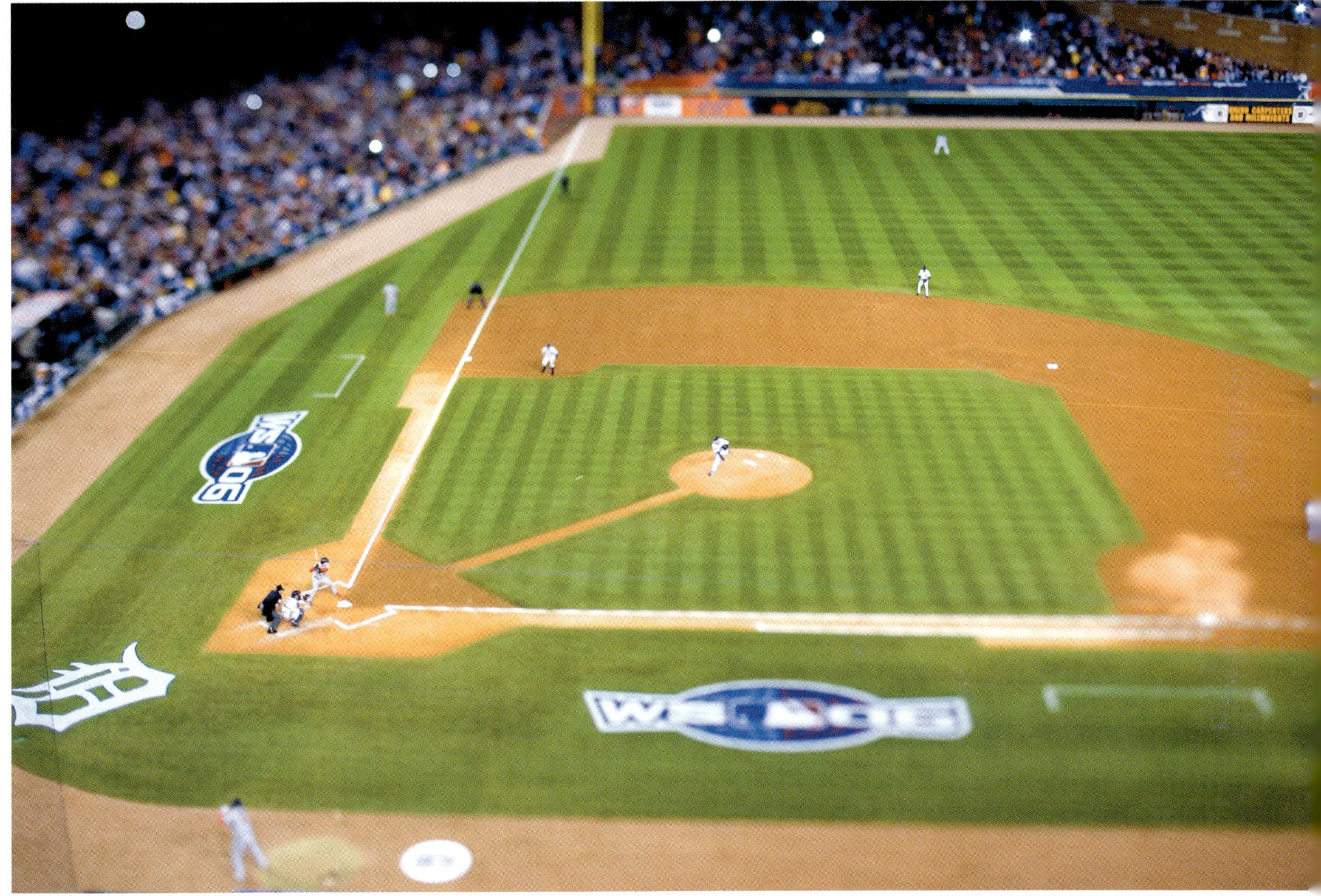

ISO 200 f/3.2 1/100 45mm

You should use a tilt-shift lens for a reason, and with a purpose—to augment or tell the story in a better way—and make sure you always choose a specific focal point to help accomplish that.

This next image, which I shot in Grand Central Station in Manhattan, is one of the rare vertical images I've made with tilt-shift photography.

It's very hard for me to make a nice vertical tilt-shift image. You'll notice that I really prefer to make tilt-shift images that have the tilt or the shift happening on the horizontal plane. In other words, everything gets more in or out of focus toward the top or bottom of the frame. I don't like it as much when it's switched so that it's from left to right.

At the time of this shot, we were still feeling raw from the events of 9/11. I felt that the American flag was a pretty important element to have as part of Grand Central, and to have it hovering above these masses of people going in and out of the station.

This lens choice allows the photographer and the viewer to appreciate the environment and the world in a very different way, I believe, than if it had been shot with a standard lens.

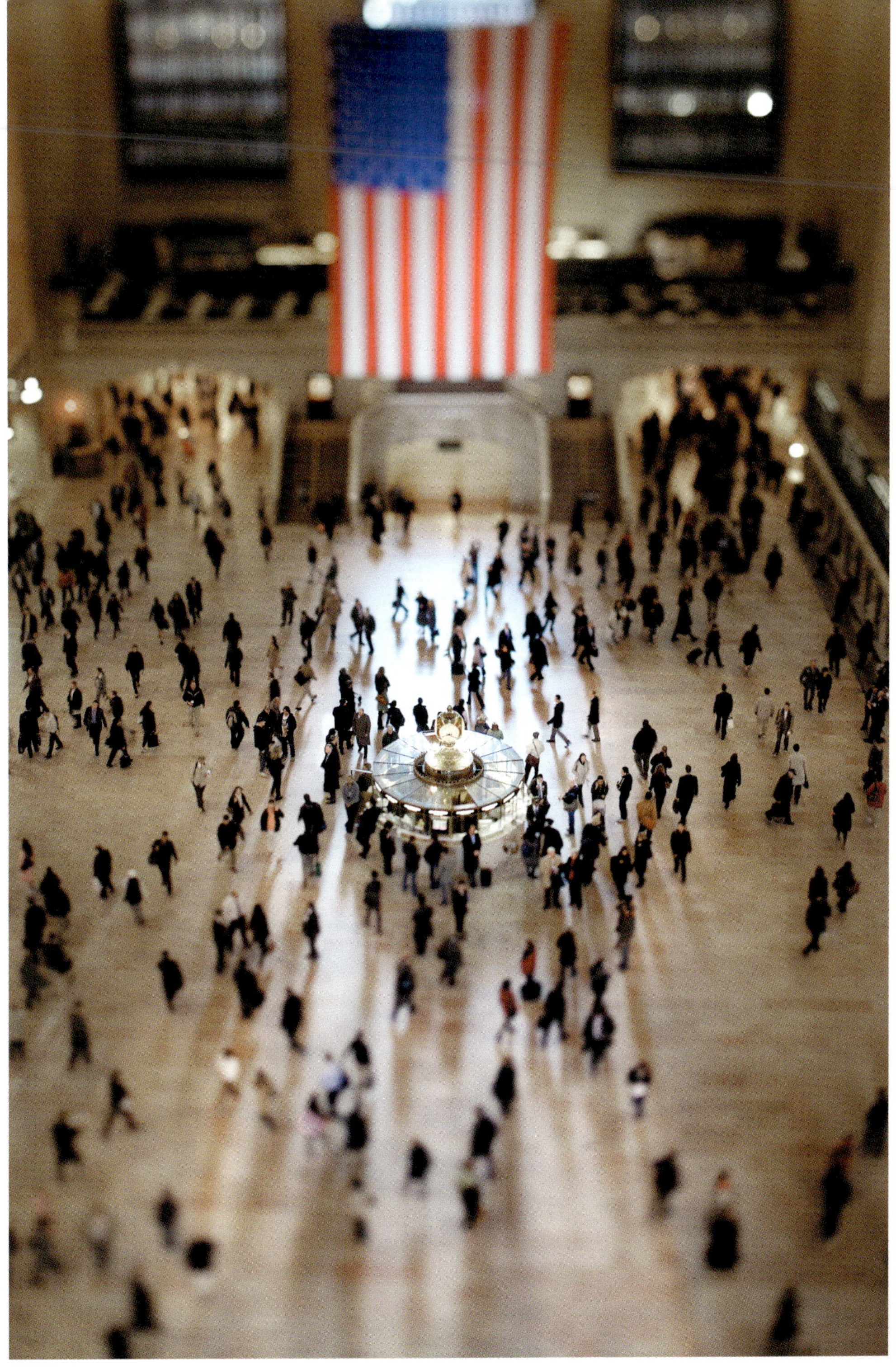

Grand Central Station, 2007. ISO 500 f/2.8 1/20 45mm

Commuters wait for a train for a New York City-bound Metro North train in Scarsdale, New York.

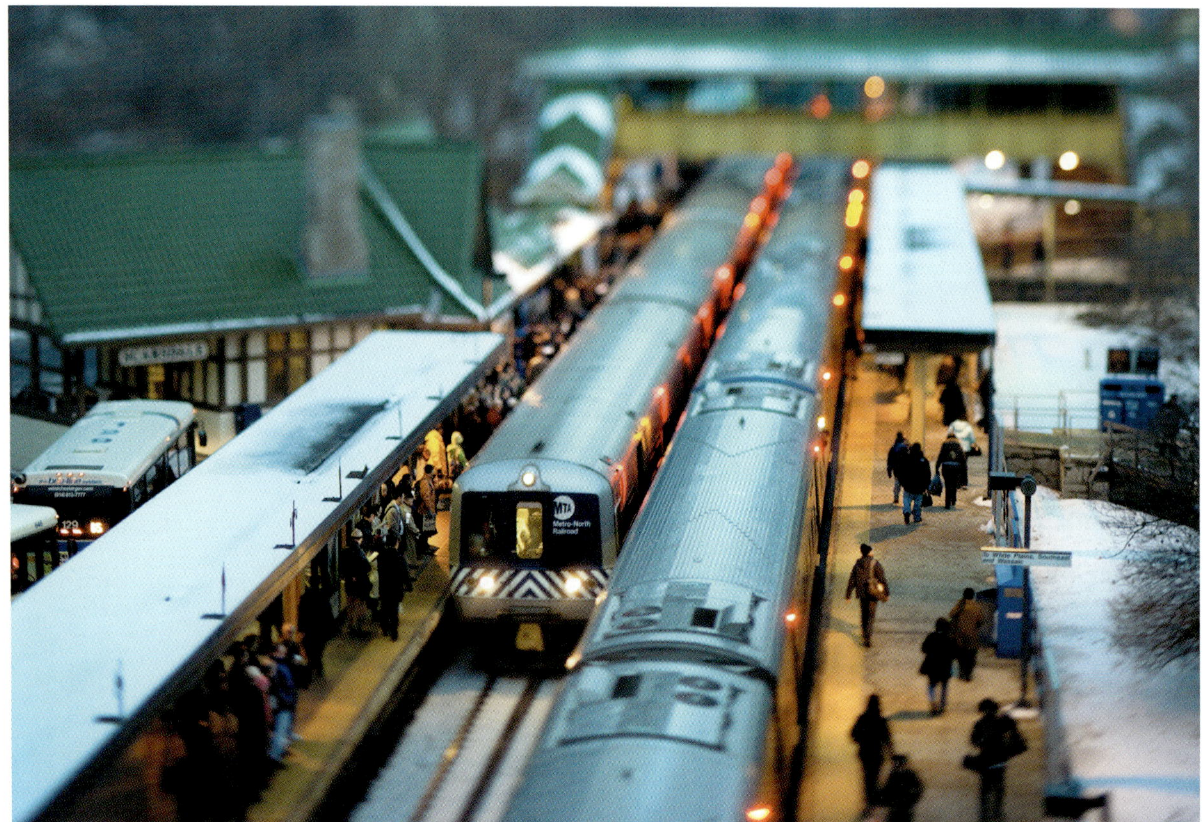

ISO 320 f/2.8 1/30 90mm

MOVING BEYOND BORING

Sometimes I use the tilt-shift technique to help tell the story of a very boring event. There's nothing special about the geometry of the train station shown in this image, or that environment. The light is flat and ridiculously boring. The only way I would shoot this with a normal lens would be with a super telephoto lens to get all the people coming in and out of the train.

The tilt-shift lens made this very mundane situation look surreal. And it made all the little people getting in and out of the train look like miniatures. The image compels you to look at one of the most boring things known to mankind: getting on and off a train. That's their commute every single day. There's nothing exciting about it. The train usually shows up on time. People know exactly where they want to stand on the platform.

My challenge as the photographer was to try to make the scene a little more interesting, and that's where the tilt-shift effects make you stop, freeze, and look, and study the image.

This photograph was very painful to make because we had to be there at 3:00 a.m. in order to get that color palette. We also had to be there to meet the cops to get the scissor lift up on the bridge before sunrise, so that we would be ready to shoot before daylight.

I could have decided to get there at 9:00 a.m., but those extra hours of sleep would have cost me the pre-dawn light and color. I would have missed the window of time when the ambient light balanced with the artificial light. And I would have lost that special brief moment just before that natural light overtakes the artificial light.

My challenge as the photographer was to try to make the scene a little more interesting, and that's where the tilt-shift effects make you stop, freeze, and look, and study the image.

Keep in mind that you can shoot with more depth of field and a smaller aperture, but you'll get more things in focus and the effect will be minimized.

KEEPING UP WITH A SUBJECT

Again from the commuting series, this is an image of the intertwining highway overpasses in downtown Los Angeles, shot from a helicopter. As I've mentioned, one of the biggest challenges with tilt-shift lenses is that you have to focus them manually; there are no autofocus tilt-shift lenses. So when you're moving in a helicopter, it's very hard to pull off focus, especially when you're trying to follow a subject. But when you do manage to do it, it makes for a very unique image.

I was trying to follow a very small bus, which you may or may not be able to see, and it was indeed a challenge. What you will notice here is how the tilt-shift effect is lessened because it was shot at f/5.6 versus f/2.8. So keep in mind that you can shoot with more depth of field and a smaller aperture, but you'll get more things in focus and the effect will be minimized.

Nevertheless, when you shoot wide open, there's absolutely no room for error—in fact, what I've tended to do is to use the live view function on a digital SLR camera and apply 10x zoom to the exact point of focus; that guarantees me that what I'm trying to get in focus is tack-sharp. Sometimes doing it with your eye through the ground glass of the viewfinder isn't enough. That's where the live view function can really come in handy.

Commuters make their way by car amidst the morning traffic flow on the freeways surrounding the Los Angeles, California metropolitan area.

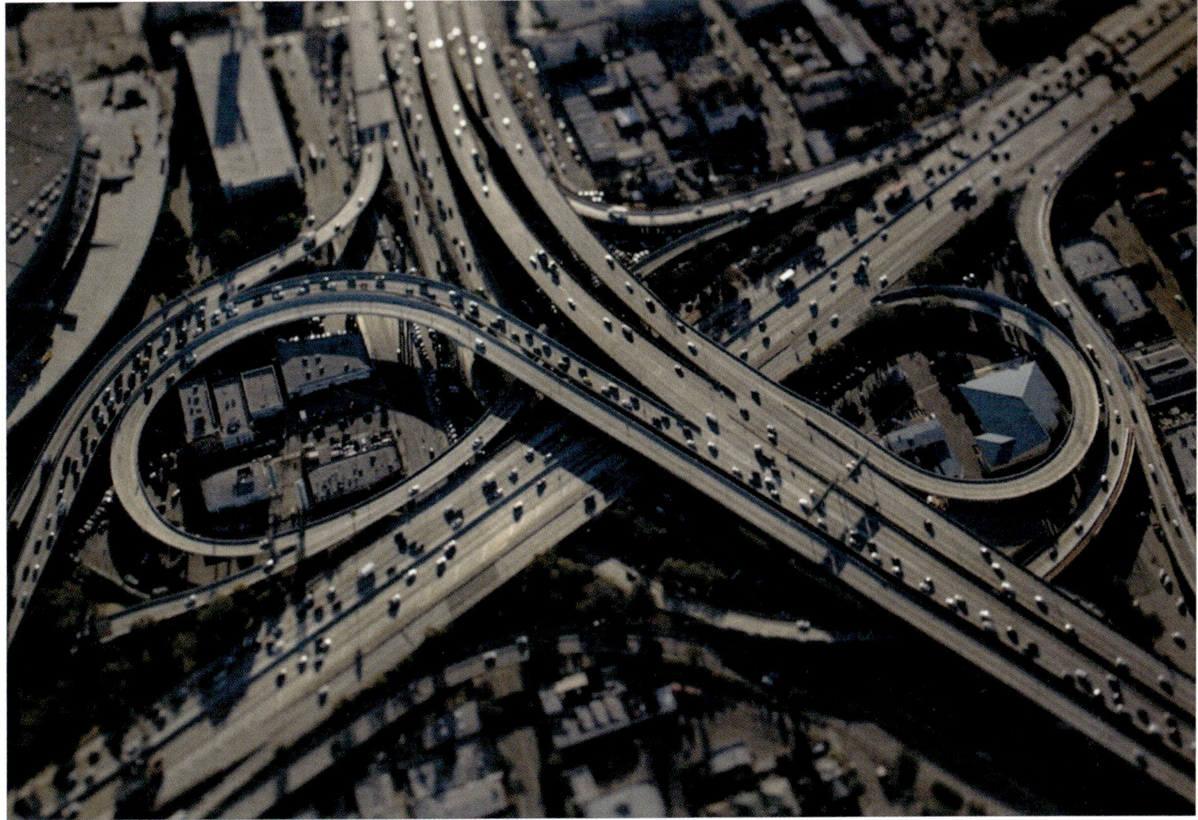

ISO 200 f/5.6 1/1250 45mm

WHEN LUCK MEETS PREPARATION

This is definitely one of my favorite images, mainly because it was an extremely lucky one. I made this shot at the Kentucky Derby in 2007 with a remote camera; in other words, I had to prefocus the camera and guess where the perfect point would be at the end of the race. I was actually shooting with another camera at the finish line a few hundred yards away, and a radio trigger remote fired off this camera.

What makes this image particularly lucky is the fact that I focused a few hundred yards past the finish line. It is there, at about 150 yards beyond the finish line, that the winning horse, Street Sense, and his jockey, Calvin Borel, can be seen in perfect focus. It was a moment when the stars magically lined up and I was very fortunate. Had he pumped his fist in victory a half-second earlier or later, the picture would not have come through.

When magic like that happens, I personally thank my lucky stars, and then tell everyone else that that's exactly what I had planned and that there was no luck involved (I'm joking, of course).

The one thing I did differently is that I used aperture priority mode. This is very unusual for me because the weather at Churchill Downs is unpredictable. It tends to get rain or patchy clouds, and in this case that's what we had.

I wasn't sure exactly what the exposure would be at that golden winning moment, and this was a remote camera that we had to set up hours in advance. I set it to the automatic exposure mode and applied some exposure compensation to ensure that the exposure wouldn't be inaccurate as a result of the tilt-shift lens, as it usually is. I got the image.

The 133rd running of the Kentucky Derby in Louisville, Kentucky, in 2007.

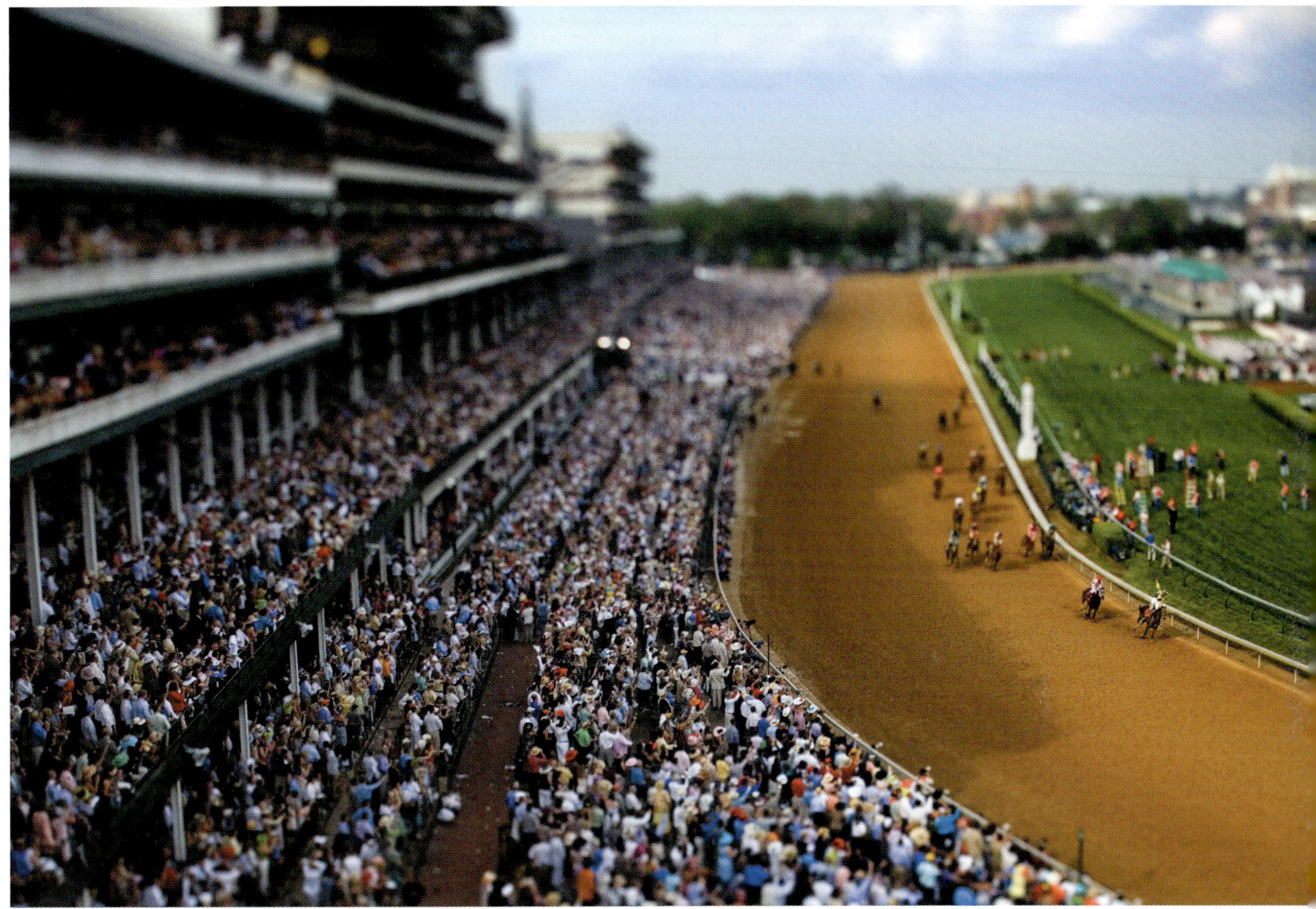

ISO 160 f/4 1/800 45mm

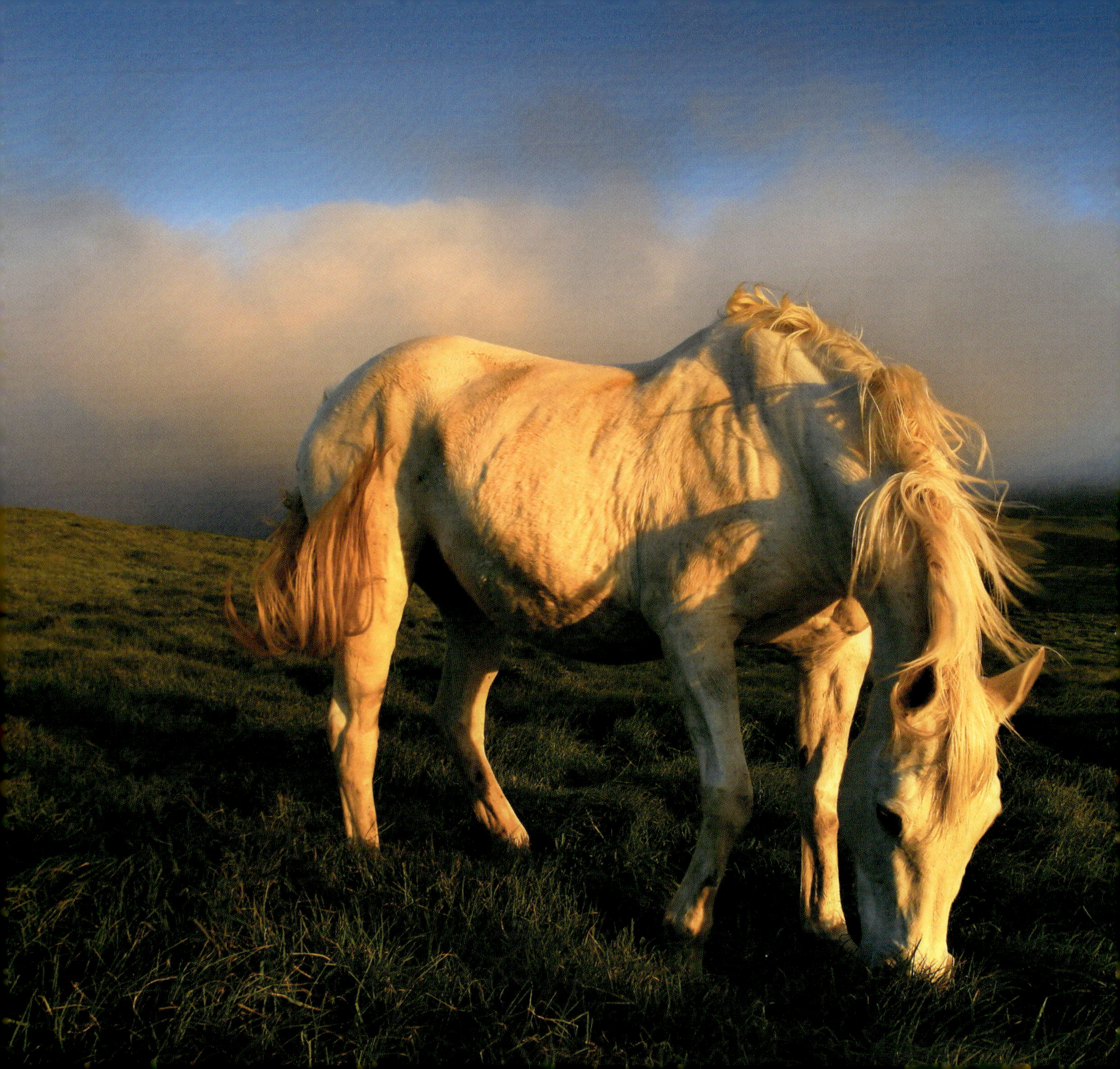

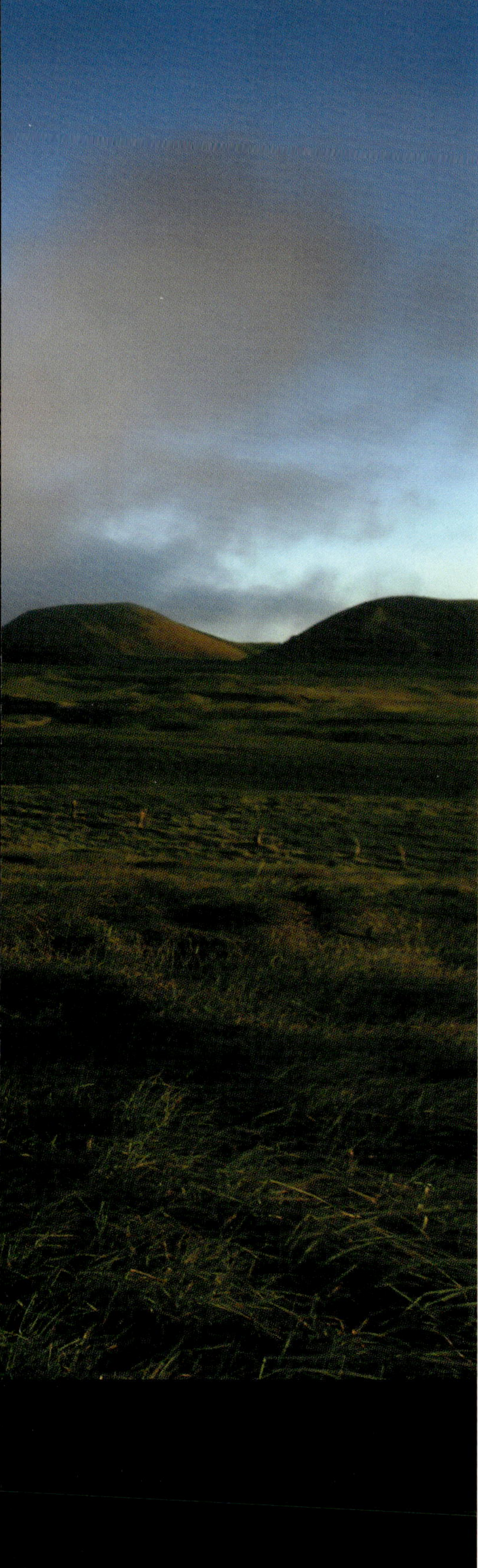

CHAPTER 11

SEEING AND USING LIGHT

On August 14, 2003, New York City experienced the largest blackout in U.S. history. I was on the beat that day, and all the traffic lights were out. It was pure gridlock within minutes.

I drove against traffic for a few minutes and gave up, because it was not only dangerous, but also kind of pointless. I called my editor.

"I need to get in a helicopter, and I'd really like to get a shot of the New York skyline silhouetted against the sunset."

"Sorry, Vince," he said. "We can't put you up in a helicopter every time you want to go. It's too expensive."

◀ A lone horse grazes at sunset in Waimea on the Big Island of Hawaii.

ISO 200 f/6.3 1/320 16mm

So I kept trying to make images. At the time I had an early digital camera that didn't do very well in low light, let alone no light. I kept calling the editor, trying to convince him to put me in a helicopter.

I called him for the sixth time and said, "Jim, when's the last time you saw the New York City skyline against the sunset with all the lights out? It's only happened once or twice before."

I reminded him of the famous black-and-white image of the southern part of Manhattan made during the 1965 blackout and finally sold him on it.

We chartered a helicopter, but when I showed up, there was no helicopter. There had been an issue with a credit card as well as the reality that people were paying $2,000 a seat to fly out of the city. Luckily, this is where it pays to know people and treat them well. I was able to get access to a helicopter for 30 minutes.

I photographed midtown Manhattan from the East River with only the headlights and brake lights on 42nd Street as my light sources. You can see a little bit of FDR Drive as well as a tugboat at the bottom of the frame.

After landing, I ran back to the *New York Times* passing by all these incredible scenes of people in the middle of the street, in front of their brownstones with flashlights. It was a very special, weird moment when New Yorkers were all part of the same melting pot for real, because it was incredibly hot and humid, sticky and disgusting.

I ran up to the *New York Times* offices through the stairwell, got the image to the paper, and it made the front page—not this particular version of it but a different one, with the sun still up.

The next morning, the editor I'd asked six times for the helicopter asked me for a print of the image for his office. I made a print for him that very day, but I put it in my locker and waited for him to ask me six times before I gave it to him.

As it turns out, I did a lot of traveling after that so it was about six months later when he asked me for the sixth time for the image and I told him I'd had it in my locker for months.

He chuckled, as he understood the humor in it. And if nothing else, it made for a good story.

Long exposure around Manhattan of street scenes during the East Coast blackout.

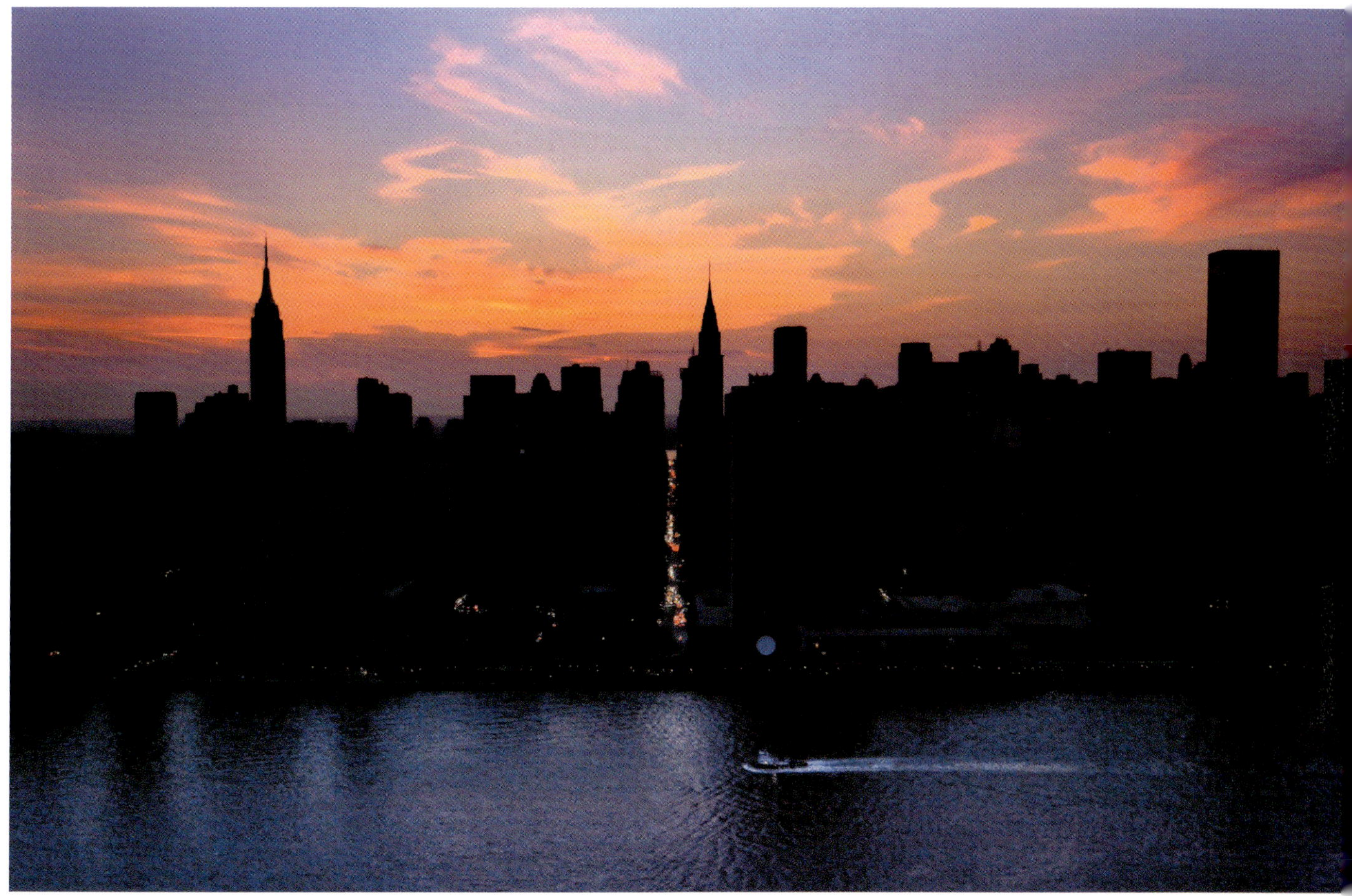

ISO 400 f/2.8 1/160 23mm

Natalie Coughlin, of the USA team, wins the bronze medal in the Women's 100-meter freestyle during the 2008 Summer Olympics.

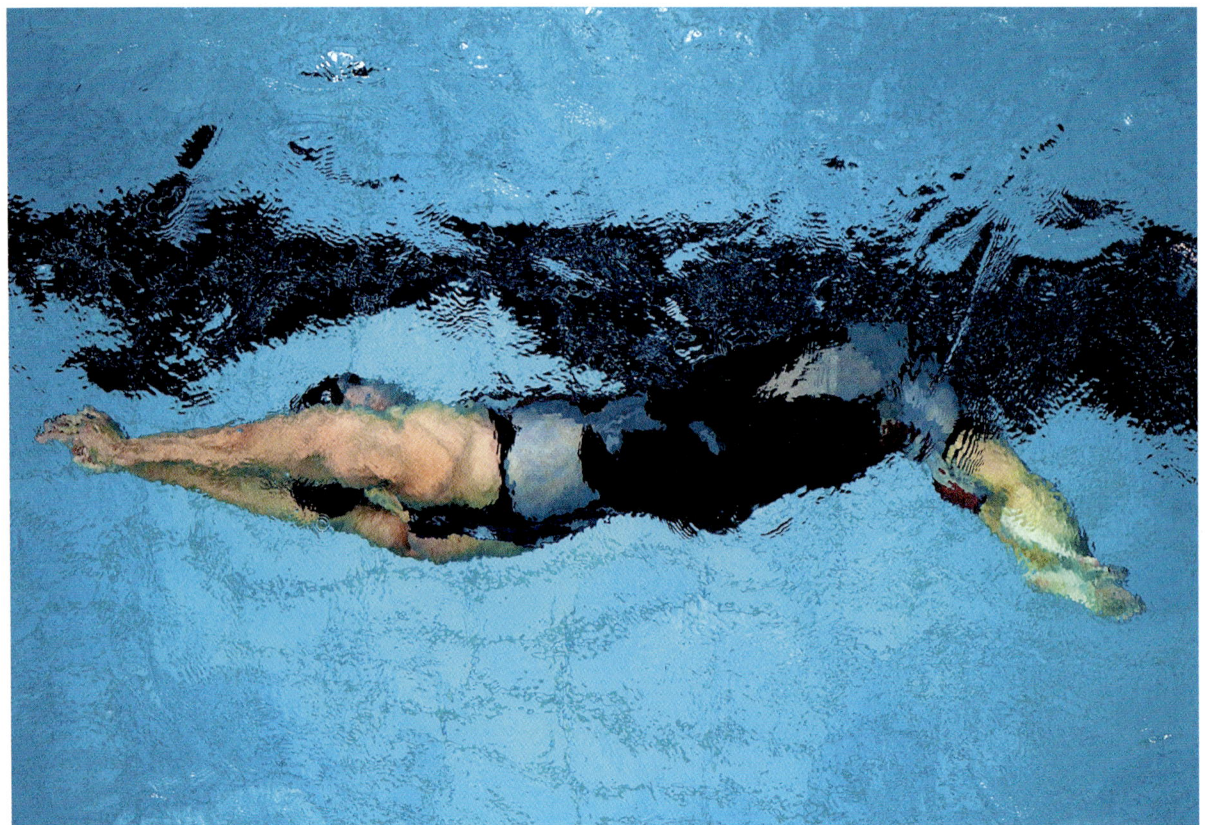

ISO 800 f/3.2 1/1250 400mm

It's the ability to see light and how it's shaped and changed by the world around you that helps elevate a snapshot into something more.

THE IMPORTANCE OF LIGHT

Although it was the lack of light that resulted in the drama of the previous photograph, light is actually the most important factor in any photograph. If you really want to break it down, the etymology of the word *photography* is "recording with light." So without light, you can't have an image.

Most of us learn photography first by studying *lensing*, or learning what lenses to use. We then get into how we frame images. We study timing and when to depress the shutter release. As we get more sophisticated, we see compositions in layers with a foreground, a middle ground, and a background.

But eventually you get to a point where you realize how important it is not only to know how to expose any given scene, but also to be able to see and evaluate the light itself. And when it comes to light, there are so many factors that you could write several books about it.

Some of the main considerations include the angle of light—how high is the light? Is it a high-noon light? Or is the sun kissing the horizon? What's the color temperature of light—is it a warm light? Is it a cold light? Is it a fluorescent green light? And think about the fall-off: How quickly does the light die? Does it get darker very quickly, or is it a shaft of light that stays pretty consistent? Is it passing through something?

Then you'll learn about negative fill and fill—is the light bouncing off of something, filling in the shadows? Or is it bouncing into something black, thus sucking out all the shadow detail?

It's the ability to see light and how it's shaped and changed by the world around you that helps elevate a snapshot into something more.

MOVE YOURSELF, NOT THE LIGHT

One of the single most important pieces of advice I can share with photographers is if they want to learn about light, they should find one single light source.

For those who don't have much money, use a household light bulb. What's the easiest thing to do with it? Take some aluminum foil and form a cone so that you have your light pointing in a single direction. Put that light in one location, put your subject on a stool, and have that subject stare right into the light or just a little bit away from it.

Then don't move your subject or the light, but instead move yourself.

By leaving the light and the subject exactly as they are, you force yourself to move relative to the two of them. That's when you'll start to learn about light, and how you can shoot using the same identical light with the subject staring in the exact same direction. And depending on whether the subject is three-quarters, frontal, backlit, or side lit, it's an absolutely different image.

Next, alternate your exposure as well when your subject is backlit, and blow out the light coming at you and flare it into your lens. Or close down and capture that detail. Then you'll start to understand how important your exposure relative to light is.

Some people are obsessed with changing the light itself—the intensity, the diffusion, the fall-off, and the angle. They forget that just changing your position is often change enough. And, that's a better way to learn because unless you have lighting crews with you for assistance—most of us work with available light—you'll learn that your relationship to the light and the subject is a huge and important decision.

DISSECTING THE LIGHT

One of the things I like to do once I've lost the natural light for the day is to go ahead and do a series of portraits. In this case, I took the surfer in this photo up to the pier and did a portrait session with artificial light. We used two Elinchrom Ranger strobe packs, one with a beauty dish off to the side of his face. You can see it's a very nice soft light, yet it's quite focused. In the back we had a second light running off another Ranger battery-operated unit that rim-lit him. It was just a bare head with a grid—a spot grid that really creates that nice rim light around him. What you're seeing in the air is just all of the mist coming off the shore.

We shot everything at 1/5 second at f/4.5. This allowed us to balance the ambient light with the strobe light, so you get a bit of warmth in the image. That's where you see a little bit of that fill on the side where you don't have the key light. Had I shot it at 1/250 second, it would have gone completely black.

Although this was shot with strobes, the principle of seeing where the light and the shadow fall applies whether you use flash or available light. It's still about the light, regardless of where it's coming from.

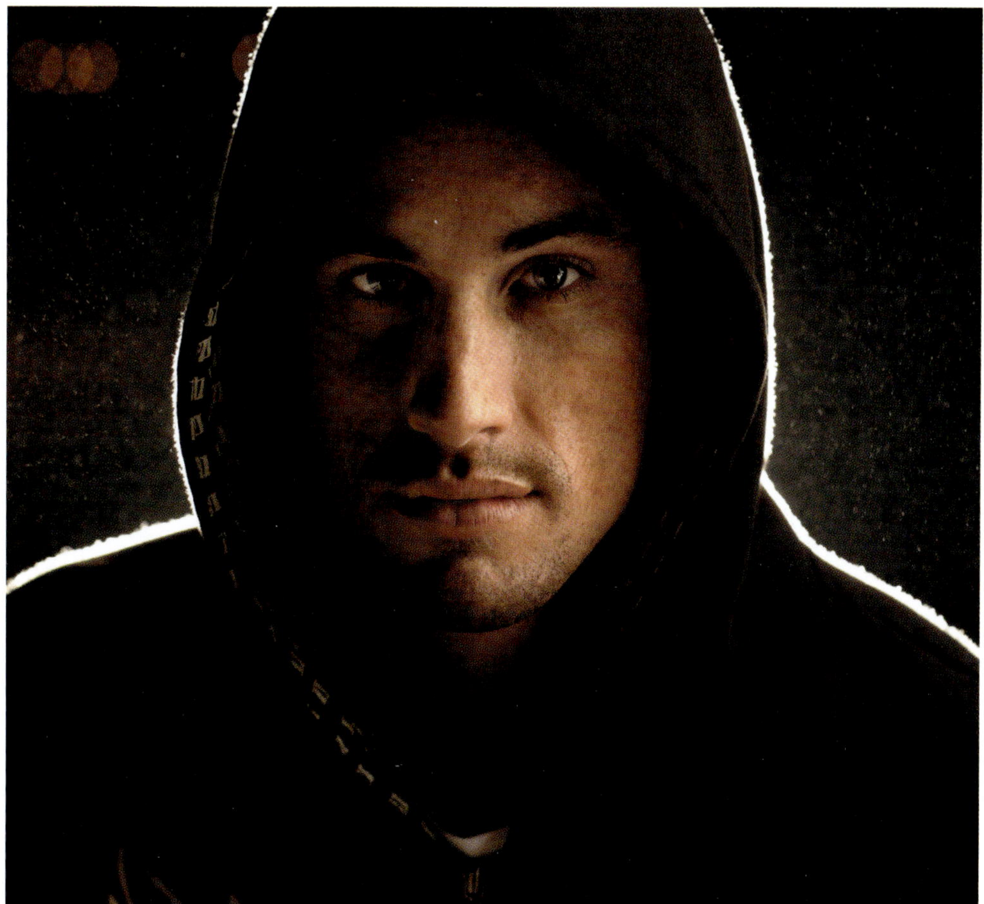

Portrait—Ventura, California, 2006. ISO 50 f/4.5 1/5 85mm

The general rule is that a heavier person will look better side lit, because you will see only half of them. Simple stuff. For a person with a long nose, being side lit is a disaster. For a model, frontal light is acceptable, but most people look horrible staring into a frontal light. Light from below makes a person look like a ghoul; it's the lighting used in horror films. You never light from below unless you're trying to make someone look scary.

Everyone has problem areas on their face. The angle from which you are shooting combined with the angle of light can make someone look really good or really bad. That's where the art of lighting really begins.

When people think about light, they are often just concerned with getting the perfect exposure. But exposure is more than just a correct setting—exposure is an incredibly creative tool.

I could expose a subject with a window behind them and make them appear as a silhouette; or I could open up to see the detail in the shadows of their eyes and face, and thus blow out (overexpose) the background and get an absolutely different result. That's what is so important to understand: how to use light and exposure is an aesthetic decision. There's no such thing as a perfect exposure. The exposure is only perfect when it fits with what you are trying to achieve with the camera.

But, the point is, the rules that apply to a good portrait and someone's face will apply to every single thing you shoot, whether it's a car, a wedding couple, a rock, or a tree. It's all about how you expose the image, how diffused the light is or isn't, the angle of the light relative to your subject, your angle relative to the light and your subject, and diffusion of the shadow. It's all the same principle.

The best thing I can share with you is what my father taught me. In life there's only one light source: the sun. Learn with one light first and master that. And, then and only then, learn how to use a second or third light. But if you can't light well with one light, you will never be able to light well with ten lights.

Matt Taylor, a lifelong surfer, catches some early morning waves in Ventura, California (2006).

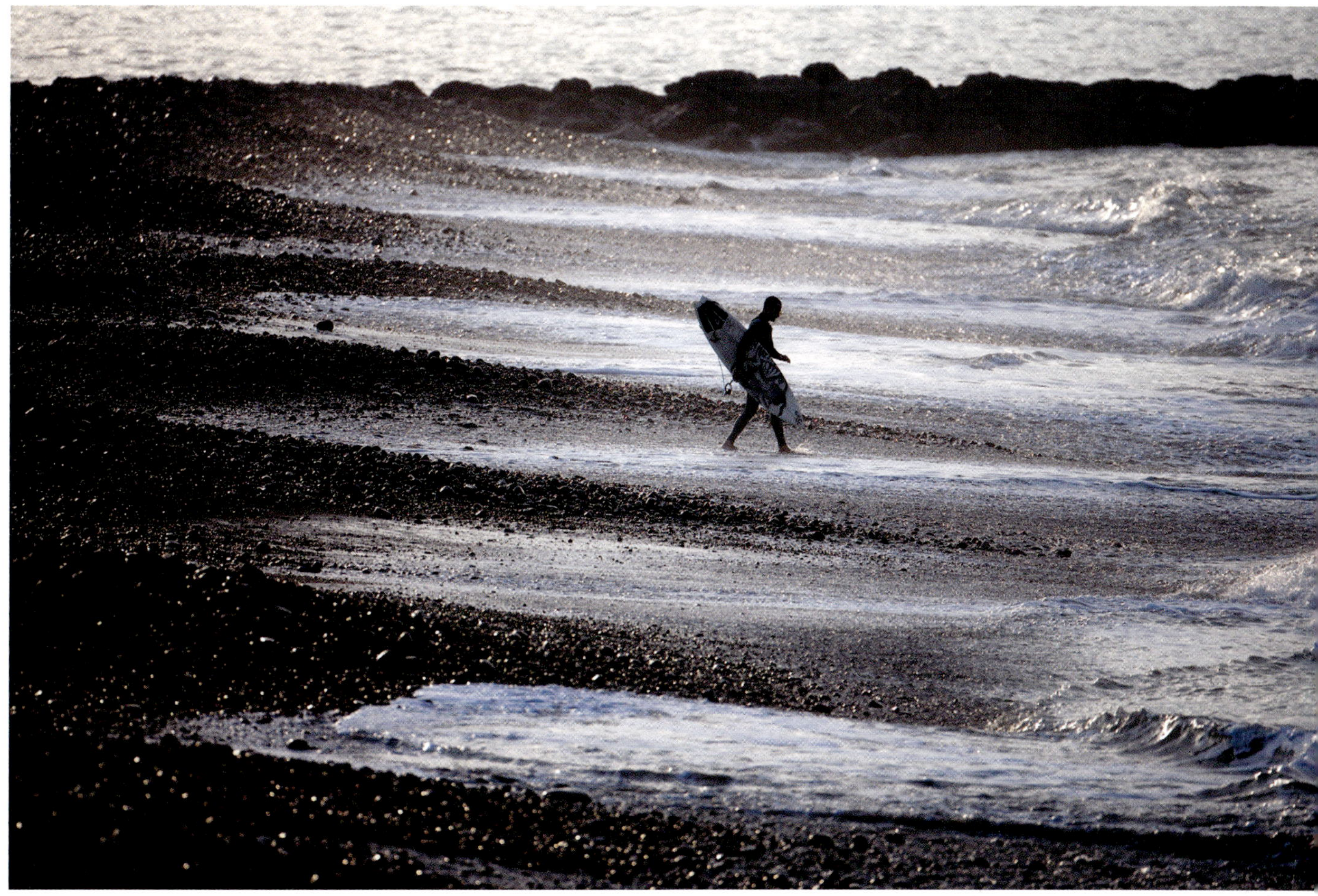

ISO 100 f/4 1/320 500mm

I had to anticipate the light, the gesture, and the moment, and hope that they would step into the spot of light.

THE ART OF ANTICIPATION

I made this image with light at sunset while photographing in Times Square. There were shafts of light coming through the very tall buildings. This girl was being playful with her boyfriend. The light around them was very angular; it was very harsh.

I had seen the light, and now I was hanging with them for a little bit and simply waiting for them to step in the spot of light. When they did, everything around them was dark because they were being hit by this spotlight of the sun.

I couldn't tell them to do that. I had to visualize what would happen if they stepped in that spot of light and just wait patiently for the moment and the light to come together.

This is where 20 years of experience comes into play in the form of a visual anticipation. I had to anticipate the light, the gesture, and the moment, and hope that they would step into the spot of light.

And when they did, I had to pounce on it, because they were in the light for only a few seconds, and then they shifted back into the shadows. That's when photography is a game of anticipation and experience.

Exploring the patterns of New York City's street life in a 12-week column for the *New York Times*.

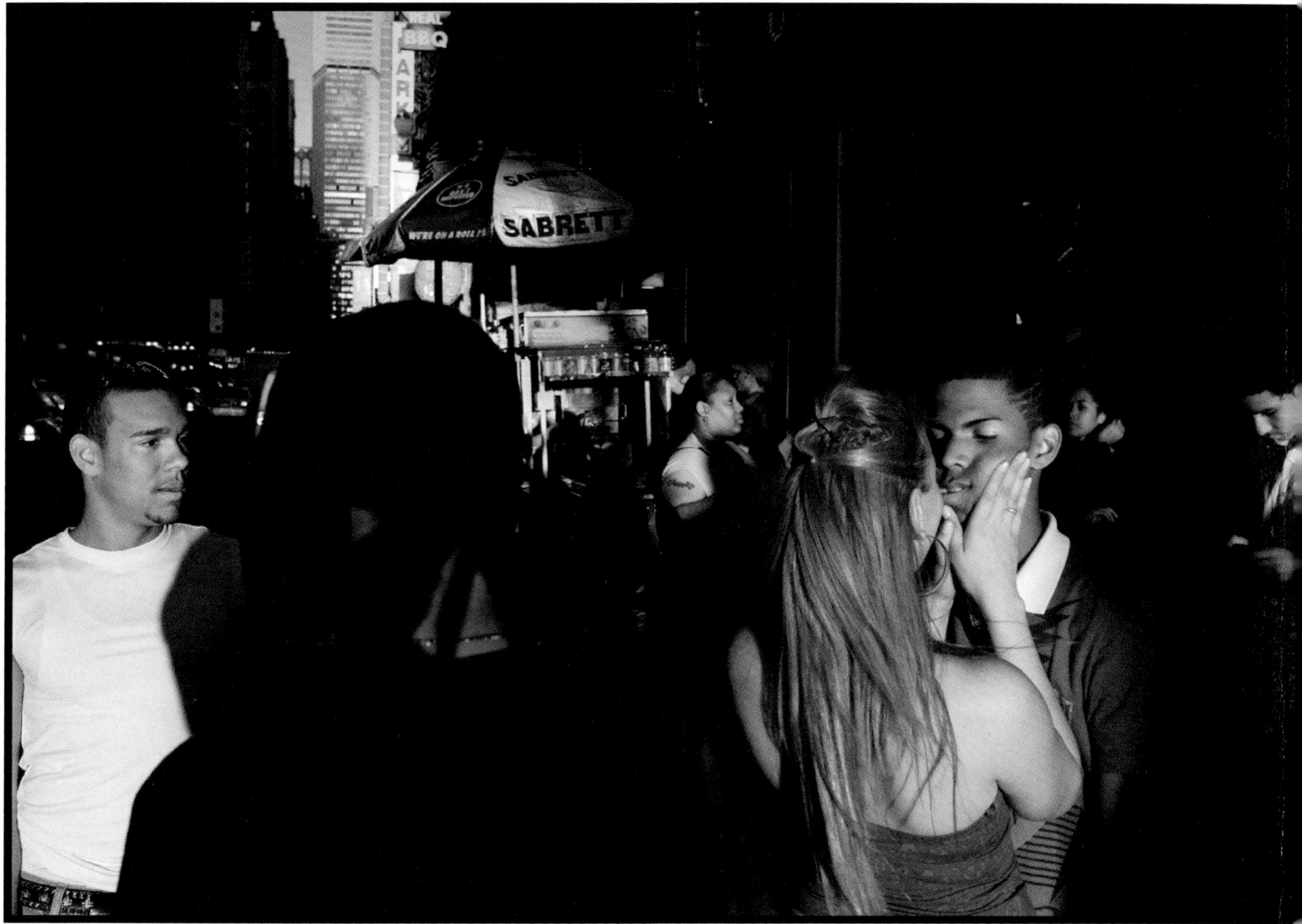

ISO 320 1/180 28mm

A lone taxi drives a narrowly plowed street in Flatbush, New York (2002).

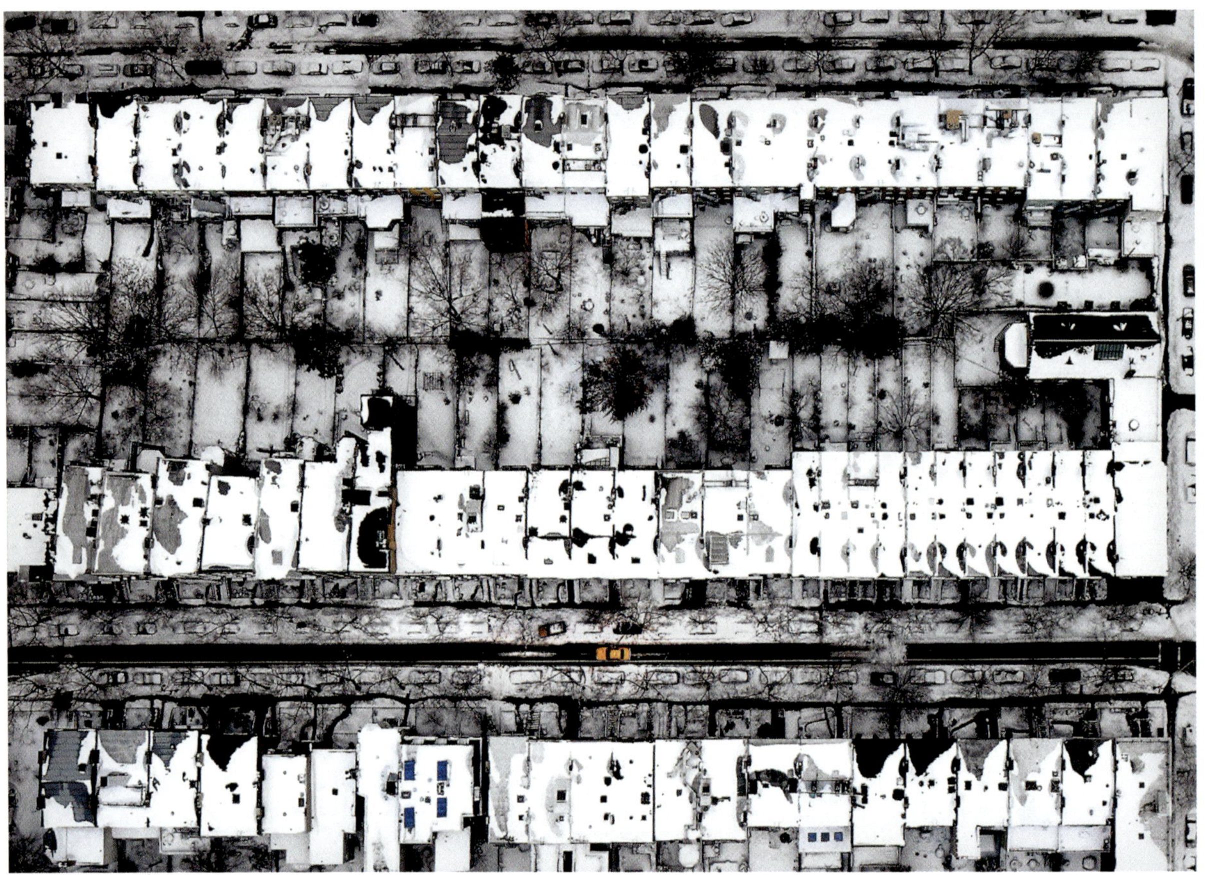

ISO 800 f/2.8 1/800 24-70mm

THE MAGIC OF OVERCAST

This was shot during a huge snowstorm that dumped a few feet on New York City. This is a very different type of light that I love, overcast. Most photographers are unhappy with this quality of illumination because there's no directional light, but I consider overcast light to be a giant soft box from God.

When you have overcast or very diffused light that's very even, you learn that you need to rely a lot on geometry and color, or lack of color, to help make your frame. There's always an opportunity to silhouette someone against a beautiful overcast sky, but for the most part the light tends to be very even and does not have much direction to it, especially from the air.

Why this image speaks to me is because it makes the extraordinary out of the ordinary. There's no news value or anything special about a cab driving up an empty street. It happens about a thousand times a minute in New York. But what you have is a perfect geometry of buildings with one stripe down the lower bottom third, adhering to the rule of thirds.

Everything is monochromatic. Everything is black and white. If you look really carefully, you'll see little colorful windows popping out of the buildings. But for the most part, the entire image is black and white naturally with the snow and the trees. The one spot of color is that one lone cab on the street.

Overcast light is a very different kind of light, but one that is just as capable of delivering a great result.

When you have overcast or very diffused light that's very even, you learn that you need to rely a lot on geometry and color, or lack of color, to help make your frame.

Amid all the chaos in the world, here were these two kids with their younger sibling flying a kite, which for me symbolized hope and freedom.

USING A CLASSIC APPROACH

Very often with digital cameras, you can't afford to have the sun flaring into your lens and keep the tonal range unless you have a really great sensor, or the air is a bit diffused as it is in Los Angeles. If flare happens, you lose contrast and color saturation. However, there are times when you do want to point the camera toward the light.

For this photo I waited for the sun to drop beneath the hill, and then used one of the oldest tricks in photography, which is to create a silhouette. It's one of the best ways to obliterate a distracting background or to make an image that pops, especially when you've got a gorgeous colored sky. Simply expose for the sky and allow the shadows to go dark from underexposure.

With respect to lens choice, you don't want to go so wide that the people become too small, or so tight that you can't appreciate how the sky changes color from yellow to pink to blue.

At the time, this photograph spoke to the only sign of hope I saw after 9/11. Every image I was shooting was one of death, destruction, and misery, and this is one of the images I kind of threw out there as a sign of hope. Amid all the chaos in the world, here were these two kids with their younger sibling flying a kite, which for me symbolized hope and freedom. That's the significance of this image to me. It's not a masterful image, by any means, but at the time it was taken, I thought it was necessary.

A young man flies a kite as the sun sets over the Punj Puti refugee camp in Quetta, Pakistan.

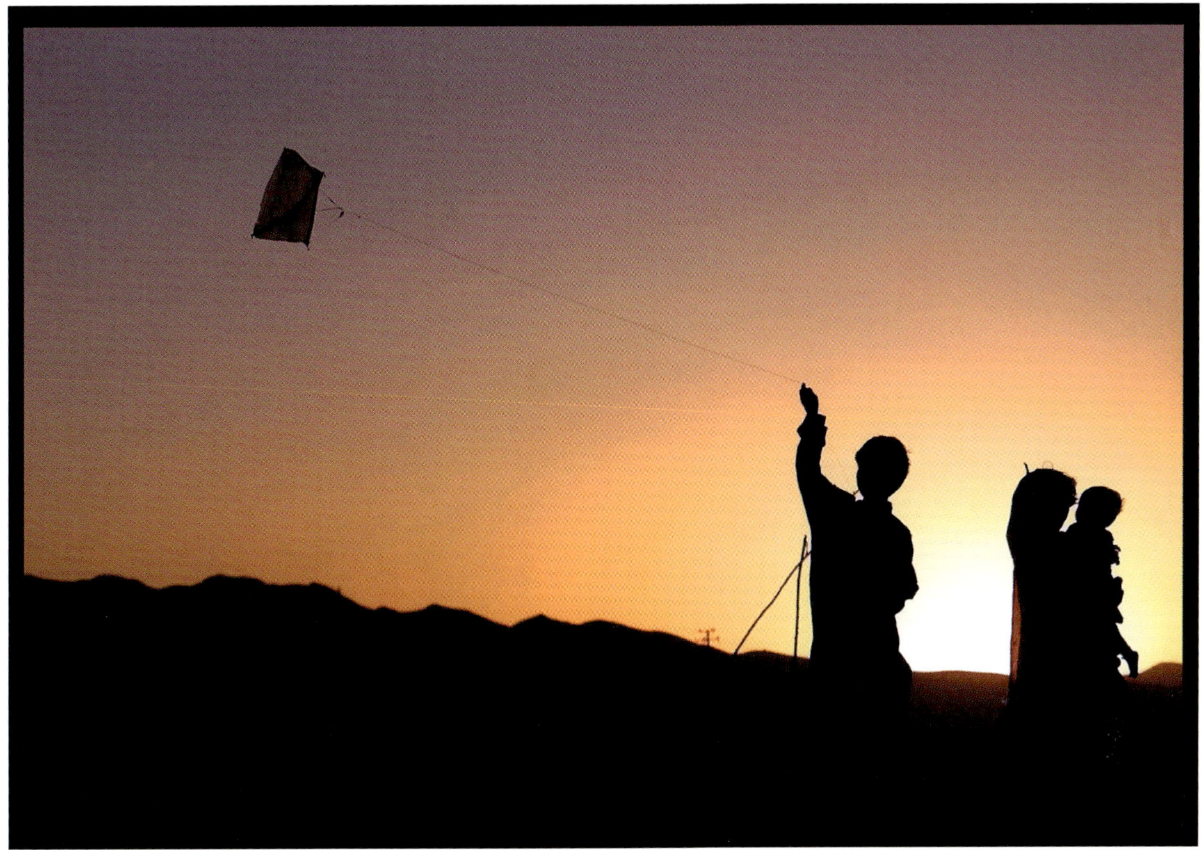

FACING TECHNICAL CHALLENGES

This is an image of the *RMS Queen Mary 2,* which at the time was the largest passenger ship ever built by man, and here she was pulling into New York City. It was shot from the roof of Grand Central Station looking down 44th Street, just one block from where the New York Times Building was at the time, and I think it shows the juxtaposition of this incredible large-scale ship with the downtown life of Manhattan. It's a very unique New York moment; I think a big part of what any photographer does is to try and juxtapose elements to kind of show either a similarity or a difference, and it worked out quite well in this case.

In terms of technique, this was actually a pretty challenging image for two reasons. On the one hand, the exposure was all over the place. This was shot very early in the morning with the sun behind my back, and as you can see, the sun is hitting the hull of the ship but not any of the streets in the foreground.

You've got to remember there are lots of tall buildings in Manhattan, the sun rises of course from the east, and we're shooting looking straight west. So the good thing that I did was to shoot this image in Raw mode. Had I shot this in JPEG, it would never have worked, but the Raw image allowed me to hold the detail in the highlights and also to pull out the shadows later, and that was pretty important.

The second thing I did involved a lot of luck. I shot with two cameras just to be safe—always a good idea. On the one hand, I shot with an 800mm lens, as this is what I thought would be my main image or where my main image would come from.

Using a PocketWizard wireless radio transmitter, each time I made a frame on my main camera, the PocketWizard would trigger a second frame. I used a 70–200mm lens, a significantly wider lens than the super telephoto I was using on my main camera. The idea is every time I fired a picture from the main camera, I would get two images for the price of one.

But while I had been practicing all morning using the 500mm lens on small tugboats and police boats, when the *Queen Mary 2* arrived, it filled so much of the 500mm frame that I knew I was in really bad shape. But I kept shooting because I knew that my other camera was going to have a backup image, and that's the image you see here, the image that showed up on the front page of the *New York Times.*

In a westbound view up West 44th street, the *Queen Mary 2,* the world's largest passenger ship, makes its way to Pier 92 as its maiden voyage to New York from Southhampton, England, comes to a conclusion (2003).

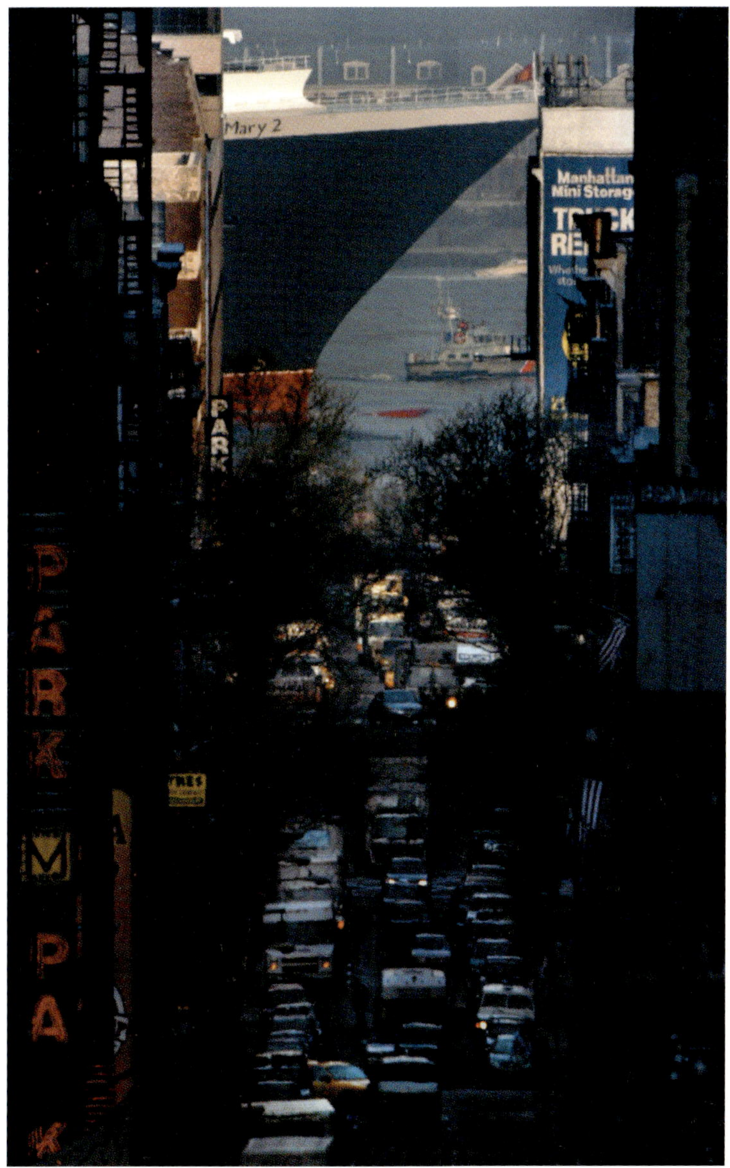

ISO 500 f/10 1/640 800mm

RESPECTING THE PROCESS

Just as you have to learn the basics of aperture, shutter speed, exposure, and how to use your camera and lenses, you have to learn how to see and use light. You need to respect the techniques before you can actually accomplish what they're intended for.

It's important to understand that you've got to learn your scales before you can improvise as a musician. The same idea applies to photography. But I think the most important part is to understand light, accept it, and to enjoy learning about it. Because there are few things as fun as seeing and discovering a wonderful quality of light and using it to serve your vision.

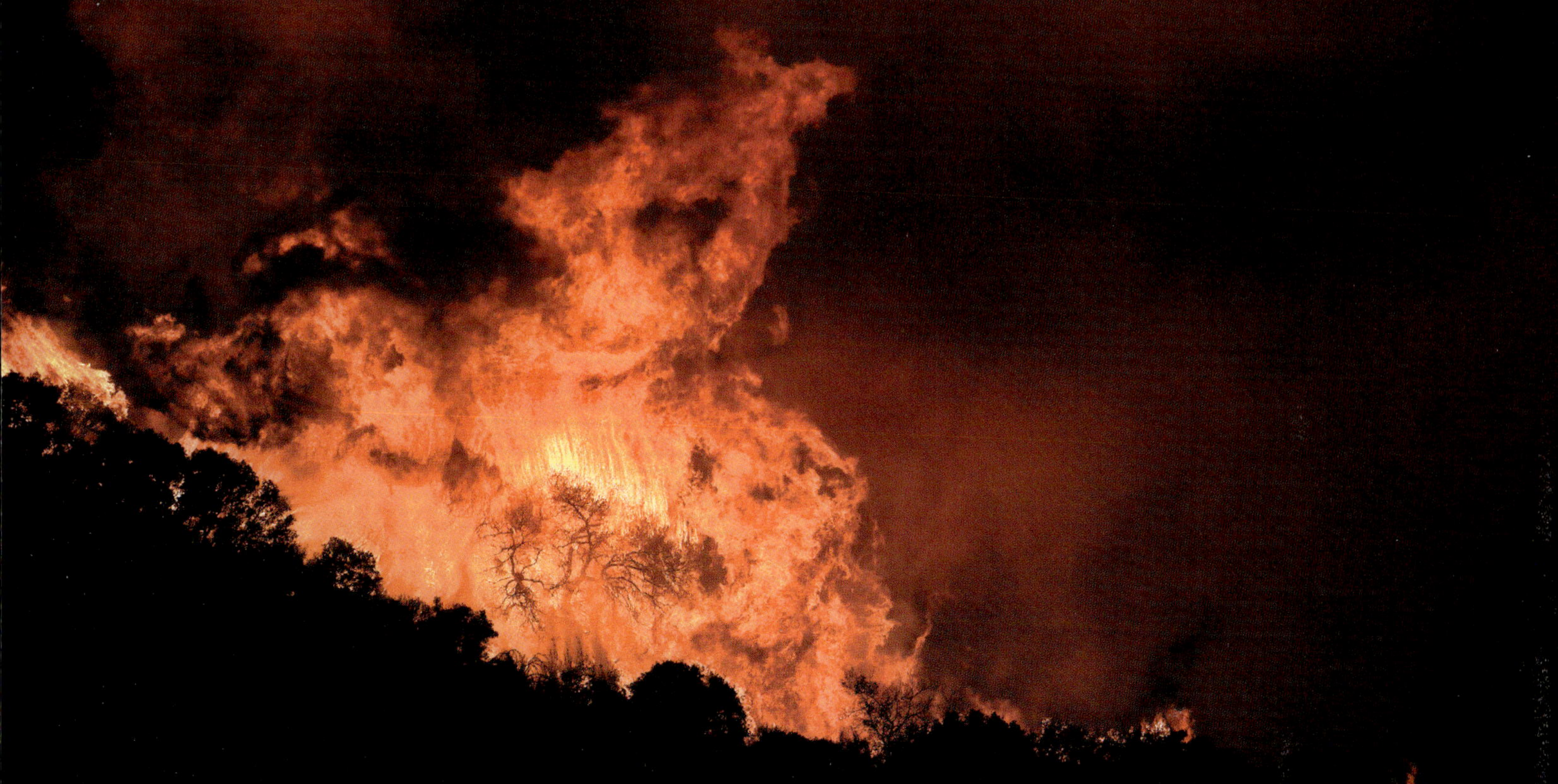

Hotspots flare up as firefighters battle the Zaca Lake wildfire north of Santa Barbara, California, in 2007.

ISO 200 f/4 1/1250 500mm

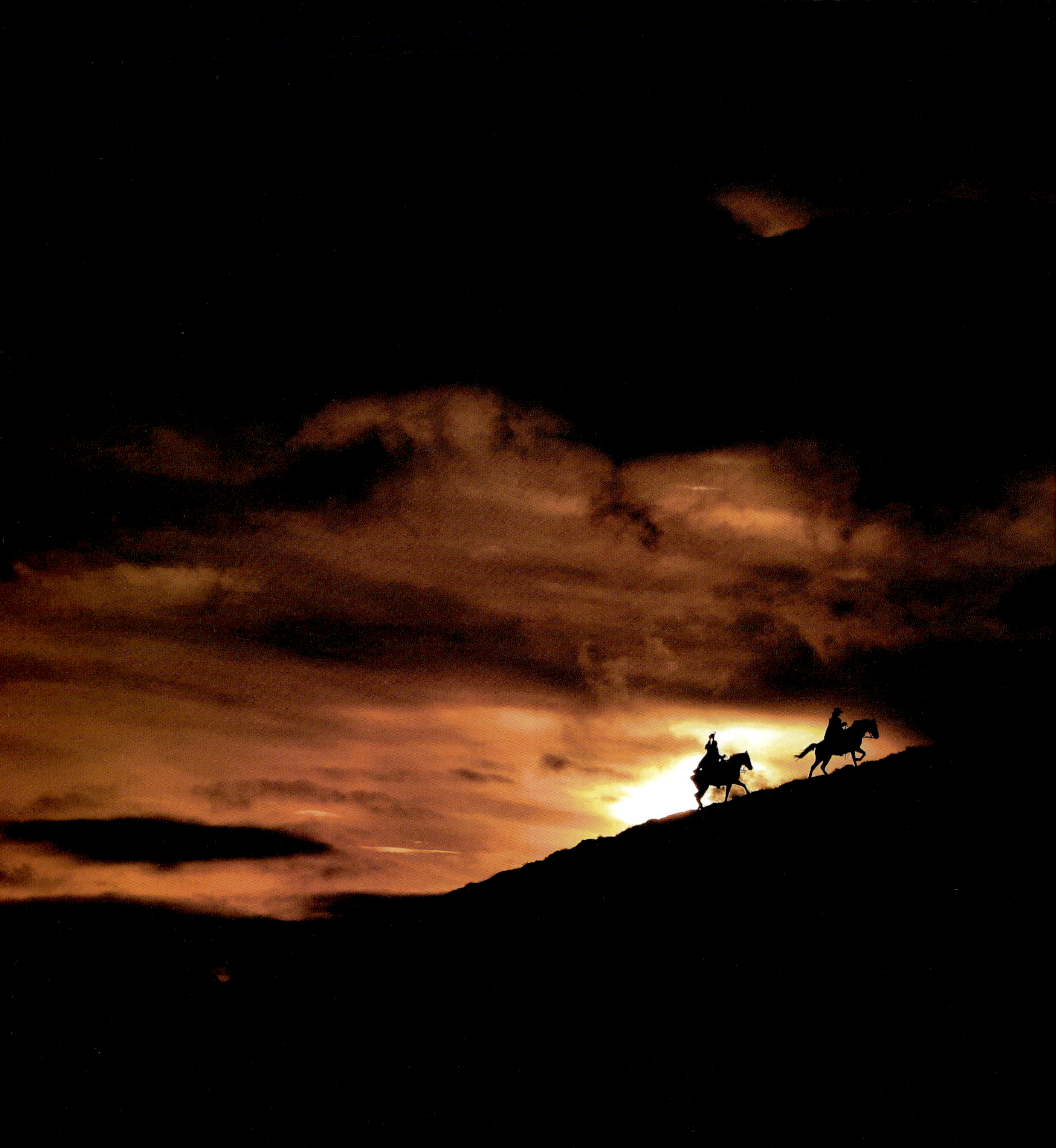

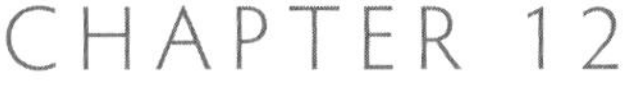

CHAPTER 12

THE PANIOLO

The paniolo shoot in Hawaii had all the elements of a dream job.

I got the call from Canon; they were looking for a photographer to illustrate the brochure for their new Canon EOS 30D and said, "We need seven shots. You can go anywhere in the world. Here's your budget." It was one of the few times that this will ever happen in my life.

And while it had all the elements of a dream job, it was still an assignment, so there was quite a lot of pressure to decide where to go and what to shoot.

We decided to photograph the paniolo, some of the first cowboys in the history of Hawaii. We went to Waimea, on the big island of Hawaii, and I can tell you from experience that it is one of the few places that I would say is heaven on Earth, as well as hell.

◀ Big Island, Hawaii (January, 2006).

ISO 100 f/8 1/3200 100mm

A lone horse grazes at sunset in Waimea on the Big Island of Hawaii.

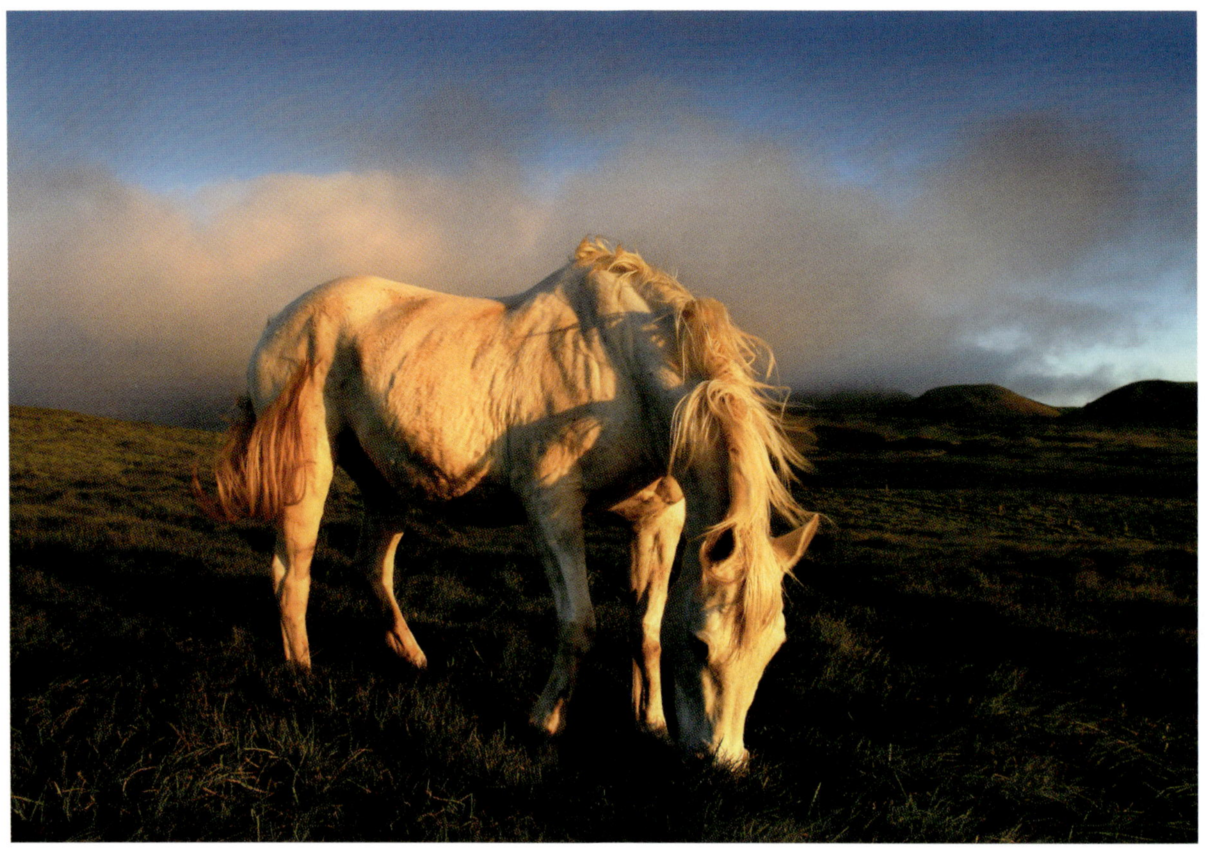

ISO 200 f/6.3 1/320 16mm

WINDOW OF OPPORTUNITY

Take it from me, never photograph in Hawaii in January. Although you'll likely find the most beautiful light you've ever seen, you'll also have to face the harsh reality of the rainy season, when it pours 80 to 90 percent of the time.

The "dream job" proved incredibly frustrating. There were many times I thought I was going to lose this assignment or come back with nothing.

When I made this image of the horse, it had been raining for three straight hours. It was yet another day of torrential downpour. This was one of the last of the scheduled shoot days. Pressure was high. Frustration was extreme.

I'd already shot as many pictures as I could in the rain, so I had exhausted that option. I had accepted the weather and just shot through it. But after a few thousand photographs of horses and people in the rain, I realized that this was likely going to be the biggest downer of a campaign ever.

I had considered other locations on the island, but quickly realized that even if the light was great when we left for the spot, it would likely be raining by the time we got there.

So I had to accept the fact that I couldn't control nature. I just had to let it go.

Then I saw a little opening in the sky and we bolted for the four-by-four Gator vehicle. When you get that five-minute opening in the sky, you can't be busy pounding the dashboard of the car venting your anger and frustration. You make sure your team is ready and you jump at the opportunity.

We drove following the light, which was nothing more than a patch of brightness hitting the mountains.

As we got closer to our destination, I saw the horse. It looked golden. The light was incredibly gorgeous because of all the cloud cover. The darkened sky accentuated the lush green grass that was the result of all those weeks of rain.

Two cowboys from the Kahua Ranch in Wamea ride their horses past a rainbow at sunset.

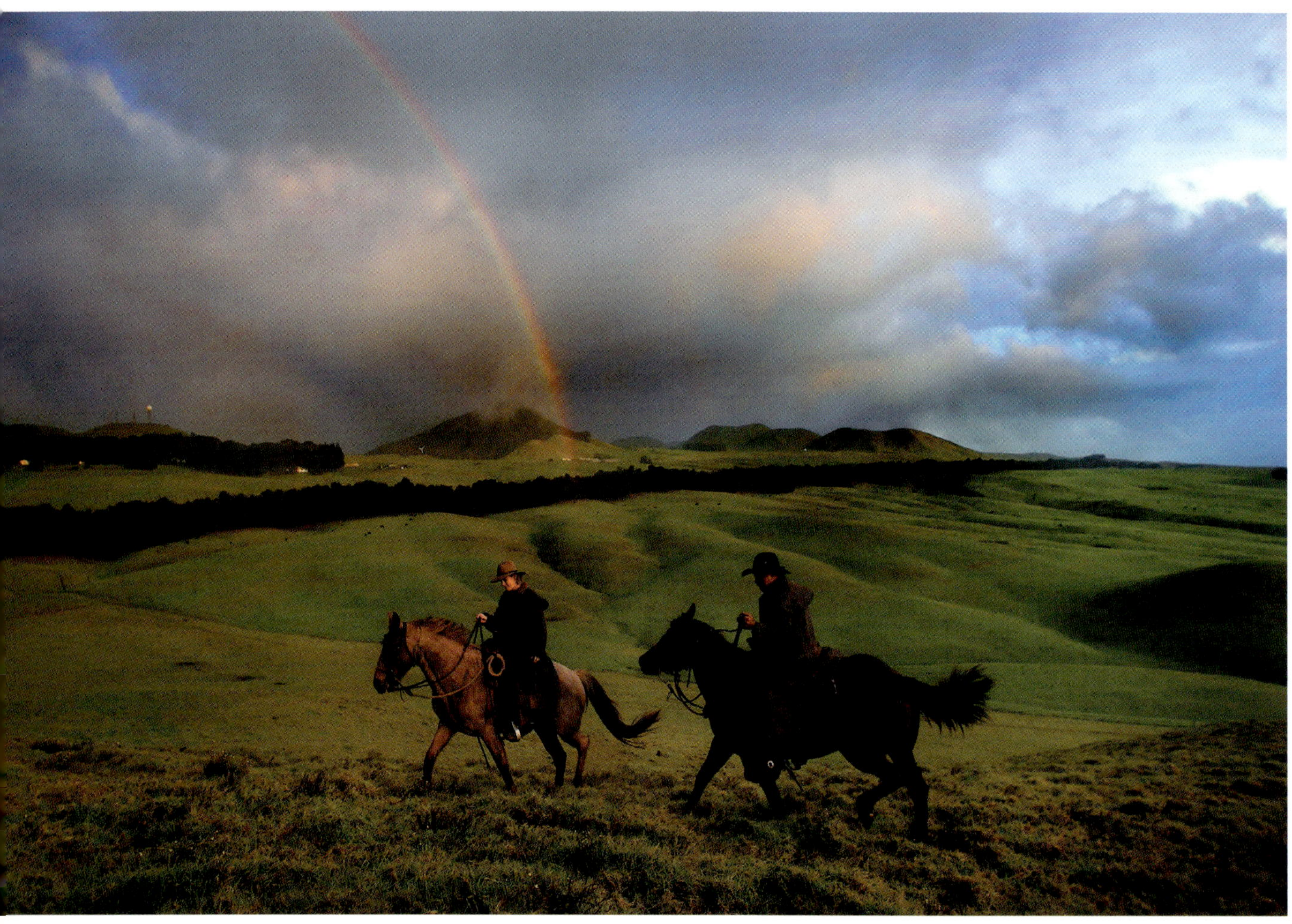

ISO 100 f/4 1/160 14mm

I used a wide-angle lens for the image because it allowed me to include the beautiful sky in the background. Had I shot this with a tighter lens, I would have compressed the horse into the background and lost the lovely quality of the sky.

I then looked behind me and saw the clouds moving swiftly across the sky. Suddenly we were racing down the hill, and I saw another shot.

I picked up my radio and communicated to the cowboys on horseback, "I need you to go from the bottom of the ridge to the top of the ridge." I made them repeat the movement fives times. All the while the light was rapidly changing and retreating.

As it started to rain again, we rushed up the hill where I spotted a rainbow. The rain was collecting on the front element of the lens, but all I could do was wipe it away and keep on shooting.

In a little less than an hour, the window of opportunity for photographs with that beautiful light had closed.

When you get that five-minute opening in the sky, you can't be busy pounding the dashboard of the car venting your anger and frustration. You make sure your team is ready and you jump at the opportunity.

A COMMERCIAL APPROACH

Even though this was a commercial assignment, it was my first one so I was very hands-off in terms of directing. I tried to make it as documentary as possible. With rare exceptions, I waited for moments to happen.

Today as a filmmaker, and as a commercial photographer, I would be much more controlled and plan ahead, with an entire team to pre-light and pre-think these photographs. And I would probably not have any of the stresses that I had back then.

I was just making the transition from editorial to commercial, so this editorial approach was my strength at the time—and I was right to do it this way. I would just let moments happen, capture them, and maybe say, "Do that again," or "Let's change it a little bit to this way."

Now, instead of waiting to discover a moment, I'll say, "I'm going to want a shot of him with his white hat and white shirt against the blue. Let's make it happen."

Now I know how to work both ways, and I can make a photograph look as if it had been shot spontaneously even if it's completely constructed. Back then I didn't know how to make a constructed situation look natural. I've evolved.

You have to learn how to make constructed situations appear natural because when you do a big commercial project, you have so many people involved. It's extremely expensive, so you learn to accept that everything has to be planned.

You don't have the option of thinking, "We'll figure out what we'll shoot when we get there." That approach doesn't work for a commercial shoot. You have a shot list; you have a location list; it's been scouted. Nothing is left to chance. But to make the shots look unplanned, you have to develop the sensibilities of a photojournalist.

That's the art. It's a very fine line, and a very difficult skill to develop. I think sometimes it's harder for people with a commercial background to do it, because they haven't documented the real. But in some ways it's easier for them because they know the exact pose that's going to look perfect, whereas a photojournalist needs to feel it out and find it.

An aerial view of the volcanic terrain in Waimea on the Big Island of Hawaii.

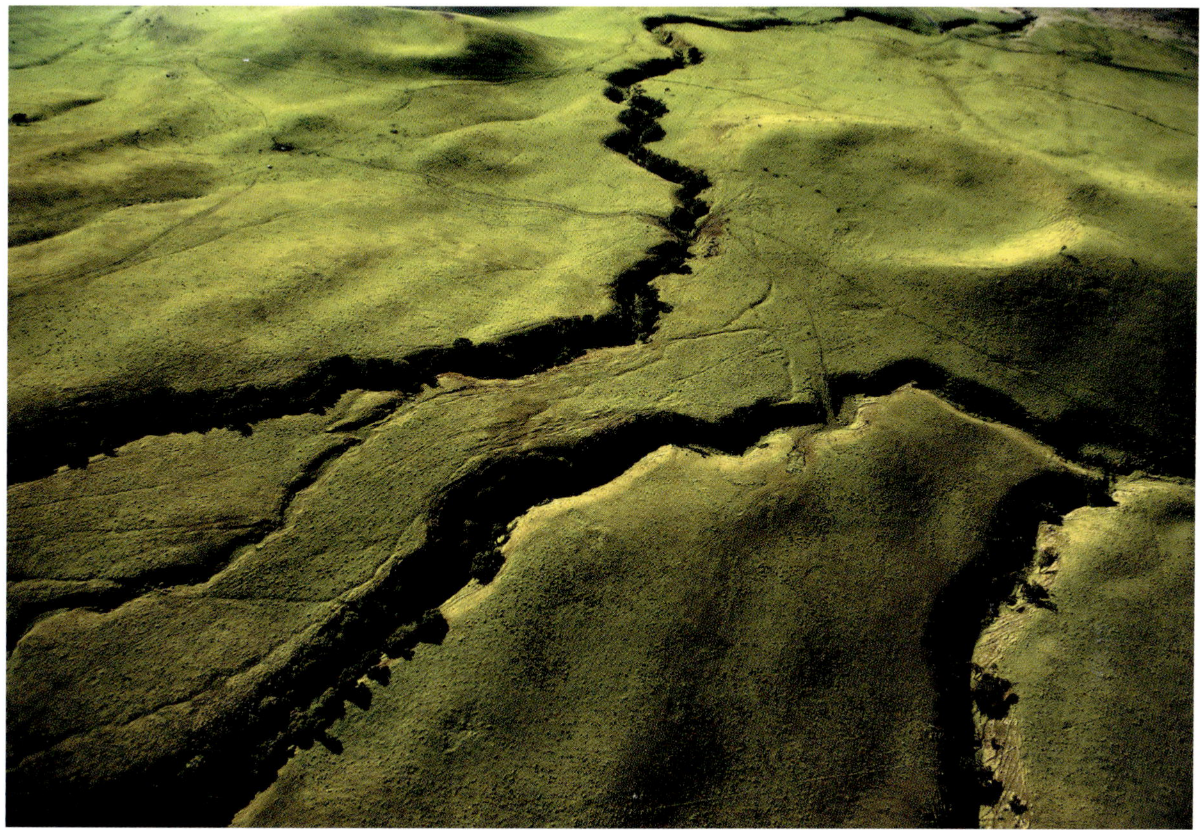

ISO 100 f/4.5 1/500 24mm

Instead of placing the cowboys in the middle of the frame, I put them at the right third of the frame, and the result was a much more balanced composition.

RELYING ON OLD TRICKS

Here is a classic vista picture that uses one of my favorite tricks. On days with patchy clouds, you'll see patches of light and shadow, and when your subject matters are in shadow—in this case, the two cowboys—they in effect become silhouetted. It's a really cool technique to pull off.

Naturally when they were in the sunlight, the look was very different, but in the shade they became silhouetted. If I had opened up the exposure for the shade, I would have blown out all of the beautiful color around them. In this case, I exposed for the highlights—the lit areas—and allowed the shadowed areas to turn utterly black.

I also used the rule of thirds for building the composition. Instead of placing the cowboys in the middle of the frame, I put them at the right third of the frame, and the result was a much more balanced composition.

I shot this image with a 16–35mm lens, which allowed me to get this incredible panoramic view. I also shot everything in manual mode, not autoexposure, so the cowboys would be silhouetted.

Shooting with a zoom was a practical choice because I couldn't keep up with the cowboys on foot, and instead had to be driven around in the four-by-four while standing with my head poking out of the sunroof. The zoom lens allowed me to make those small but critical last-minute changes.

Two Hawaiian cowboys ride their horses through wide open ranch land.

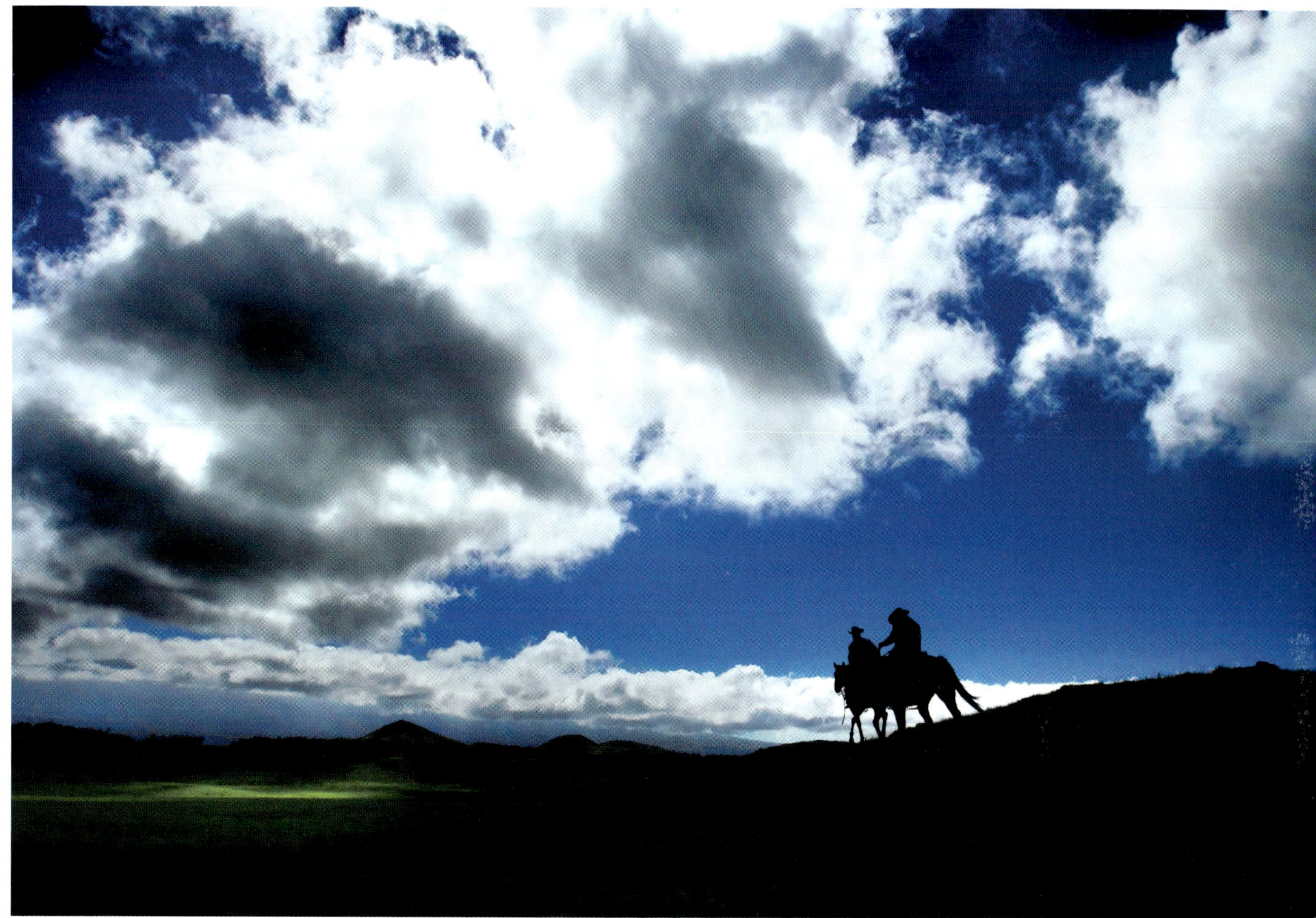

ISO 100 f/10 1/250 16mm

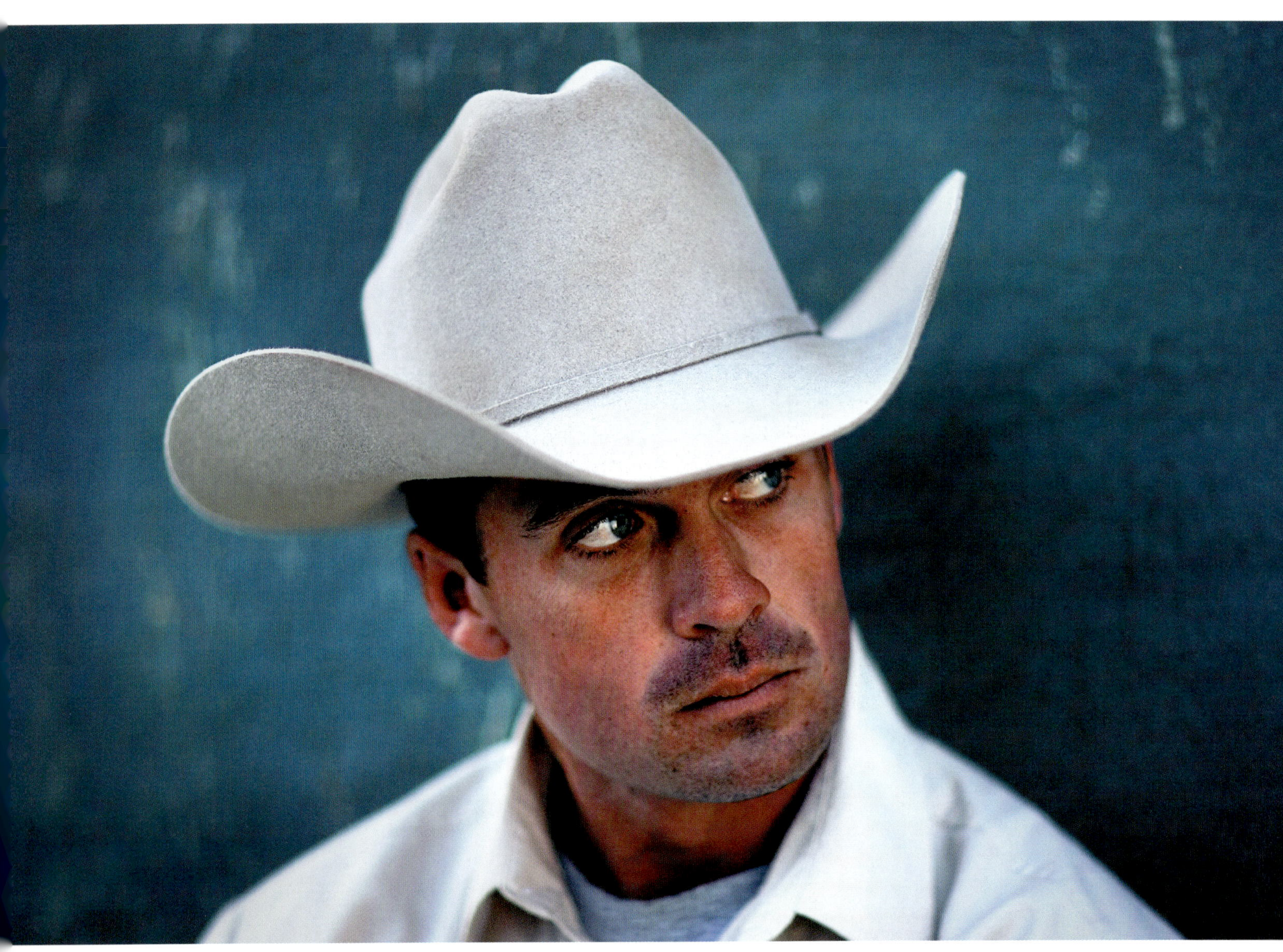

A portrait of a Hawaiian paniolo in Waimea.

ISO 100 f/1.2 1/640 85mm

BACK TO BASICS

To make this portrait of one of the cowboys, we went back to basics. As I do for many portraits, I kept it simple not only in terms of how I shot it, but especially in terms of wardrobe.

I had my subject in a white hat and a white shirt against a simple blue background, and I shot with an 85mm f/1.2 lens wide open. It is one of my favorites of all the portraits I have ever taken, and the lighting setup couldn't have been simpler.

It was an overcast day; we had a big white reflector and all natural light. I didn't need to have fancy lights or lots of equipment to make this portrait. I just had to focus on making it unique by simply art-directing the clothing and the background, with the added bonus of the color of his eyes matching the color of the background. It all came together.

Because I was using the 85mm f/1.2 lens wide open, I had to be critically accurate with my focus. I didn't have much latitude with respect to depth of field.

Although my cameras have multiple autofocus sensors, I choose and detect focus using the one autofocus sensor that is positioned closest to my subject's eye. With the lens wide open, the depth of field is incredibly narrow, and it is not possible to keep both eyes in focus.

As I do for many portraits, I kept it simple not only in terms of how I shot it, but especially in terms of wardrobe.

Aerial view of cattle in Waimea, Hawaii.

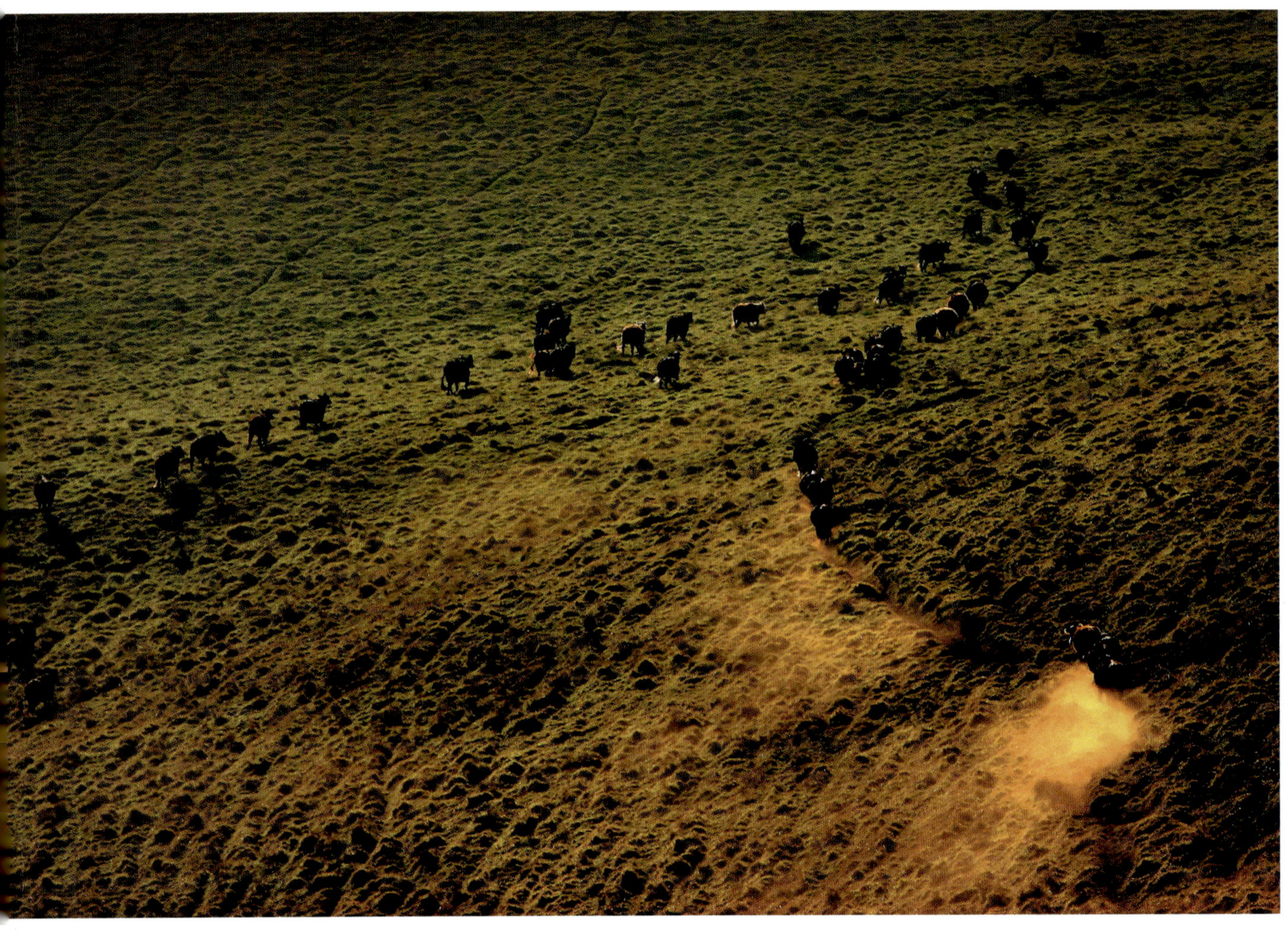

ISO 100 f/4 1/1250 200mm

If I had shot into the light, I would have gotten a very different result than if I had shot with the light behind me or off to the side.

UNDERSTANDING YOUR LIGHT AND LENS

This shot was made from a helicopter at sunset. One of the most important things to keep in mind in photography is where you are relative to the light source. During a sunset, the light comes from a constant position; if I had shot into the light, I would have gotten a very different result than if I had shot with the light behind me or off to the side.

We shot toward the setting sun that created an incredible glow, when these cows started running away from the helicopter and the dust started to pick up. This is known as the "V nature," the geometry in a picture that kind of draws your eye in an otherwise unspectacular image. These little elements between the backlight and the V nature of that geometry make for a much better image.

By using a 70–200mm lens at the 200mm position, I was able to take advantage of its compression at that focal length and accentuate the V the cows were making as they were running away.

ALWAYS LOOK FOR THE CLOSER

For almost any series you work on, I recommend always trying to have a beginning, a middle, and an end. As you get more advanced, you can begin to break down that formula, but when you're getting started, always try to have a basic structure to ensure you tell a complete story.

This photograph is an example of an ending image. Being a cowboy has this very mythical aura about it, and the reality is it can be a very lonely job. Here he is at the end of the day, the cowboy by himself, bringing the horse back to the stables. I shot it very backlit, with an 85mm f/1.2 wide open, to create a very lonely, dark mood that I think is crucial for this series.

One of the most important lessons that any photographer who has been doing this for a while will tell you is that you need a lot of patience, and you can never give up. When the situation looks dire—and that was the case at different points with this job—it's important to stay ready and be prepared to make it happen even if the moment of opportunity is brief and fleeting.

On this shoot, as with many others, fear was the number one enemy: fear of failure, fear of creating a boring image, fear of missing the moment. Learning to manage those fears was and is a constant struggle. But as this assignment demonstrated, I couldn't control everything.

The irony is that when I started to accept that I couldn't control everything, I started taking chances. I rolled the dice even further and achieved a higher degree of success. When I was ruled by fear, I played it safe and my images suffered for it. It's when I overcame my fears that I started to become a better photographer.

A cowboy takes his horse into the stable at the end of a long day.

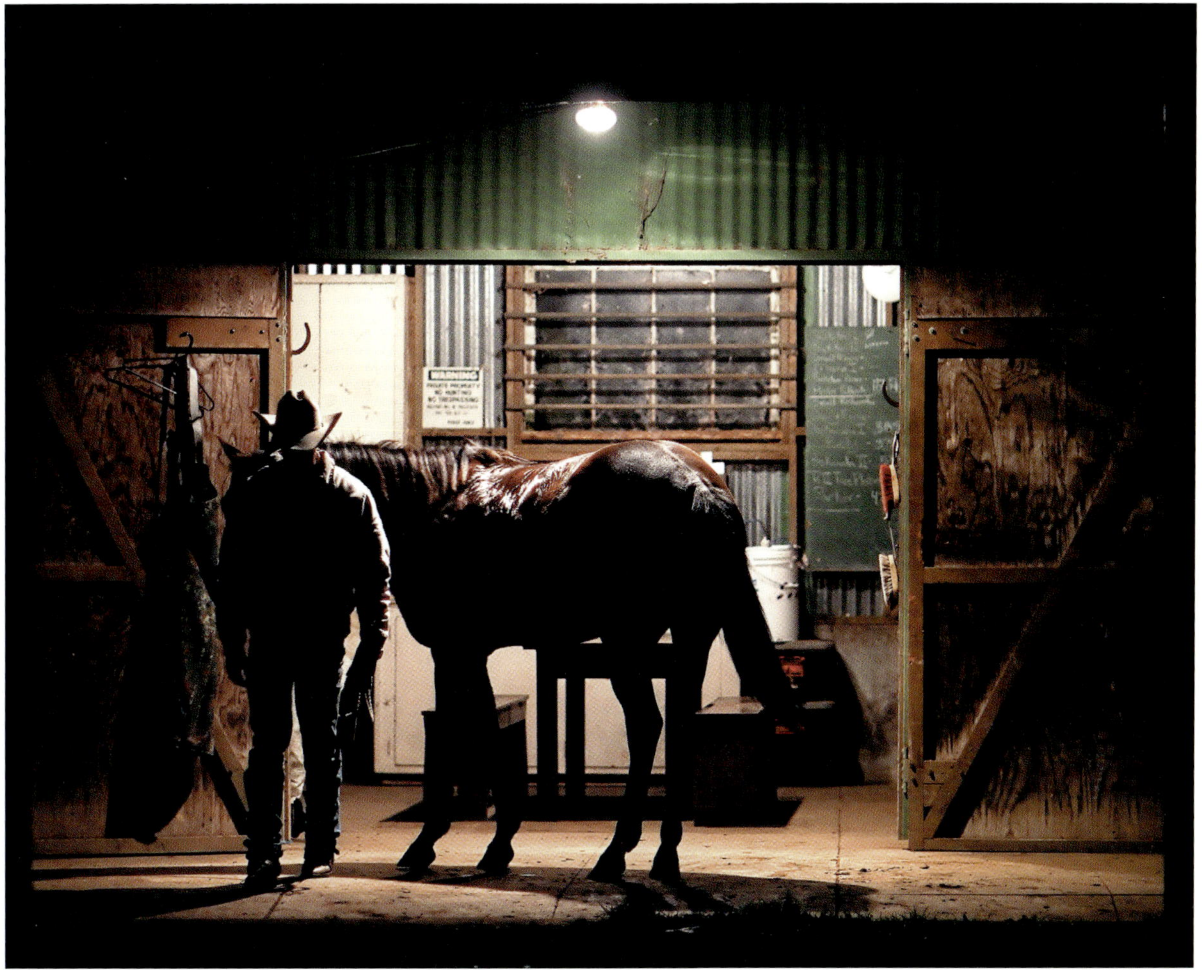

ISO 640 f/1.2 1/80 85mm

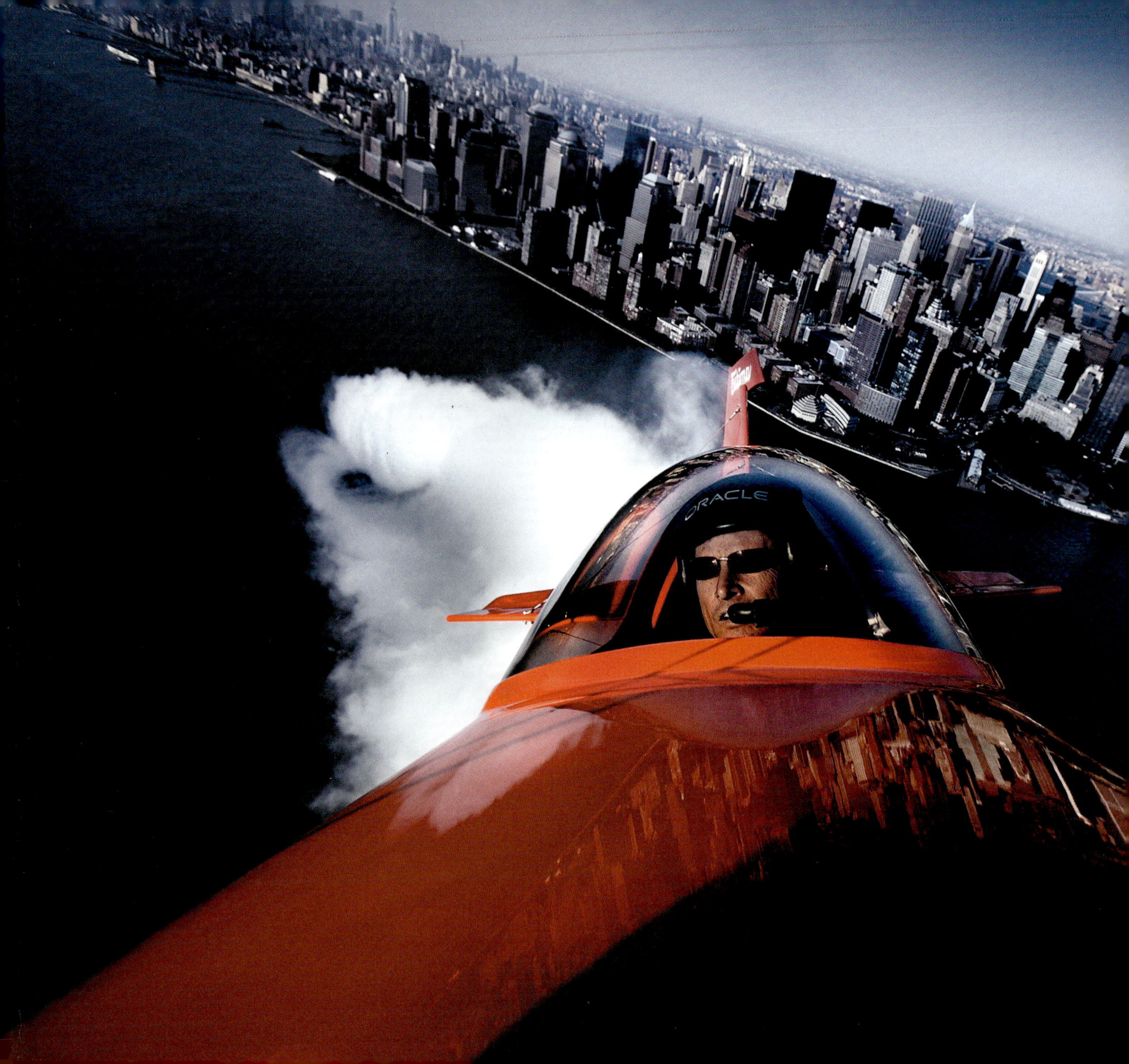
ORACLE

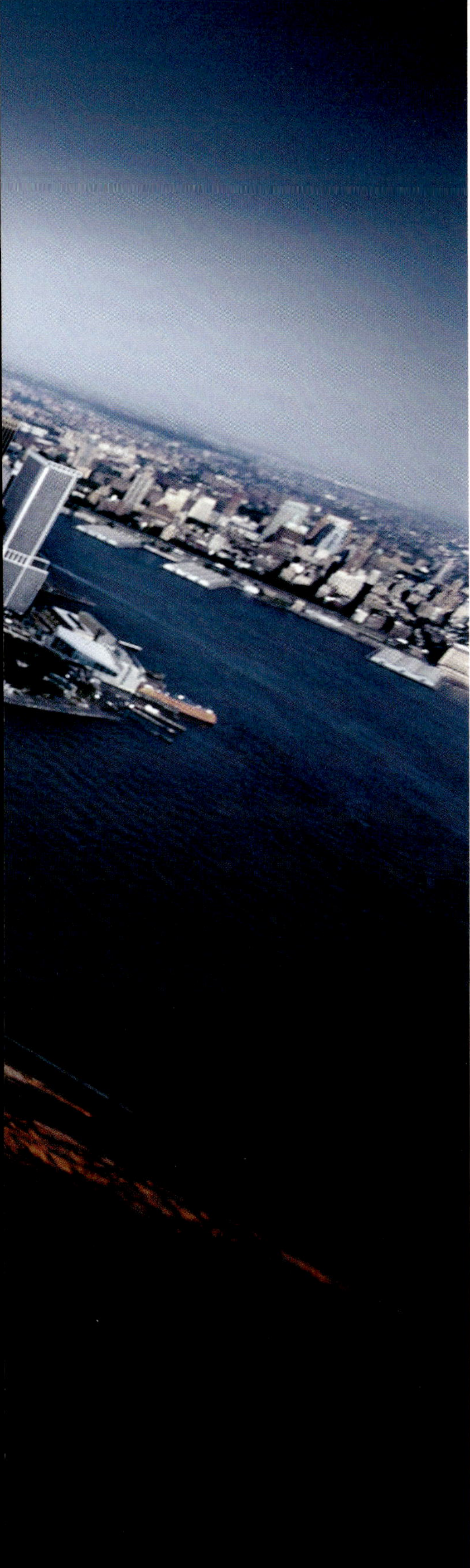

CHAPTER 13

NEVER MAKE A MEDIOCRE IMAGE

The reality for any photographer is you are only as good as your last photograph.

It doesn't matter how good the image was that you shot last year or last week; you're always in pursuit of the next image. And that pursuit of the next great image is about finding something new and different that you didn't know, or haven't seen yet, or haven't thought of yet. It's just a way of life.

◀ Airshow pilot Sean D. Tucker of Team Oracle flies south of New York City.

ISO 320 f/6.3 1/1250 16mm

It's very easy to go through your career making predictable photographs. You take few risks and face few discomforts, and that can be your approach to photography. There's nothing wrong with that.

But there's something inside of a lot of people, including myself, that refuses to take those predictable images—that refuses to take the same images over and over again. Instead you make the choices that cause discomfort and create uncertainty. It's only when you take this kind of risk that you discover the images you've never seen before, ones you can't expect.

It makes me feel very alive, and reignites my love for how beautiful and unpredictable life is.

STRIVING FOR THE UNATTAINABLE

I'm a photographer because the single worst thing I can imagine in life is going to the same office every day at the same hour, sitting in front of the same computer and desk. What keeps me ticking is going out and discovering new people, new places, and new things every day, and it's a tremendous privilege.

I think for that privilege, you have to sacrifice a lot—not only the comfort of that desk, but also the comfort of the predictable image. You have to strive for the images you think are unattainable, the images you're not sure you can make, because when you do make them, even if it's two or three times a year, it keeps you going. It keeps me going.

It makes your career interesting, and also helps build a healthy respect for the photographers who push the envelope and go into areas that are unexplored, or where images are difficult to make.

It's far too easy to do what's predictable with a camera, and for me that is far too boring. I can't take that image. I've shot it 100 times or I've seen it dozens of times. I want to find an image that I've yet to see or take.

The first BMX competition of the Olympics in the summer of 2008.

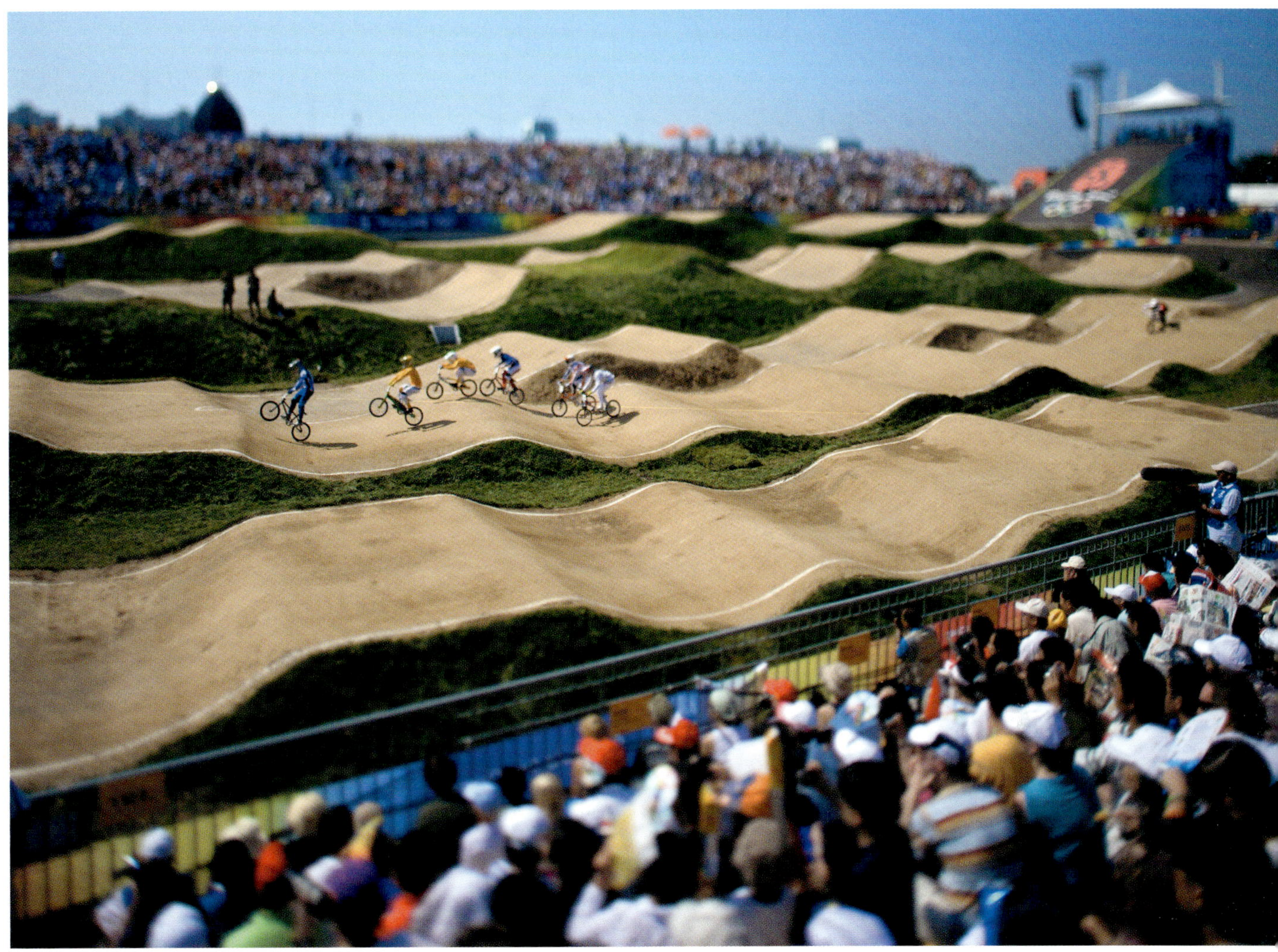

ISO 50 f/3.5 1/800 24mm

THE PERILS OF PRAISE

Because I began as such a young photographer, I often received praise.

"For your age, you're so far ahead of the game."

"Attaboy. Nice stuff."

"Man, I wish I had your talent when I was your age."

I knew innately that the praise was not helping me. Praise does not help you grow. Praise slows you down. Praise lets you rest on your laurels.

Instead of pursuing praise, spend your time studying your failures.

Making that choice forced me to study what I was doing, and to learn ten times faster. When you examine your failures or where you have fallen short, you are forced to think about what you are doing and how you are doing it.

So I welcome criticism. I have to admit I have a pretty thick skin. But whether you do or not, I think that when you receive criticism, you always have to analyze who it's coming from.

Does this person know what they're talking about? Do they have an agenda? Do I respect and admire their work?

Do a little bit of research. Don't listen to just anybody, because most people don't really know what they're talking about. But if they do know what they're talking about, even if they're from a very different field than you are, there's almost always something to be taken from it. It helps you grow.

THE ROLE OF EGO

This isn't about having an ego or not having one at all. Ego needs balance. If you don't have enough of one and you're too insecure, you get stepped on. You need enough ego that you won't take no for an answer. You have to persevere. You need enough ego to be able to talk about yourself, to sell yourself as a photographer. It's what gets you in the door, gets you the project.

You also need enough ego to have confidence. You need enough ego to say, "I can shoot this, even though there are 70 other photographers over there and I'm the only one here." That's ego. It's almost arrogance, but it pays off.

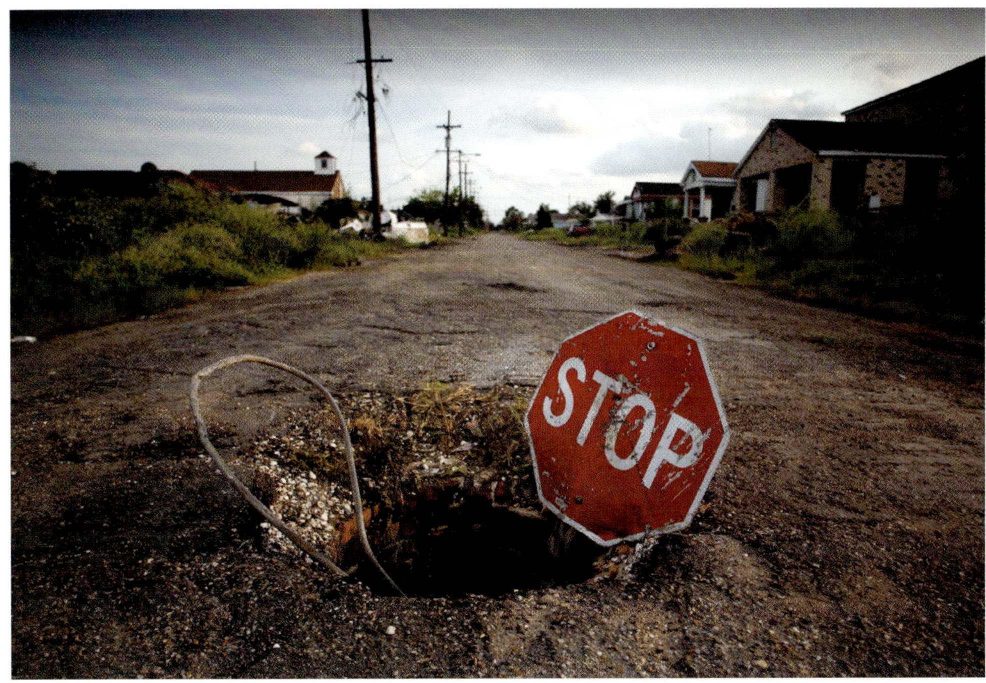

Hurricane Katrina. One year later.

ISO 100 f/3.5 1/1000 24mm

Where ego should have no place is in how you treat other people, how you treat other photographers, and how you act. It's a tricky balance.

I hate talking about myself. When my son was going through the kindergarten admissions process in New York, the school interviewed the parents, which I thought was the most asinine thing. I didn't mention anything in my interview about winning a Pulitzer Prize. I refused to. It just felt wrong. This is my kid trying to get in a school, not me.

But the point is, ego is necessary. Humility is necessary. Perspective is necessary. It doesn't matter how famous a photographer you are, you're still a human being like anyone else.

Recently when I went to pick up my laundry, a guy walked up to me.

"Are you Vincent Laforet?" he asked.

"Yeah."

"Oh, I really like your blog."

That tells me that I'm doing some good stuff in my blog. That's *all* it tells me, and I appreciate it. It's an affirmation when people actually take the time to compliment you or thank you. That's the best thing you can ask for.

But ego is dangerous, too. Confidence and arrogance in a job like mine can get you killed, literally, especially when you're in war zones. Again, Katrina reaffirmed this in a way that nothing else ever did. It isn't about me. It's about the pictures and the stories I'm telling, the people I'm photographing. It's about them. And I really understood that in Pakistan and Katrina as I never had before.

LESSONS LEARNED

Over time, no matter what the size of your ego, you're going to learn some lessons as a photojournalist. One is that the event trumps you and your work. And it's going to happen —over time the world will teach you that it's not about you.

The second thing you learn as a photojournalist is how we're all equal human beings on this earth, and that gives you a very unique perspective.

I have been in the presence of and photographed some very important, wealthy, and successful people. When you meet them and spend time with them, you see beyond the veneer. You see how insecure they can be, how some of them are so unhappy even with all their wealth. You come away from this realizing that beneath the surface, we're all the same.

I feel good when I've taken an image that has helped someone. I'm not sure true altruism really exists, but I think working for a newspaper can get you pretty close. When you're documenting things, it kind of brings you down to earth a little bit—or a lot. I ultimately find that the best photojournalists are the ones who care, because they're able to connect with the people they're photographing.

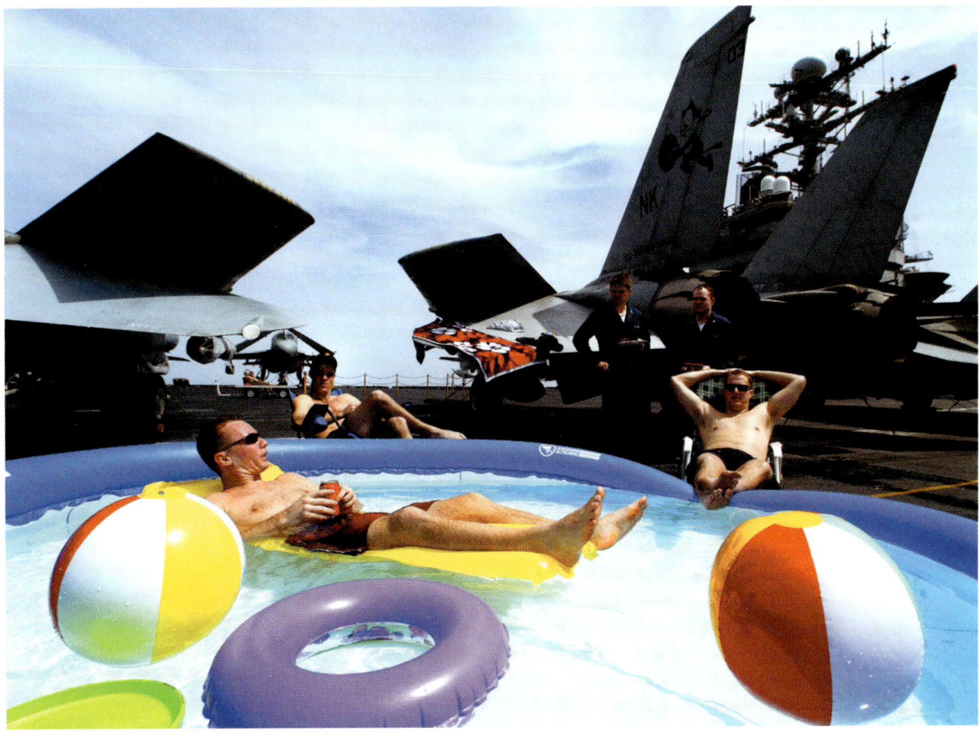

Aboard the *U.S.S. Abraham Lincoln*, in the Persian Gulf, in 2003. The pilots and most of the 5,500 crew members took part in the "Steel Beach" picnic on their second day of rest, prior to resuming their eighth month of duty at sea.

f/7.1 1/1000 14mm

And the best way to connect with someone is to be genuine and to really understand, or admit you don't understand, to be real. If you've got a huge ego and you're arrogant, dismissive, or uninterested in them, they see right through you.

I tell people that if you're a photojournalist or a street photographer and you're uncomfortable photographing someone, everyone within 100 yards can feel it. I think it's intuitive. But on a more practical level, it's probably the way you look at people, the way you comport yourself, the way you move.

ON PERSISTENCE

Finally, this game is about persistence.

People look at my career now and think that the *New York Times* or *National Geographic* are always pounding on my door. What they don't know is that even after 20 years of work, I still have to practically beg for a big project, and I often have to face being turned down.

Seven is my lucky number. I usually get turned down six times, and on the seventh time—with many big projects—I'm told yes. I just don't take no for an answer. I do it politely and very respectfully. I don't argue with people, but I don't stop asking them to hire me. If it's important to you, people will see. It's not that you're obsessed, although you may be.

The Canon 5D Mark II, the camera that helped launch my filmmaking career—I created the video *Reverie* with it—is a great example of that. That camera was not meant for me to test. Canon said no six times over four hours. The seventh time, they got so tired of me asking them politely that they finally said, "Fine, take it for the weekend. Ship it on Monday to the guy who's been chosen to shoot video with it."

That changed my career. I have David Sparer and Hitoshi Doi to thank for that opportunity.

A still image from "Reverie," shot in Fall 2008.

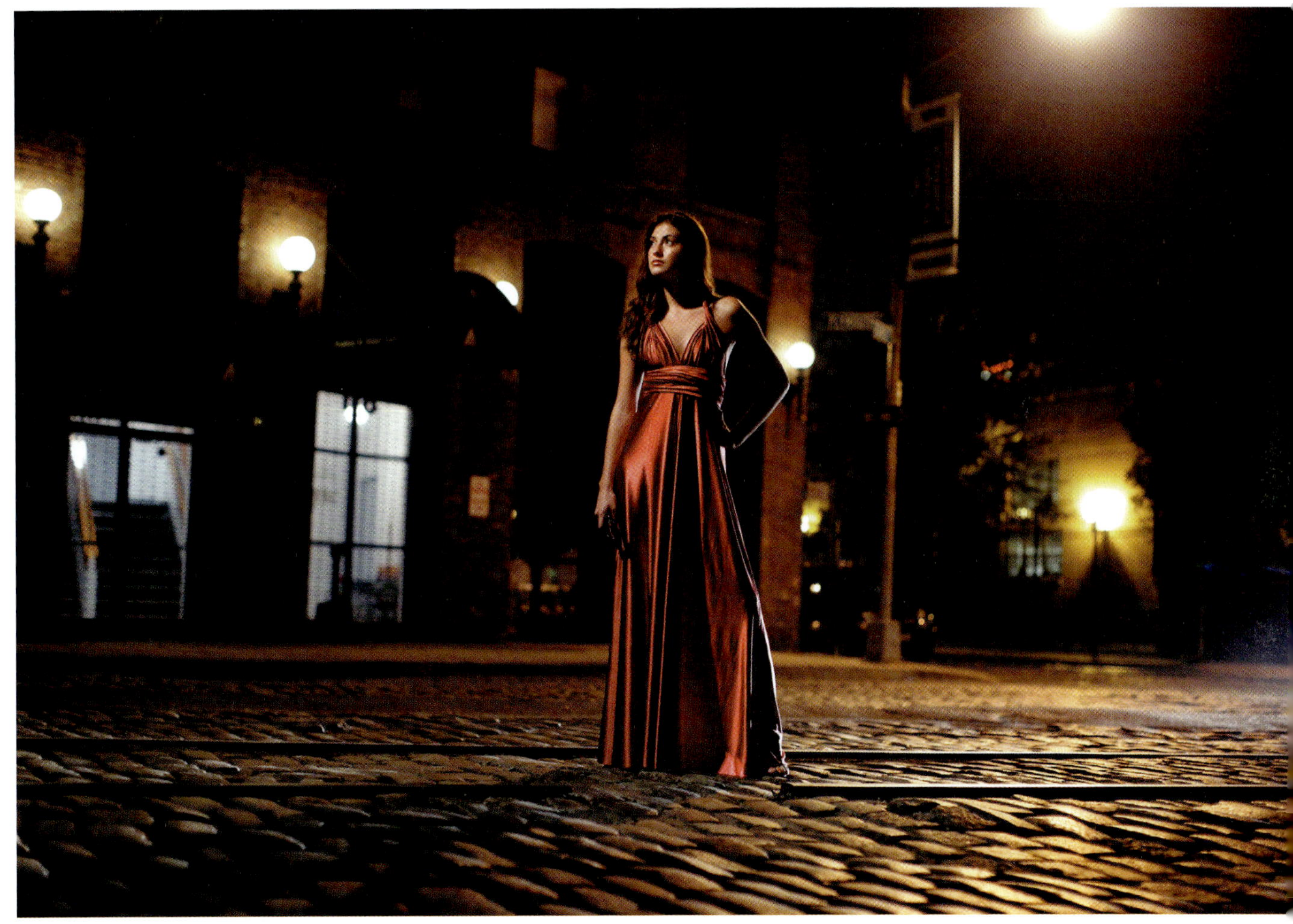

I think people, including myself, get very excited when we have eureka ideas. The reality is everyone has great ideas. The number of people who see them through to the end is incredibly small. And a lot of that has to do with perseverance.

Every success story could be written with the same narrative: "I had a great idea. They told me no. They told me it was stupid. They told me it wouldn't work. I did it anyway."

And that spirit of perseverance and stubbornness carries through into my photography.

For the Chrysler Building aerial photo shoot, we had 14 days we couldn't fly because of weather. The first day we got clearance to go up in the air, but then were told that we couldn't fly over lower Manhattan for security reasons. It was total B.S., but it's what air traffic control told us. We called the supervisor on Saturday and got his voice mail. What's the chance of getting a callback?

We sat for 45 minutes with the helicopter blades going, when finally the pilot got a call on his cell phone and was cleared to go. This photograph is the result of not giving up. It wasn't an option.

The reality is everyone has great ideas. The number of people who see them through to the end is incredibly small. And a lot of that has to do with perseverance.

Chrysler Building, New York City.

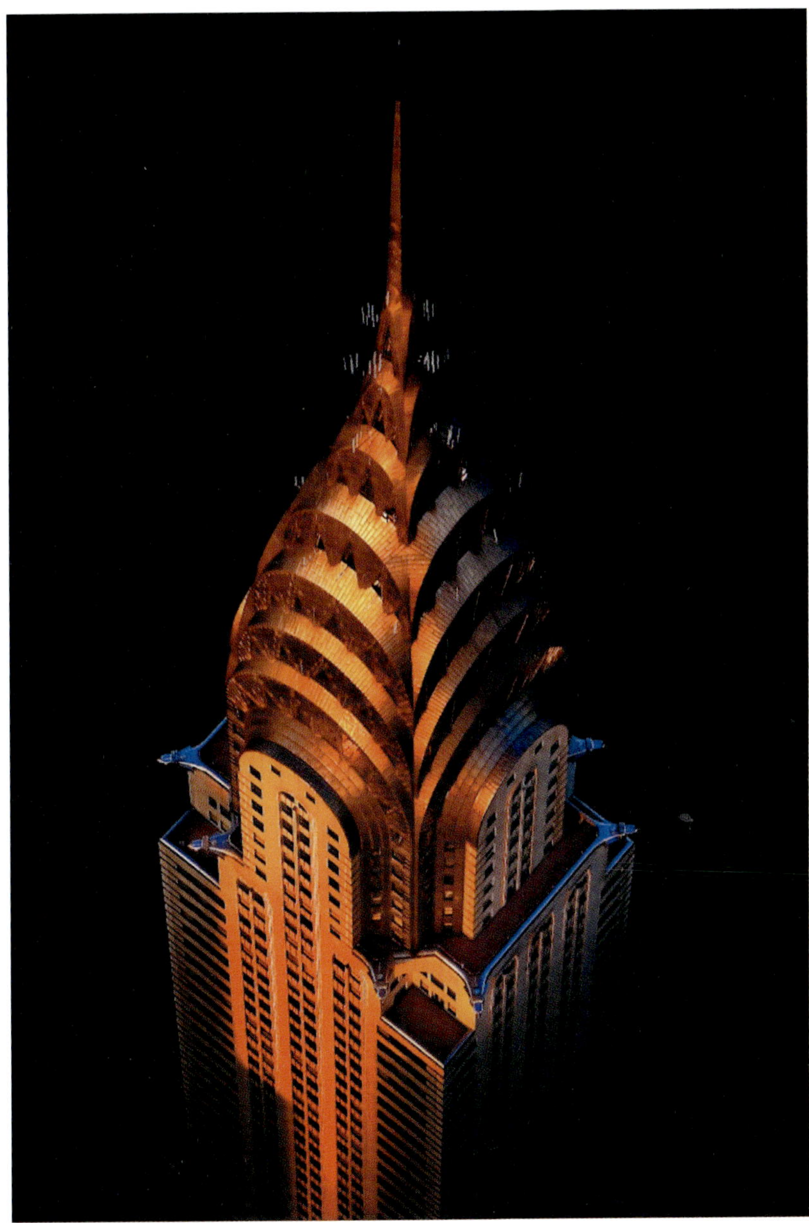

ISO 200 f/2.8 1/500 145mm

AIMING FOR THE BEST

Making great photographs is not just about aiming for the best. It's about being able to say no to all the mediocre ones or even the good ones.

You need to become a giant rejection machine saying, "I've seen it before. I've shot it a 100 times. It's not relevant to the story. It doesn't really do anything for me. Sure, it'd be good in my portfolio, but what I'm looking for is just not there."

Improve your ability to see photographs move up, down, left and right, and keep moving till you find the best one.

Ultimately, photography is about documenting everyday life, the unspectacular. But what you're looking for is something you've never seen or your audience has never seen. While we do travel the world and see amazing things, 95 percent of our job is photographing almost mundane stuff that we see every single day. The job—our profession—is to find something special in the everyday. As I photograph people and the world, I feel I'm most alive during that quest for the extraordinary.

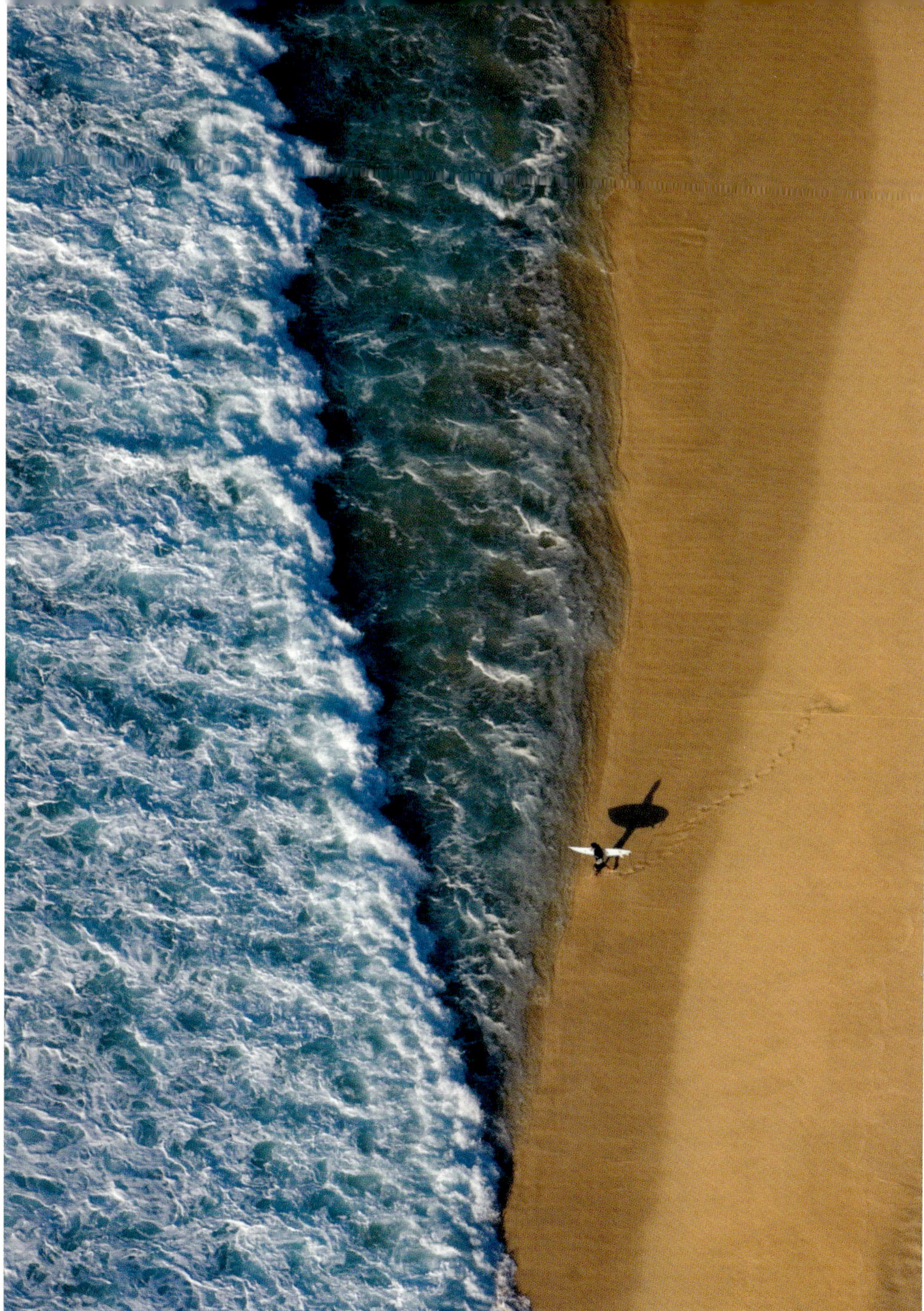

A surfer makes his way toward the Rip Curl Pipeline Masters, one of the most prestigious surfing competitions in the world.

ISO 200 f/5.6 1/2500 500mm

INDEX

G

H

I

J

K

L

M

T

U

V

W

Z

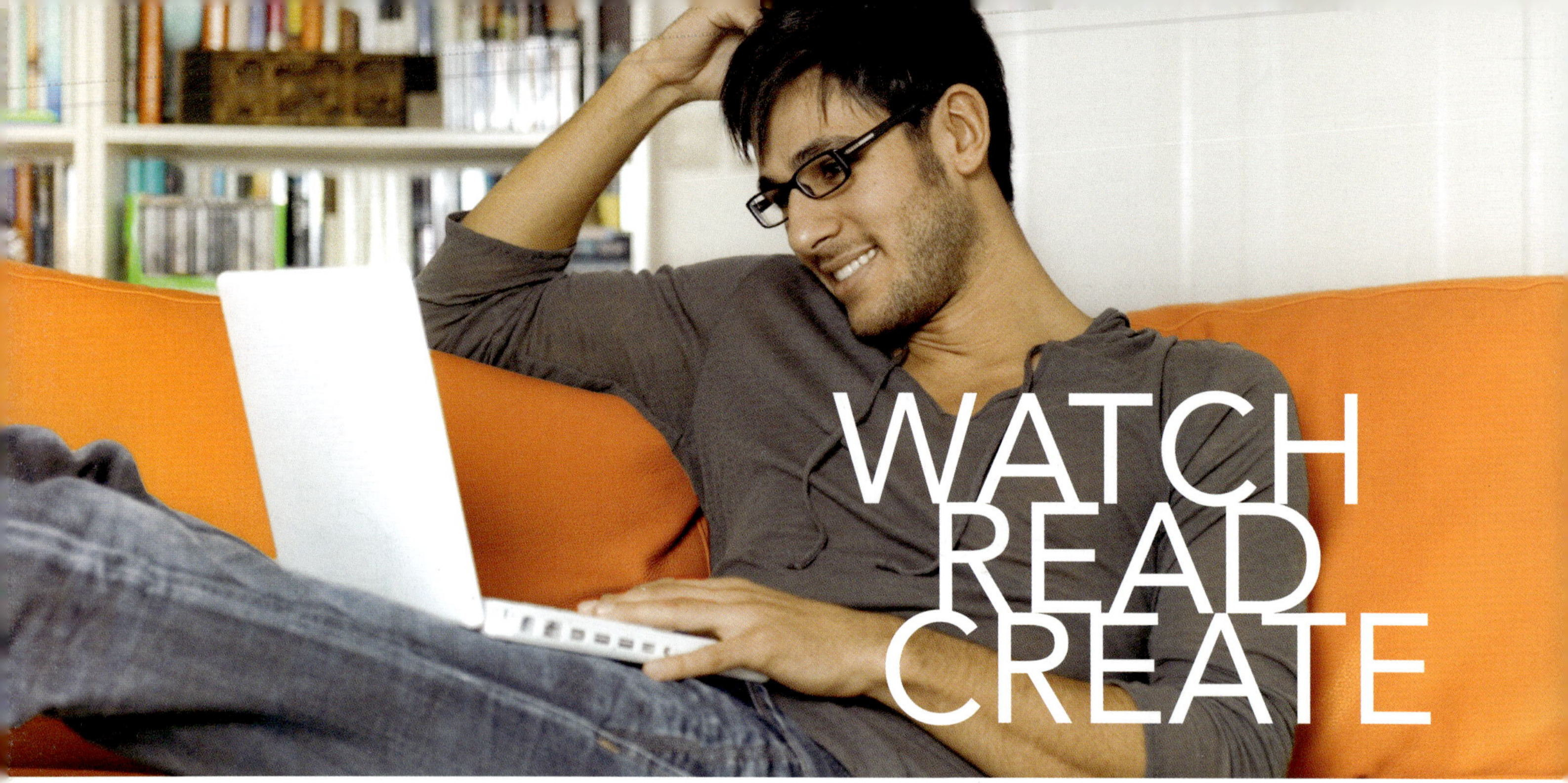